Learning Through Digital Game Design and Building in a Participatory Culture

Colin Lankshear and Michele Knobel
General Editors

Vol. 14

The New Literacies and Digital Epistemologies series
is part of the Peter Lang Education list.
Every volume is peer reviewed and meets
the highest quality standards for content and production.

PETER LANG
New York • Bern • Frankfurt • Berlin
Brussels • Vienna • Oxford • Warsaw

QING LI

Learning Through Digital Game Design and Building in a Participatory Culture

an enactivist approach

PETER LANG
New York • Bern • Frankfurt • Berlin
Brussels • Vienna • Oxford • Warsaw

Library of Congress Cataloging-in-Publication Data
Li, Qing.
Learning through digital game design and building
in a participatory culture: an enactivist approach / Qing Li.
pages cm. — (New literacies and digital epistemologies; vol. 14)
Includes bibliographical references and index.
1. Simulation games in education—Design and construction.
2. Computer games—Design. 3. Computer games—Social aspects. I. Title.
LB1029.S53L5   371.39'7—dc23   2013015641
ISBN 978-1-4331-1679-7 (hardcover)
ISBN 978-1-4331-1678-0 (paperback)
ISBN 978-1-4539-1020-7 (e-book)
ISSN 1523-9543

Bibliographic information published by **Die Deutsche Nationalbibliothek**.
Die Deutsche Nationalbibliothek lists this publication in the "Deutsche
Nationalbibliografie"; detailed bibliographic data are available
on the Internet at http://dnb.d-nb.de/.

© 2014 Peter Lang Publishing, Inc., New York
29 Broadway, 18th floor, New York, NY 10006
www.peterlang.com

All rights reserved.
Reprint or reproduction, even partially, in all forms such as microfilm,
xerography, microfiche, microcard, and offset strictly prohibited.

*This book is dedicated to my kids, Vivian and Richard,
game creators and players.*

Contents

Acknowledgments ix
Foreword xiii

Part 1: Epistemology

Chapter 1: Enactivism: A Framework for Understanding Cognition and
  Beyond 3
    Learning and Cognition 3
    An Alternative Learning Theory: Enactivism 9
    Enactivist Learning World: Games and Web 2.0 27

Chapter 2: Key Elements 34
    A Brief History of Learning by Game Building 34
    Key Concepts 36
    Essentials for Good Games 43

Part 2: Structure

Chapter 3: Enactivist Learning World 49
    Skills 49
    Systems Thinking 65
    Types of Games and Design Considerations 69

Chapter 4: Core Principles 81
    The Process of Learning by Game Building 81
    Idea Generation and Student Choice 88
    Creating Fun 93
    Prototyping and Play Testing 98

Part 3: Culture

Chapter 5: Enactivist Learning World and Culture 109
    Culture and Participatory Culture 109
    Collaborative Learning 121
    Small Group Learning 129
    Learning Communities 135

Chapter 6: Important Aspects 138
    Game Dynamics 138
    Narratives and Storytelling 142

Part 4: Value

Chapter 7: Enactivist Learning World and Value 153
    Value and Identity 153
    Affective Domain and Ethical Questions 156
    Assessment 162

Chapter 8: Vital Domains and Basic Tools 179
    Learner Motivation and Engagement 179
    The Role of Teachers and Learners 183
    So You Want to Build a Game? 187

Part 5: Conclusion

Chapter 9: Learning by Game Building in the Twenty-first Century 199

References 203
Index 211

Acknowledgments

Throughout this book, I reference projects that we have conducted to substantiate the points and ideas. By "we," I mean work I conducted with colleagues to which K-12 students, preservice and in-service teachers, and graduate students have contributed. This is truly a collaborative effort and every participant deserves recognition. Although not possible to name everyone who contributed, I will try my best.

First, this book would be impossible without the countless hours of the work produced by the participants. The graduate students and preservice teachers who were involved in my projects include students who took my game-based learning courses and other methods courses, in particular, Steve Martin, Chris Appleton, Shai Nathoo, Arkhadi Pustaka, Robert Louis, Yang Liu, Scott McEwen, Elise Vandermeiden, and Collette Lemieux.

Second, many colleagues have supported this work in different ways. James Paul Gee, a wonderful mentor and supporter, has been instrumental in my work related to digital games. I am extremely grateful for his never-ending support, including writing the Foreword for this book. Henry Jenkins at the University of South California deserves special recognition because of his continued support. Several years ago when Henry was a professor at MIT, I spent part of my sabbatical year as a visiting scholar to work with Henry and his teams on his research projects. That experience of meeting and working with like-minded people, including Erin Reilly, Eric Klopfer and Philip Tan, has further inspired my interest and passion in game-based learning, in particular learning through game design and building. Ian Winchester at the University of Calgary has been an insightful supporter. Many hours of conversation about enactivism shaped my ideas about this new paradigm. Richard Tay at the La Trobe University in Australia was part of *The Driven* project, and I thank him for his intellectual inspiration on integrating games to the field of road safety. Special thanks also go to David Wizer at Towson University, who has provided continued practical and moral support.

Third, I also want to thank the Social Sciences and Humanities Research Council of Canada (SSHRCC), Towson University, the University of Calgary, and MIT, which provided financial support to the game projects discussed in this book. In a similar vein, my department (the Department of Educational Technology and Literacies) deserves thanks for acknowledging the value of my research and for supporting my work in this area.

Fourth, I thank my series editors, Colin Lankshear and Michele Knobel, for their insightful comments and invaluable feedback. I also want to express my sincere appreciation to Lisa Twiss and Keturah Fountaine for their help in editing this book and providing suggestions. Thanks also to Peter Lang editorial members including Phyllis Korper, Chris Myers, and Jackie Pavlovic.

Last, but definitely not least, I want to express my gratitude to my special family members. My dad, a math professor his entire life, was my first mentor and role model who encouraged and inspired my career in academia. My mom taught me how to be persistent to get through the tough times. My two kids, Vivian and Richard, are both the initial and continued inspiration for my interest in digital game-based learning. In particular, I thank Vivian for her patience in editing my work at any time without hesitation. And my dear husband, Liang, deserves a very special acknowledgment for his unceasing encouragement and support that have allowed me to find and pursue my academic passions.

This book is grounded on my years of work in the field of education, and more specifically game based learning. Parts of chapter one were co-written with Bruce Clark and Ian Winchester and initially published as "Instructional design and technology with enactivism: A shift of paradigm?" in *British Journal of Educational Technology* (2010), reprinted by permission of the publisher, Taylor & Francis Ltd, http://www.tandf.co.uk/journals and http://www.informaworld.com. The Do It Yourself project discussed in this book also contains components of my paper titled "Understanding enactivism: A study of affordances and constraints of engaging practicing teachers as digital game designers" in *Educational Research & Development* (2012), 60(5), 785-806, reprinted by permission of the publisher, Springer, http://www.editorialmanager.com/etrd/ and http://www.springer.com.

This book have elements of my previous published papers: Li, Q. (2010), Digital game building: Learning in a participatory culture, in *Educational Research*, 52(4), 427-433; and Li, Q. (2013), Digital games and learning: A

Acknowledgments

study of preservice teachers' perceptions. *International Journal of Play*, 2(2), 101-116, reprinted by permission of the publisher, Taylor & Francis Ltd, http://www.tandf.co.uk/journals and http://www.informaworld.com.

The Driven project discussed in the book contains elements from the coauthored paper Li, Tay & Louis (2012). Designing digital games to teach road safety: A study of graduate students' experiences, *Loading*, 6(9), 17-35. http://journals.sfu.ca/loading/index.php/loading/article/view/102/114 reprinted with the permission from the journal.

This book also uses materials from the following papers:

- Li, Lemieux, C., Vandermeiden, E. & Nathoo, S. (2013). Are you ready to teach secondary mathematics in the 21st century? A study of pre-service teachers' digital game design experience. *Journal of Research on Technology in Education*. 45(4), 309-337. Reprinted by permission of the publisher, International Society for Technology in Education, 800.336.5191 (U.S. & Canada) or 541.302.3777 (Int'l), http://www.iste.org.
- Li, Q., Vandermeiden, E., Lemieux, C. & Nathoo, S. (in press). Secondary students learning mathematics through digital game building: A study of the effects and students' perceptions. *International Journal for Technology in Mathematics Education*.
- Li, Q. (2013, Mar.). Teaching secondary mathematics: Preservice teachers' digital game design, pedagogy, and 21st century skills. Paper presented at the annual conference of ABSEL, Oklahoma City, OK. Proceedings of the Developments in Business Simulation and Experiential Learning, 40, pp. 110-114.
- Li, Q. (2013, Mar.). Digital game building as assessment: A study of secondary students' experience. Paper presented at the annual conference of ABSEL, Oklahoma City, OK. Proceedings of the Developments in Business Simulation and Experiential Learning, 40, pp. 74-78.
- Li, Nathoo, Vandermeiden, Lemieux, C. (2012, Mar.). Practicing teachers as digital game creators: A study of the design considerations. Paper presented at the annual conference of ABSEL, San Diego, CA.

Foreword

James Paul Gee

Humans are simulators, not calculators. We learn from experience; we use images and actions from experience to give meanings to words, and we use prior experience to prepare for new ones and the actions we need to take in them. Humans do not learn well from just any old experience. They learn best when, in an experience, they have an action to take or something they want to do that they really care about. They learn best when they have mentors who make them successful before they can go it alone and help them know where to focus their attention in the midst of the plethora of details in any experience in the world.

Digital games are virtual experiences where players take actions, consider their consequences, and seek to achieve success at least partially on their own terms but with due deference to what counts as mastery by peers and mentors they wish to affiliate with and be accepted by. Human minds work a good deal like digital games: based on past experiences, we simulate experiences in our heads where we can try out different roles, approaches, and solutions to problems in order to prepare ourselves for new learning and mastery. Thinking—when it is focused on living and achieving—is like a video game in the mind, a game we ourselves design, play, and redesign.

Students learn and read best when they bring to talk and texts what have been called situated or embodied meanings, what Qing Li calls *enactive meanings*. Such situated, embodied, enactive meanings involve associating words with images, actions, experiences, and interactive dialogue—not just definitions, other words, and other texts. Students can attain situated, embodied, enactive meanings only if they have a chance to try and do before and alongside reading, and if, when they are new to an area, get text in small bits "just in time" (when they can apply it) or larger chunks "on demand" (when they ask for it, need it, and are ready to use it).

Digital games have a dual role to play in improving learning in and out of school. They can be a platform for situated, embodied, enactive learning, since they are externalized versions of human thinking and problem solving. And digital games can teach us how to teach and learn beyond games in any and all forms that recruit rich experience, good tools, and nurturing mentoring for creating innovative, lifelong impassioned learners. Qing Li's book is a thoroughly excellent guide here, one that gets theory and practice right.

PART ONE
Epistemology

• CHAPTER ONE •

Enactivism: A Framework for Understanding Cognition and Beyond

This chapter starts with a discussion of learning, knowledge, and cognition. The introduction describes several stories, one of which is a story of Sam, an elementary school teacher, and his kindergarten students, playing with Crayon Physics, *an online game. These stories demonstrate that learning can occur through learners' conscious and unconscious interactions with their environment without any specific, predetermined goals. This leads to the introduction of* enactivism, *an emerging philosophical paradigm. Such discussion is contextualized by comparing enactivism to constructivism and behaviourism. Then, leading figures in the field of education—Lev Vygotsky, Seymour Papert, and James Paul Gee—are profiled. The ideology of their work forming a foundation for digital game-based learning is discussed. This chapter concludes with a proposed model based on enactivism, integrating learning by game building and Web 2.0.*

Learning and Cognition

Prologue

I was working when my 12-year-old son, Richard, rushed up to me and said, "Mommy, can I ask you a question?"

"Sure," I answered, only half paying attention.

"Which one is better? Being a perfectionist or being a workaholic?"

"Huh?!" was my first reaction, as he looked at my puzzled face, eagerly waiting for a real answer. While I was still absorbing this bizarre question, Richard suddenly declared his thought, "I got it." With that, he dashed out, leaving me scratching my head.

Later, while having a conversation with my daughter, I mentioned this odd question posed by Richard, and she jumped on top of her chair with excitement, "I know it!!!" she exclaimed. "I know why he asked that question. He was playing *The Sims 3* (a game) and trying to choose his avatar's personality traits!"

This scenario is an example of many interactions I have had with not only my own children but also children we have worked with in schools. It is an example of how kids today are living, thinking, and experiencing a world that is vastly different from that of previous generations. The kids of this generation are growing up with smartphones, Internet, and digital games. They are tweeting, viewing YouTube, and using FaceTime. Do we understand them? Do we know what creates meaning for them and how they learn?

There is no doubt that our world is changing. The development of new technology and new media has fundamentally changed our society, thus permanently altering the way we work, live, socialize, and play. It's long been discussed that we need to prepare our students to be "tech-savvies" in order for them to have a secure future. This book is therefore written to answer such a call by offering the perspective of learning through digital game designing and building. Game designing and building can include any type of game—video games, computer games, mobile games, board games, or even in-person, live action, role-playing games. The focus of this book, however, is on digital games. Accordingly, in the remainder of the book, the term *game* refers to digital game unless otherwise specified.

This book is for *you* and about *you*, whether you are a college professor, a schoolteacher, a graduate student, a game designer, or simply someone who is interested in digital games and new ways of learning, specifically learning through digital game designing and building. It is my hope that you will find the contents of this book valuable. To help you, the reader, best relate to what is presented within this text, which hopefully will lead to personal connections, I have chosen to use "you" to represent the person designing and/or building a game for learning and "players" to represent the people who play the game.

Learning in Informal Settings

This is a book about learning with digital games, particularly *learning by digital game designing and building*. As the term suggests, while the scope of this book positions technology as an avenue through which learning occurs, essentially *learning* is the ultimate focus and therefore it begs for a discussion about learning and cognition first.

Epistemology

Consider young children coming to grips with daily life outside themselves: walking, talking, bathing, running, and falling. While practicing and acting on such tasks, they learn. It all looks random during the process, but the end result is very precise indeed. This learning is not formalized, and the children do not do it consciously. Such learning can occur at any level and at any age. It can happen when we are facing a new world into which we want to find a way or simply do find a way. For example, children often learn the accents in a language of their school chums rather than those of their parents. And in the case of children, this is often not consciously constructed, as it might be for an adult; it simply occurs through children's complex interactions with their school environment. It is possible to pass from confusion and perplexity to knowing, through intermediate phases where learning is unconscious.

Think, for example, of Inuit and how they traditionally learn without conscious teaching on the part of their family. In passing, children may notice the adult Inuit building a kayak. Perhaps the children fiddle a bit with the same materials; perhaps they do not. Yet somehow, one day, without any special conscious effort, the children may know how to build a kayak and what a kayak is good for. Nobody "taught" them or set them a task. They did not consciously construct either a theory of kayaks or their building, and they did not build a kayak before they found themselves actually needing to do so and as a matter of fact being able to do so too.

An interesting research project called Hole in the Wall further illustrates these points. In 1999, Sugata Mitra, a professor in India, started to explore the potential of computers in disadvantaged areas (Mitra & Rana, 2001). He and his team found a place near an urban slum in New Delhi, dug a hole in a wall, and installed (in that hole) an Internet-connected computer. Without giving any instruction or explanation to anyone, they simply put the computer there and left. They used a hidden camera to film the area and collect data. Nine months later, Mitra returned to the site and found some amazing things. The footage from the hidden camera showed that groups of children were curious about this new toy and played on the computer. Through this play, these children not only taught each other how to use the computer but they also learned how to access the Internet. It is important to note that absolutely no intervention was conducted in this case. Inspired by this amazing result, Mitra and his team (Mitra, Dangwal, Chatterjee, Swati Jha, Bisht, & Kapur, 2005) then repeated the experiment in 22 different geographic locations, with children who had diverse ethnic and cultural backgrounds. These children in different locations also spoke different first languages. The results were surprisingly consistent, pointing to the same conclusion: Children could learn computer skills on their own, regardless of who or where they were. When compared with the traditional classrooms, no difference was identified between the self-instructed learning experience and the traditional teacher-instructed learning experience.

In the following years, Mitra's team replicated the experiment again in different places, with subjects beyond computer literacy skills, including English, mathematics, and biology. They found that this type of self-teaching and self-learning, involving computers and the Internet, could not only teach children any school subject but also improve their social values and collaborative skills (Mitra & Dangwal, 2010; Mitra et al., 2005)

Cases like the aforementioned studies highlight how learning can occur through learners' conscious and unconscious interaction with their environment without any specific, predetermined goals. They demonstrate that even in the absence of any direct input from a human teacher, an environment that stimulates curiosity can cause learning through self-instruction and peer-shared knowledge.

This kind of learning—with no predetermined or specific goal setting, using self-motivation and learning through continued interactions with the surrounding environment—is not new. It has been exercised for thousands of years. For example, it was common practice in ancient monastic education in Eastern Asia. The famous Zen story of "burnishing a brick into mirror," originally published in the Jinde Chuandeng Recorded (Grind A Brick to A Mirror, n.d.), reflects this spirit of teaching.

A long time ago, Matsu Road was practicing meditation every day, hoping to become Buddha ("the Awakened One"). For years, he tried really hard, despite wind or rain, sun or snow, but to no avail.

One day, Master Zen Huai saw Matsu meditating in front of a temple and went to ask: "Why are you meditating every day?"

Matsu replied: "I want to become Buddha."

Zen Huai took a piece of brick and started to burnish it on the stone in front of the temple. Matsu was really surprised and asked: "What are you doing?"

Zen Huai: "I want to mill it into a mirror."

Matsu: "Copper can be polished into a mirror, but not bricks."

Zen Huai replied: "Oh, no. As long as I do it carefully and persistently, it will surely be milled into a mirror."

Epistemology

Matsu became anxious and shouted: "Master, you are out of your mind! A brick cannot be ground into a mirror! Without a good grasp of the truth, blind perseverance will get you nowhere. You will not succeed!"

Zen Huai smiled: "Precisely! If I cannot turn a brick to a mirror by grinding it, how is it possible for you to become Buddha by simple meditation?"

Although Master Zen Huai's words sound abstruse, they are similar to the ideas reflected in the stories of the Hole in the Wall project or the experience of young children acquiring accents while playing on the playground, as discussed earlier. These ideas carry an important educational ideology that is completely contradictory to our traditional formal education: Unintentional learning is important and real. In other words, learning and the environment become a united whole; learning goals and processes become a united whole; students learn with or without conscious effort.

Learning in Formal Educational Settings

You may be wondering if the premise of this book is informal learning. I can tell you it is not. While I acknowledge all that occurs outside of school, in terms of what children learn and the interaction between adults and children during this learning process, what I elaborate on here is more about the learning taking place in schools and what teachers can do to foster the type of learning that took place in India (i.e., the Hole in the Wall study) right in their own classrooms.

Let me tell you a story involving kindergarteners playing an online game in a formal classroom setting. To make sense of this story, I first need to tell you about *Crayon Physics*, the game the children in this story played. *Crayon Physics,* as the website described (http://www.crayonphysics.com/), is an online 2D physics puzzle/sandbox game. Being a sandbox game, a player can draw anything in the game, and the drawings are instantly transformed into physical objects on the screen. So if the player draws a line in the sky, it becomes a stick that eventually falls to the ground. If the player draws a circle, it turns into a ball that can roll. In short, the idea is that players can solve puzzles with their artistic vision and some creative use of physics. The objective of each puzzle is to move a ball in the game so that it touches all the stars placed in the picture. The trick is, "the players cannot control the ball directly, but rather must influence the ball's movement by drawing physical objects on the screen" (Crayon Physics Deluxe, n.d., para.

2). Although the core design behind the game embodies rich physics ideas and principles, the game contains far more beyond physics itself.

Sam, an elementary teacher, has been teaching for 16 years. On one occasion, I introduced him to *Crayon Physics*. The following adventure is an edited version of what he shared in his blog.

Sam loved the *Crayon Physics* game and was eager to know whether he could use it in elementary classrooms. When he showed the game to his colleagues, some teachers dismissed this idea because "the game would be too difficult for the students." Sam decided to try it in his kindergarten class, the youngest group in his school. His logic was simple: "If my youngest kids can use it, other grades can certainly use it as well." What would the students do as they interacted in the game environment? Sam was curious. One Tuesday morning during snack time, he put *Crayon Physics* on the Smartboard, an interactive whiteboard to provide touch control of computer applications and annotations. Projected on the Smartboard was the image of a house standing on a green yard, a ball, a star, and blue sky with white puffy clouds. Sam started to draw a black line in the sky. It turned to a stick and fell to the ground. Then he sketched a red circle. It became a small ball that dropped and rolled off the roof of a house. At this point, he started to invite these young children to experiment with these "magical pens." The 5-year-olds got excited and started to play this as a sandbox on the Smartboard. Shapes, letters of the alphabet, and crazy scrawls were created and sent in a free fall, to the ground, to the roof of the house, to the top of a rock….. Occasionally several students frantically scribbled at the same time, jumbling the screen with huge piles of objects. All the children were clearly enjoying this new *Crayon Physics* center.

Then one student changed the dynamic of the center. A rock he sketched on the screen bumped into the ball, causing the ball to roll and eventually hitting the star shape. The game rewarded the boy with a happy sound and a map appeared. Apparently, his random action accidentally revealed to the students that this is actually the "objective" of the game. Instantly, the children who were watching and the children who were playing understood what had happened. These children cheered loudly with delight, "Mr. Sam, he got to the next level!" all of a sudden, the free spirited play became a purposeful "game" because now they had discovered this goal of the game. No longer were they interested in merely drawing shapes to see what happened. Rather, they were excited to share ideas and exchange advices. When one student drew on the Smartboard, six or seven students would stand near her watching and acting as consultants, discussing possibilities, giving advice, and providing suggestions. The children were excited each time they found a solution to achieve the objective. It became quite a sight to watch these five-year-olds experiment with different physical objects, explore strange landscapes, and play collaboratively, all the while solving problems through discovery, playing, and experimenting. Sam was quite surprised and expressed, "I was amazed at what outcomes can be achieved when you are given minimal instructions, especially when it is in a gaming environment."

Sam's story matters here because it starts to capture authentic and powerful learning that occurred in a learning world, a world that involved games. This learning world seemingly had no apparent specific learning goals to start with, yet it had resulted in significant purposeful learning. Students learned, for example, ways of identifying and discovering the game objectives and collaborating with each other, along with characteristics of different physics objects such as balls or sticks in this process of playing. In this book, I intentionally use the term a learning world rather than a learning environment to reflect enactivism, the philosophical grounding of this book that is discussed next.

An Alternative Learning Theory: Enactivism

Enactivism

The previous observations of learning, highlighted in the text of young children's learning to walk and talk, or Inuit people's learning to build a kayak, or Sam's kindergarten students' learning to play *Crayon Physics*, all lead to an important point: learning and cognition, unlike what we typically think, can start without learners' conscious actions or prescribed objectives. Indeed, quite the opposite occurs when students learn and know through fully immersing themselves in a complex world where they play, experience, and interact with each other and the environment.

Such observations challenge traditional views about learning and knowing, calling for new worldviews. In this chapter, I introduce an emerging philosophic paradigm called enactivism. I argue that education based on enactivism can help us prepare students to assume roles as effective workers, citizens, and self-fulfilled people in the 21st-century global civilization.

You may find the following discussion about enactivism more abstract than the rest of the book. This is because it deals with theoretical perspectives. However, it is important to include such discussion because understanding good learning theories helps you build a strongly supported foundation for good teaching. Understanding educational theories also helps you better understand yourself and others, students and teachers included, in terms of limitations as well as abilities. Knowing your own and others' beliefs helps how you act and think. This being said, you can skip this section if you do not find it applicable to your situation. This will not affect your understanding of the book's main ideas or purposes. You may even wish to return to this section once you have read the rest of the book, for what is discussed here may help you better frame the suggestions made, and in the end, being able to conceptualize enactivism may help you better plan the actions you will take either in or out of the classroom. It may also come to pass that knowing who is responsible for much of the educational and technological advancements being made today could serve you well in future endeavours.

Now, going back to the topic of enactivism, we see that it has roots in both the phenomenological work of Merleau-Ponty and Bateson's biological views (Fenwick, 2000). It has flourished particularly well in the field of mathematics education in the last couple of decades. Enactivism, first introduced in Varela, Thompson, and Rosch's book, *The Embodied Mind* (1991), provides a more encompassing philosophical stance than other viewpoints (Davis & Sumara, 1997). A fundamental difference between enactivism and other commonly discussed philosophical views is that it rejects dualism and focuses on the importance of embodiment and action to cognition. Such dualism separates mind from body, self from environment, or subject from object (Davis & Sumara, 2006). The main ideas of the following discussions about enactivism in this chapter are originally published in the *British Journal of Educational Technology* (Li, Clark, & Winchester, 2010) with reprint permission from the journal.

An Example

Enactivism is a philosophy based on two important premises: 1) cognition and environment are inseparable, and 2) "systems" enact with each other from which they "learn." Let's consider a simple event: Jean is learning how to make a peanut butter and jam sandwich. Understanding that this event of making a peanut butter and jam sandwich is not just about the bread pieces, or the peanut butter and jam, or just Jean herself as separate entities. It is not even just about putting jam on the bread, the motion of her hands putting two pieces of bread together, or the room. It is all of the above. Her physical process of making the sandwich shapes her understanding of the event. That is, Jean learns to make the sandwich through her personal enactment with the physical world. Most importantly, when Jean makes the sandwich, she draws upon specific experiences from her personal history to understand her present world. For example, she may have been told, by her mom, that she needed to learn how to make a peanut butter and jam sandwich for her lunch. She might have found, based on her previous experience, that toasting the bread pieces before putting peanut butter and jam on them would make the sandwich taste better. This is part of her personal history that helps her make sense of this event. Likewise, Jean may notice that holding the bread in one hand and the knife in the other would make the job easier. Jean's learning to make a peanut butter and jam sandwich is connected to her experiences, mirrors her structure (e.g., cognitive), and is embedded in her action.

Perhaps Jean is a student in China who is learning English from her teacher through this activity, so she may have to use chopsticks instead of a butter knife to spread peanut butter and jam. Or she may have to use a butter knife but is not sure how to use it. Peanut butter and jam may be stored in bowls instead of jars. In this scenario, Jean's limited personal experience with butter knives affects her understanding of the event. Further, intertwined cognitive, social, and physical systems all shape how she enacts.

Or, suppose Jean is an astronaut from NASA. She is making a peanut butter and jam sandwich in a space shuttle in outer space for the first time. Spreading peanut butter and jam on bread thus becomes a brand new concept even though she may have rich experience with making these sandwiches in a North American context. The simple act of taking out two pieces of bread and putting them on a table in our normal sense is no longer possible. In outer space, where gravity is lacking, bread pieces would fly around instead of sitting nicely on a table. Therefore, what appears to be a trivial action of putting bread pieces on a table in one setting, in this case on Earth, turns out to be an event that needs a tremendous amount of conscious thought in another setting, outer space. Such trivial actions are often called habit or tacit knowledge.

In daily life, we are heedless of a lot of tacit knowledge. Walking, for instance, is quite natural for adults. We do not need to consciously think much about our walking action when we stroll around a park on a beautiful day. Yet when observing a child who is just starting to walk, we can see that the process of learning to walk takes a lot of conscious effort. This suggests that, often, we realize only a small part of our bodily sensations, attend to only the surface of our thoughts, and recognize only fragments of our acts. It tells us that our body, mind, and this world that surrounds us cannot be separated.

Although this may seem contradicting to common wisdom, what follows is that learning is more than simply paying attention to a series of conscious events and changing some intentional decisions. Instead, learning is a complex matter, enmeshed in a convoluted network of people, such as students and teachers (Davis, Sumara, & Luce-Kapler, 2008). It involves the incarnation of varied perceptions, of applying, of abstracting, and of acting that engages both conscious and unconscious understanding and abilities.

Many predominant educational theories, objectivism and constructivism included, view cognition as the representation of a pregiven world by a pregiven mind. Enactivism, in contrast, rejects such representative views and claims that cognition emerges from embodied actions (Davis & Sumara, 2006). That is, we learn from processes of perception and action, which gives rise to recurrent sensorimotor patterns. We know from the enactment of our world and mind contextualized in a history of the variety of actions we perform. For any learning to occur, it requires both a body and a world (that is, the context).

Roots

In the beginning of this section, I mentioned that enactivism is grounded in two important views: the phenomenological work of Merleau-Ponty and the biological perspectives of Bateson. Consistent with Merleau-Ponty's view of ontological embodiment, enactivists think that meaning depends on the learner's conscious determination. According to the conceivers of enactivism (Varela et al., 1991), our body is not only a lived structure to experiences but also the setting for cognition. Embodiment, therefore, refers to the "developing process" of our interaction with the real world. It is not simply our beliefs or behaviors; rather, it is our ways of living and experiencing the world through our sensory and motor processes and perceptions. Knowledge is not only embodied, meaning there must be a learner to enact, but it is also situated where the context allows for the enactment of the learner actions (Menary, 2006).

The idea that cognition is embodied has been discussed widely and tested with numerous examples and experiments. For example, in the 1990s, Proffitt and colleagues (Proffitt, 1999; Proffitt, Bhalla, Grossweiler, & Midgett, 1995) from the University of Virginia conducted a series of psychological experiments exploring perceptions. They asked participants to judge how steep a mountain was before and after they exercised. Each participant would run a distance that he or she felt challenging. These exhausted participants then estimated the steepness of a different mountain immediately after they came back. For both shallow (5 degrees) and steep (30 degrees) mountains, participants viewed the mountain steeper after running than before their run. Later, the research team manipulated various factors with this experiment. They recruited different groups of participants and explored their perception under different conditions. They found that mountains looked steeper when people carry a heavy backpack. People who were less physically fit perceived the mountain steeper than those who were physically strong. Older people viewed the mountain steeper than younger people.

In a similar vein, some studies examined people's judgment of other people rather than nonliving objects like hills (Williams & Bargh, 2008). These researchers found that people who are holding a warm drink tend to view others as more warm and friendly; however, their perception changes when they hold a cold drink. More studies were conducted that explored the relationship between human emotional states and cognition. Utilizing the hills-appear-steeper studies as a catalyst, Riener, Stefanucci, Proffitt, and Clore (2011) asked participants to estimate the slope of a mountain in one of two conditions: one group listened to happy music (e.g., major key, upbeat) while the other group listened to sad music (minor key). The participants listening to the sad music perceived the hill steeper than the participants who listened to the happy music, demonstrating the close relationship between our emotions and perceptions. Examples like these illustrate clearly how our body and mind are connected and inseparable.

Origins of enactivism can also be traced to biological perspectives involving systems theory and cognitive theory. Renowned researchers in these areas include Bateson, Capra, Maturana, and Varela (Bateson, 1972; Capra, 2002; Maturana & Varela, 1987). The idea of autopoiesis heavily influences these theorists' thoughts. Autopoiesis refers to the auto-production process explaining the circular organization of living systems. In other words, enactivism does not view living systems as simply observation objects or interacting systems. It views them as closed systems that are autonomous, self-contained, self-referencing, and self-constructing (Maturana & Varela, 1980). They produce themselves endlessly, adjusting to their complex surroundings in an autopoietic manner. From this point of view, cognition is continuous with what other living systems (e.g., human, animals) do when they encounter a new situation that they adjust to in all their complexity. This may or may not be a cause of conscious construction but rather noticing, slowly, the light that dawns over the whole in the context of their need(s). One can go from a state of complete lack of understanding, puzzlement, bafflement, or mystification through a series of unconscious stages, until suddenly one can do whatever it is, individually or collectively.

All living systems, including plants, animals, and humans, have to be involved in cognition, and cognition is active rather than passive. Cognition, contrary to our common ideas, is a human and social as well as biological phenomenon. Our mind, body, and the world are inseparable. Learning is a complex process of learners adjusting to their dynamic environments and affecting each other; therefore, this causes not just mental but also biological changes.

A central idea of enactivism is *co-emergence*. Co-emergence focuses on the concept that the change of both a living system and its surrounding environment depends on the interaction between this system and the environment. For example the learner can never be separated from the environment in which she or he lives and learns. Hence, the learner's knowledge of his or her world depends on the environment in which the learner lives and the actions of which the learner is capable. When a system and an environment interact, they are structurally coupled and they co-emerge (Reid, 1995). It is important to note that there is no dichotomy (i.e., the learner and the environment), because any system and its context are inseparable.

Comparing Philosophical Paradigms

To better understand enactivism, it is useful to compare this new paradigm with other frameworks. Specifically, I compare enactivism with objectivism and constructivism, two views that have dominated the field of education in the last several decades. Objectivism, constructivism, and enactivism can be summarized as follows: "The objectivist says: 'I observe', the constructivist says: 'I think', and the enactivist says: 'I act'" (Begg, 2000, p. 2). In the following sections, I discuss these paradigms by examining their ontological and epistemological assumptions. These assumptions relate to ontology, which is a field of study focusing on the nature of reality, and epistemology, which studies the nature of knowledge and thoughts. To better orient you, I list the assumptions of each paradigm in Table 1.1, a table originally published in the *British Journal of Educational Technology* (Li et al., 2010).

It is important to emphasize that both objectivism and constructivism offer significant understanding of the learning process. At first glance, these two perspectives appear to be completely different. Yet, diving down deeper, one can see that objectivism and constructivism share similar assumptions. These assumptions lead to the limited application in education, and consequently, can profoundly misinform teaching practices (Davis et al., 2008). A noticeable such shared assumption is that cognition sits inside the individual's body, isolated from the world and other people. For both objectivism and constructivism, reality, or the real world, is separated from the mind, even though objectivists and constructivists have different views about where reality is located. Enactivism, on the other hand, rejects such a dualist view that divides self from world, mind from body, or subject from object. Therefore, enactivism emphasizes knowing while objectivism and constructivism focus on knowledge (Begg, 2000).

Holding an objectivist or an enactivist view would have different implications for classroom practices. Objectivism considers teachers as the experts who hold the absolute truth and knowledge to be transmitted to students. Lectures predominate as classroom practice and students simply replicate and try to master factual knowledge and skills. Enactivism asserts that teachers are not the only source of knowledge but coauthor knowledge with students through the design of a complex learning world. Rather than focusing on telling, teachers would guide students' attention toward the intended possible goals.

Table 1.1. *Comparison of Objectivism, Constructivism & Enactivism**

	Objectivism	**Constructivism**	**Enactivism**
Reality (real world)	• External to the knower • Structure determined by entities, properties, and relations; • Structure can be modeled	• Determined by the knower • Dependent upon human mental activity • Product of mind • Symbolic procedures construct reality • Structure relies on experience and interpretation	• We and the world are mutually specifying and co-emerging • Reality is dependent on the consciousness of the knower who determines the meaning (i.e., double-embodiment)
Mind	• Processor of symbols • Mirror of nature • Abstract machine for manipulating symbols	• Builder of symbols • Perceiver/interpreter of nature • Conceptual system for constructing reality	• Placed in embodied everyday experience • Cannot be separated from nature • The mind interprets and affects nature
Cognition	• Interpreted mechanistically • Governed by and reflect external reality • Independent of human experience • Mental is separated from physical • Action is the only access to cognition	• Interpreted mechanistically • Cognition is a process of organizing and interpretation of one's subjective experience • Mental is separated from physical	• Interpreted biologically • Cognition is a complex process of enactment of a world and a mind. • Mental and physical are inseparable and co-evolve
Knowledge	• External • Is a "thing" that can be acquired • Cognitive/conscious knowledge only • Knowledge is mental • Do not consider emotion	• Embedded inside inner self, internal • Is a "thing" • Constructed by the learner • Cognitive/conscious knowledge only • Knowledge is mental and physical but essentially human • Do not consider emotion	• Neither internal nor external, it depends. • Is not a "thing" but a domain of possibilities • Emerges from our ongoing interpretations necessary for successful action in an ever-evolving world • Both cognitive and

Epistemology

				• nonconscious knowledge • Knowledge is both mental and physical, not restricted to human. • Knowing is knowledge • Includes emotion
Dualism	• Inner vs. outer • Self vs. world/other • Subject vs. object • Mind vs. body • Knower vs. known • Action vs. mental	• Inner vs. outer • Self vs. world/other • Subject vs. object • Mind vs. body • Knower vs. known • Action vs. mental		• No dualism • Inseparable
Causal relationship	• Change the environment causes behaviour change • Same stimulus leads to same response	• Response is unique for each individual		• Learning and environment co-evolve constantly • No outcome can be exactly predicted or determined (taking the universe as a whole)

*Objectivist and constructivist assumptions in this table are adapted from Jonassen (2001), reprinted with permission from the *Educational Technology Research & Development* and the *British Journal of Educational Technology*.

Similarly, the distinction between enactivism and constructivism leads to different practices in classrooms. For constructivism, teachers establish learning environments in which students construct knowledge with teachers' facilitation. Although teachers and students negotiate objectives, such objectives are predetermined. Students' learning focuses on promoting their multiple interpretations of reality based on personal experience. Instructional strategies concentrate on student-centered activities, because it is the students who control the process of learning. Enactivism, in contrast, emphasizes co-evolving goals as opposed to predetermined objectives. Instead of focusing on a "single best sequence" of lessons for learning (Jonassen, 2001), teachers in enactivist classrooms build a rich learning world with abundant stimulation but enough limits to guide students toward possible co-evolving goals. Further, the physical, biological, and electronic systems are carefully crafted to merge together, resulting in a rich learning world. Learning activities are neither learner centered nor teacher centered, because the world and we are mutually specifying and co-emerge.

Foundations to Digital Games

Holding to the practice of establishing new ideals in education within theoretical frameworks, I briefly introduce three leading figures, Lev Vygotsky, Seymour Papert, and James Paul Gee, whose work has profoundly influenced the field of digital game-based learning. Note that research into digital games in education has gained popular interest since the 1990s, when computers started to enter many classrooms, and video games, in general, became more common. This was also the time when constructivism gained its momentum and began to dominate education research. Current work related to digital game-based learning, therefore, is often grounded on constructivism of its various versions.

Lev Vygotsky

Lev Vygotsky's writing has informed most contemporary theoretical discussions in education including social development theory, activity theory, sociocultural constructivism, distributed cognition, situated learning, and even enactivism. Vygotsky's work was primarily related to the exploration of the role of cultural artifacts, including tools, language, and people, as a resource for drawing the best out of everyone's cognitive potential. His theoretical contributions could be categorized into three main themes: cognitive development, social and cultural processes, and mediating tools and signs (Engestrom, 1999).

Dismissing the idea that development preceded learning (Holzman, 2010), an important concept Vygotsky developed was the Zone of Proximal Development (ZPD). He believed that proper activities occurring in children's ZPD could lead to cognitive development. ZPD refers to the skills or knowledge levels that are not fully developed but can emerge if appropriate support, that is, scaffolding, is provided (Vygotsky, 1978).

Vygotsky's (1976, 1978) possibly less well-known work was related to the exploration of "play" and the role of play in human development. In one of his writings (Vygotsky, 1976), Vygotsky explained that amongst various activities, play was most influential in children's development. During play,

Epistemology

children would immerse in an imaginary world in which they would develop and follow rules. Such processes would help the children's development of conceptual abilities and abstract thinking. Applying his famous concept of ZPD, Vygotsky discussed how a ZPD was constructed through play to advance children beyond their current skill or knowledge level. He argued the importance of play in child development process. Play, according to Vygotsky, would create a ZPD for children, enabling them to act beyond their own age and regular behaviour. Vygotsky's pioneer writing provided a foundation for digital game-based learning research and development (Vygotsky, 1978).

Seymour Papert

Inspired by constructivist theories, Seymour Papert coined the term *constructionism*. According to Papert (1993), constructionism stresses that learning occurs when learners actively reconstruct knowledge rather than it being transmitted from others. Further, cognitive development is best facilitated when learners are actively engaged in construing meaningful products. Constructionists emphasize learners' physical engagement with materials and their creation of artifacts of understanding. "Learning by game building" is one of the most representative approaches of constructionism, focusing on providing students the opportunities to construct their own games and new relationships with knowledge in the process. In this view, building is both a personal and social act, through which students learn and socialize. Learning environments that encourage learners to design and build, therefore, can and should be established to optimize motivation and structure without subverting personal discovery, exploration, and ownership of knowledge (Papert, 1980, 1993).

Papert has explored children and computers since the 1980s. His classic book, *Mindstorms* (Papert, 1980), added affective aspects of learning. To Papert,

> the child programs the computer, and in doing so, both acquires a sense of mastery over a piece of the most modern and powerful technology and establishes an intimate contact with some of the deepest ideas from sciences, from mathematics, and form the art of intellectual model building. (Papert, 1980, p. 5)

In *Mindstorms,* Papert proposed the idea of microworlds to be knowledge incubators. Microworlds, as Papert argued, should be designed as simple and accessible systems that offer possibilities (such as activities, games, art) to not only make the experience matter to learners but to also contain all needed concepts to be experienced by learners in the world. Unlike in schools, microworlds would focus on artifacts building, allowing trial and error ways of knowledge construction. Most importantly, students would be encouraged to learn through tinkering or exercising bricolage.

In his book *The Children's Machine* (1993), Papert stated that constructionism assumes that the best learning occurs when learners find themselves the specific knowledge they need. Attempting the "reconstruction of constructivism" (Papert, 1993, p. 143), he said that constructionism emphasizes the importance of physical constructions in learning, including the virtual constructions of digital artifacts. Papert developed his famous Logo programming language in 1967. Novice programmers, like young children, could learn math and science or other subjects through programming in Logo. The signature figure of Logo was an on-screen turtle. This turtle could be animated through programming, which provided immediate feedback to students with respect to their programming syntax.

James Paul Gee

James Paul Gee is a linguist and cognitive scientist. Inspired by his own experience of playing video games with his then 6-year-old son, he started his game-based learning research. Primarily grounded on his own rich experiences, Gee has been exploring how video games can offer better learning theories in cognitive science. Emphasizing situated learning, Gee argues that digital games can offer a particularly appropriate context to promote learning through embodied experiences. Players in video games are immersed in a world of action, and learning is enhanced through such action-rich and carefully scaffolded experiences (Gee, 2008b).

Gee's work provides a vision and framework for people who are interested in educational uses of digital games. Unlike many researchers in the field of educational games, Gee takes a unique approach by extracting best learning principles from video games. Neither supporting nor arguing against the use of digital games in classrooms, he believes that the focus of educators should be the application of effective learning principles that good digital games have adopted, with or without using games as the bearer to realize these principles (Gee, 2008a, 2009).

Epistemology

In 2003, Gee published his book, *What Video Games Have to Teach Us About Learning and Literacy*, which has become one of the most important works on video games, learning, and cognition. Examining specific video games along with how the games are played, he discusses how a series of learning principles are manifested in the process of people playing and mastering video games. In the book, he summarizes a total of 36 learning principles for creating effective learning environments. These 36 principles are grouped into three categories centered on learners. The categories include the following: empowered learners, problem solving, and understanding. The empowered learners category includes "codesign," "customize," "identity," and "manipulation and distributed knowledge" principles to stress that we need to empower learners by actively engaging them to design and customize their own learning, as well as to take on new identities. The problem solving category constitutes the following concepts: "well-ordered problems," "pleasantly frustrating," "cycles of expertise," "information on-demand and just-in-time," "fish tanks," "sandboxes," and "skills as strategies." These principles emphasize the idea of careful scaffolding and ordering of problems in order to construct a safe and authentic context for learning. In his third category, understanding, Gee discusses both "systems thinking" and "meaning as action image." Systems thinking, to Gee, means considering contents as systems with embedded values and following naturally reinforced rules. In this way, students learn from their experiences instead of from lectures.

Gee's theory related to identity is worthy of further discussion because it is an important concept related to gaming and learning. Gee points out that in a digital game environment, a player can have three kinds of identities: his or her real-life identities, virtual identities, and projective identities (Gee, 2008b). He posits that a player's real-life identities refer to his or her identities as a person we see daily, such as a male student in a high school who loves to play basketball. When the student plays a video game, his avatar becomes his virtual identity. For example, my son Richard's virtual identity in the *Sims 3* game is his avatar Pooga, a middle-aged, workaholic, environmental engineer. The projective identity is the identity that the player wants the avatar to be, how it acts, and what it believes. The kind of person Richard wants Pooga to be, and the ways Richard wants Pooga to behave, become the projective identities—of Richard's real identities projected on to his virtual Pooga identities. When Richard assumes this virtual identity, he develops greater understanding of environmental engineering through his immersion and investment in the new role. Similarly, learners must have a solid knowledge base of the roles and responsibilities of the identity that they desire to embody.

Previously, I briefly introduced three leading figures whose work has largely shaped research related to digital, game-based learning. People play digital games, regardless of their gender, age, socioeconomic status, race, education, or occupation. The popularity of digital game play across these various population groups has therefore resulted in digital games gaining increased attention in the field of education. The work of Vygotsky provides the philosophical grounding for many theoretical perspectives including sociocultural constructivism. Papert's writing and his development work create the base to offer opportunities for children to learn through digital game design. Gee's contribution affords a theoretical framework for us to consider how to design interactive learning experiences, game based or otherwise. Together, their work provides a foundation for the field of digital, game-based learning.

As discussed at the beginning of this chapter, the information presented here is more theoretical than the rest of the book. While I understand that the theory and historical roots of my perspective may not be for everyone, I felt compelled to share my knowledge in the hopes of better informing you about my perspective on teaching and learning with digital games. Going forward, you will find more real-life scenarios and ideas applicable to the classroom.

Summary of Projects

Throughout this book, I frequently relate the discussion with some of the projects we conducted in recent years to support my arguments or to provide concrete examples. In an attempt to paint a coherent picture, I have provided brief information of these projects in Table 1.2.

I summarize each project here to contextualize what comes later. Details of the projects are depicted in various parts of the book. Software we used in the projects includes Scratch, Kodu, and Gamestar Mechanics. Further description of the game design software is provided later in Section 4 of this book.

The Call of Math project involved first-year students at a Canadian university enrolled in a secondary mathematics methods course as part of their degree program. I was the instructor, and the game-design process started with a two-hour introduction session where the students played and

Epistemology

evaluated free online games (e.g., *Crayon Physics*). After an hour of play, each student worked in a small group to create a lesson plan. The only requirement was that the lesson had to use one of the games to teach an algebraic concept. Since many students were nongamers, such activities enabled them to become familiar with this media. For students who were gamers, this exercise gave them an opportunity to reexamine digital games through the eyes of teachers, focusing on educational values rather than just the entertainment value of the games.

Table 1.2. *Learning-by-Game-Design projects*

Project	Core Participants	Contents learned by participants	Context	Contents of the games developed
Call of Math	Secondary math preservice teachers	Math Methods	Curriculum course for preservice teachers (F2F*)	Secondary math
Why Read If I Can Build	Grade 6 classes	Math and science	Normal Elementary classes (F2F)	Math and science
Do It Yourself	Practicing teachers	Game based learning	One F2F graduate class and one online graduate class	Varied (e.g., math, social studies)
The Driven	Graduate students	Game based learning	Graduate students taking independent studies	Driving rules
Run for Math	High school math students	Math	High school math classes in a self-directed learning environment	Math
Games in Motion	Elementary students	Math and science	Summer camp classes	Math and science

*F2F: face-to-face

A few weeks later, the students had a three-hour class focusing on game design and paper prototyping. At the beginning of the class, students were asked to adapt their favourite movies into board games. In small groups, students came up with their game design, paper prototyped their ideas, and then play tested each other's games. During this session, no computer was used. While play testing a game, everyone in the class was engaged either as an observer or as a player. The designers were asked to refrain from talking or showing but were instructed to simply observe what players were doing. I gave verbal feedback after each game was tested.

In the middle of the semester, the students began to develop their own game ideas. I introduced the software Scratch in a class and allowed the students to play with it for about one hour. An online forum was also created for these students to discuss ideas, help others, and share resources. For example, I provided a link introducing the software Kudo in this forum and encouraged students to explore it. They had the freedom to use any software platform, but Scratch was the only one being introduced in a face-to-face class. At the end of the semester, they spent two hours showcasing and playing each other's games as a celebration.

During this process, I provided no instruction on how they were to choose an algebraic topic. They were also not required to research the uses of games in teaching mathematics. Two researchers attended classes regularly to collect data and provide some technical support (Li, Lemieux, Vandermeiden, & Nathoo, 2013).

Do It Yourself was a two-year project conducted with practicing teachers who enrolled in my graduate course. The game design process in this course was similar to the structure of the Call of Math project, except the content was not focused on secondary mathematics. As a result, practicing teachers were allowed to design lessons and games focusing on the learning of any subject, ranging from elementary mathematics, to high school chemistry, to babysitting. The practicing teachers were encouraged to design games for their own students or students of their colleagues. In this project, no one chose to modify existing games (modding), although it was allowed.

In the Why Read If I Can Build project, three elementary teachers and their 86 Grade 6 students participated. This project focused on math and science and lasted one school year. Amongst the three teachers, one teacher, Sam, was a graduate student who participated in the Do It Yourself project the year before. Through his participation in the Do It Yourself project, Sam acquired not only theoretical knowledge on game-based learning but also practical programming skills using Scratch. In the Why Read If I Can Build project, Sam served as the expert on the teacher team: He was not only the main driving force for the implementation of the game project but also the technology consultant for all students during the project.

At the beginning of the project, I worked with the teachers, mainly Sam, to design the game integration process. We decided to start the game activities using Gamestar Mechanics. That is, we introduced the ideas of game design through Gamestar Mechanics, where design principles were integrated into game play. For about three weeks, students worked together to play and build games using the Gamestar engine. They were also encouraged to publish their newly built games to the Gamestar community. While working in small groups, the students were intentionally mixed together to better match their different skill sets and to promote higher level collaboration.

Then, Scratch was introduced, first by showing the "Scratch Intro Facilitorial" video (http://youtu.be/jxDw-t3XWd0), which provides basic information about Scratch. Students were given one class period to freely explore the Scratch websites. In the next two weeks, for one hour each day, students worked individually or with a partner on small Scratch challenges that Sam created. These challenges were based on the Scratch "cards" (http://info.scratch.mit.edu/Support/Scratch_Cards), and samples of these challenges are discussed later. Each teacher was provided with the answers to the challenges. These activities allowed students to gain basic programming skills with Scratch.

Next, students were divided into teams of three, and each team explored the Math Fair websites (http://www.mathfair.com/, http://www.galileo.org/math/puzzles.html). Each team tried to solve the different online puzzles and problems and later determined which puzzle or problem they would program in Scratch. This game-building process lasted two months, where for about one hour per day and four days a week, class time was devoted to building the games. After all the games were completed, students were given a class to publish their favourite Scratch and Gamestar games on a communal website where they could share their work with each other and create an archive of games. Each week, at least two researchers went to the school to observe the classes, and we met with the teachers regularly.

The Driven was a four-month project where graduate students designed games to teach drivers road rules. All but one student in education were teamed with engineering students who had strong backgrounds in programming. The only student who worked alone had a bachelor's degree in computer science and was pursuing a master's degree in educational technology. During the project, no workshop or any formal instruction was provided. However, students were provided readings to help them better understand game design and learning. The whole group met monthly to share initial game design, play test game prototypes, brainstorm ideas, and get feedback.

A preservice teacher who participated in the Call of Math project initiated the Run for Math project. Her involvement in the Call of Math project inspired her to test how digital games could be used in secondary mathematics classrooms. She worked with five teachers to implement the project, involving a total of 40 students in a Canadian high school practicing a self-directed study model (Trump, 1970). In this six-week study, students self selected themselves to be either in a treatment group or a control group. For the control group, students learned mathematics through the traditional self-directed learning approach. Students in the treatment group were offered an alternative project: building a game to teach others specific math content. Choosing one of the mathematics units determined by the mathematics department, these students could work individually or in small groups to design and develop their games to demonstrate their learning. Approved units included those from precalculus mathematics and consumer finance courses.

The students in the treatment group completed a five-stage project: Kodu tutorials, game planning, building, reflection, and celebration. The first stage required students to complete the tutorials in Kodu, introducing the basic Kodu software programming. The second stage asked students to write a game proposal with a storyline, target audience, and a student-developed list of mathematics components to be included in the game. Teachers approved the proposals before students moved to the game building stage. Upon completion of their game, students were asked to produce a written summary, delineating a game description, an outline of the mathematics involved, and a detailed solution set for mathematics problems included in the game. Finally, students celebrated by sharing, evaluating and playing each other's games. Before the project, I met with the preservice teacher to exchange ideas and adjust the instructional activities.

The Games in Motion project was conducted during a two-week summer camp (Li, 2010). The focus of the camp was mathematics and science with an overarching theme of "Mission to Mars." Three adults, besides myself, were involved in the daily coordination of the camp:

- The camp instructor was a high school science teacher who had no prior knowledge of game-based learning and was mainly responsible for preparing and implementing all teaching activities.
- The teacher assistant was a student enrolled in a preservice teacher education program and was responsible for other activities such as supervising lunch breaks.

Epistemology

- The volunteer was a high school student helping with various miscellaneous activities such as photocopying and distributing worksheets.

I was the fourth adult in the classroom as the researcher and the technical supporter. I worked with students every day, providing them technical support for using Scratch.

Daily activities included watching movies related to the "Mission to Mars" theme, participating in hands-on mathematics and science experiments (e.g., building rockets using papers and other materials), and creating artistic works (e.g., designing a "Mission to Mars" badge and spacesuit). Scientific concepts such as Isaac Newton's three laws of motion were integrated into various activities. The students were asked to work individually or with a partner to develop games to teach others one of Newton's three laws.

Due to limited access, students were able to work in the computer lab for only one hour per day during the first week of camp, and half an hour per day for four days in the second week of camp. The only formal, whole class instruction related to game design and building was my five-minute presentation on the second day of the camp, introducing Scratch (Li, 2010).

In summary, the six projects described here followed a similar pattern. That is, regardless of where they were conducted, a minimal amount of formal instruction was provided. Unlike traditional classrooms, students in these projects were given ample opportunities to explore, to play, to take risks, to discover, to fail, to test, to build, and ultimately, to learn through such actions.

Enactivist Learning World: Games and Web 2.0

Creating a Learning World

In the previous section, I argued that enactivism provides a better and more comprehensive worldview than other theoretical grounding. This being said, one might wonder where (and how) the theory of enactivism meets actual classroom practice. This section attempts to answer such a curiosity. In this book, I purposefully use "a learning world" instead of "a learning environment" to distinguish enactivist approaches from constructivist approaches.

The adoption of enactivism implies that teachers are focusing on the creation of a learning world, a world that, in many ways, mirrors the complex system of the world surrounding us (Li et al., 2010). In this learning world, students are immersed in rich and stimulating experiences. The world provides ample spaces for free exploration and at the same time has enough restrictions. Such constraints are built in intentionally to foster students' development toward the set of intended possible objectives. Authority is reframed; students are no longer passive receivers of knowledge. Instead, they become coauthors of their learning environments, their learning, and their ways of knowing and knowledge. Doing is highly valued and becomes the center of all activities.

One promising example of such a learning world is one that incorporates digital games and Web 2.0 technologies. In a game designed as complex environments of interrelated parts mirroring our real world, students are engrossed and controlled by the design of the game to act in specific ways. Such a game environment can produce a multimodal space that reflects not only the complexity of the cyberworld but also the ramifications of the social relationships and identities in our modern world. This space, with situated meanings, allows students to solve problems through embodied experiences. Here, as players and creators, students interact, enact in and with this environment, co-evolving with not only the cyberworld but also the real world. They learn by doing in the confined world manifested through software and social systems. They develop situated understanding through persistent experimenting, constructing, failing, and continued problem solving.

For instance, we can develop a learning world where students create games that teach specific content. Students work with teachers to design this world. This means that students are coauthors and codesigners of the learning goals they want to achieve, the instructional activities in which they want to engage, and the evaluative tools that will be used to measure their achievements. In this learning world, students are presented with enough structure and scaffolding to ensure sustained focus on certain content. Yet, this world provides great freedom and openness so that students can actively explore the content with enthusiasm. Through their experience of game building and sharing, students accept powerful values connected to their virtual and real identities (e.g., as designer, as teacher). In this world, students build mental models, play games, develop and evaluate outcomes, and revise their actions, all of which guide them toward the intended possible objectives (Li et al., 2010).

In order to provide a concrete example of an enactivist learning world, I describe our work during the Why Read If I Can Build project in Grade 6 classrooms. Curriculum was carefully integrated into various aspects of the learning activities that helped to establish the learning world. Students not only played games, but they also adopted the dual identities as game designers and codesigners of their own learning. Students' learning and engagement were further enhanced by the well-timed scaffolding provided, allowing them to solve challenging problems with the right tools. We immersed students in complex situations where they needed to work with their peers to identify problems, explore possible solutions, and experiment with their ideas. Such complex situations were a combination of planned activities and unexpected, naturally evolved affairs. Learning (on both the student and teacher sides) was exploratory and experimental, just like the environments in which mathematicians and scientists work daily. Instead of strictly following the preplanned sequential instructional events, teachers understood the fluid nature of this learning world, and they worked with students, at their own pace, designing and planning different activities.

To show how daily events can evolve and be integrated into teaching activities in an enactivist world, let me share with you another story of Sam. Part of this story was originally published in the journal of Educational Technology Research and Development, see Li (2012). Sam, who was taking a graduate course at the same time he was involved in the project, was assigned the task of designing and developing an educational digital game. With his Grade 6 students in mind, Sam designed a game called *Myth-Givings: Sparta vs. Athens*, aiming to teach sixth-grade social studies on Greek religion, art, culture, and society. *Myth-Givings* was a two-player role-playing game where the environment allowed the players to explore. Through such exploration, they would learn about Ancient Greek culture and society.

As educational game designers, we try our best to avoid so-called chocolate-covered-broccoli games (a term used to describe games where the play is framed as a *reward* for the uninteresting task of learning). Sam was no exception. In his own words, he "pureed the broccoli," that is, the content, in his design of the game so as to organically embed content learning into the game play. The *Myth-Givings* game included a rich set of information to assist students navigate game challenges. Such design enabled students to build knowledge through game play, with or without them noticing they were learning. In addition to embedding the content, Sam also encouraged personal inquiry into game-related topics by inspiring students' natural curiosity. In Sam's design document, he described details of his game:

> Like in the card game *War*, *Myth-Givings* involves two players who compete for resources: The player who receives the highest score wins a virtual gift, something the player needs to advance. When meeting all of his or her needs, a player could see the surplus and use the income to construct buildings or develop an army, on his or her way to victory. The game contains three levels: 1) gathering resources, 2) building a city, and 3) ending the game. In Level 1, players try to acquire basic resources as much as possible because resources appear very infrequently and special foods are rare. At the second level, building a city, players spend their resources building a city with few affordable options at the start. They have to consider strategic advantages for the end game and balance between special foods and resources. The third level, ending the game, gives player two options: 1) to complete a temple by using the resources gathered, or 2) to conquer the other player's kingdom by developing buildings and the military with the resources collected.

Sam believed this game building project created a wonderfully complex real-life situation for his sixth-grade classes. He invited students to help with the game design process, from testing to programming. Students became really engaged and proud. Many told their parents the following: "This is the work we are doing to help Mr. Sam with his UNIVERSITY HOMEWORK!"

In a play-testing session, Sam identified a problem: Athens seemed to win a lot more often than Sparta, despite the design intention of each side winning an equal number of times. Seeing this as an excellent opportunity to engage his students in complex problem solving, Sam presented them with the following concern: "Athens seems to win more. What should I do?" Students were excited that they were now trying to solve Mr. Sam's problem, an authentic problem that was much more exciting than those offered in the textbook. Sam and his students started to brainstorm and talk. After much discussion, students made the connection between Sam's problem and their current mathematics curriculum, which involved probability and data management.

During this process, many students realized that the first thing they needed to do was to identify the problem. Was it true that Athens had more chance to win? How could we find out the answer? After careful consideration of these questions, students decided to use the four-phase

Epistemology 31

scientific procedure: establishing a hypothesis, collecting relevant data, analyzing data to test the hypothesis, then disproving or confirming the hypothesis.

The hypothesis here was that Athens and Sparta did not have an even chance to win, so the students designed their first experiment to test this hypothesis. They decided on the sample size (e.g., how many rounds of games to play), identified the data collection methods (e.g., first collect data individually and then collectively), and chose the appropriate analysis approaches. The result of this experiment showed that Athens won 87 times while Sparta won only 73 times. This is not 50/50, and therefore the game was not balanced; this confirmed their hypothesis. Identifying this problem logically led students to explore what caused the problem.

Through further analysis of the game, the students suspected that the frequency of certain cards' appearance (cards are the mechanism in the game to provide a player with resources) caused the problem of an uneven chance to win. This second hypothesis guided the students to design a second experiment. They soon realized that this experiment was more complicated than testing the first hypothesis because there were many cards, and the cards did not have an equal chance of appearing in the game. Sam gave students ample in-class time to discuss and debate what strategies to use. Finally, students chose to compare the frequency of cards to the tables in Sam's original design. After several rounds of data collection, refinement, and analysis, they identified that five of the "loser" cards—because of their low score—did not appear for Athens but appeared twice as frequently as they should for Sparta. The discovery of such cards allowed Sam to identify the bug in the game and revise his program to solve the problem. The students helped retest the game afterward, and the results showed that Athens and Sparta were winning an equal number of times (Li, 2012).

This story demonstrates how everyday experience can be organically folded into meaningful instructional activities to create authentic learning opportunities. An equally important lesson learned from this story is how learning co-evolves and does not follow predetermined trajectories. Sam originally designed a game to encourage students to learn more about Ancient Greece. He initially involved his students in his game design attempting to inspire their curiosity about the social studies content. An unintended result, according to Sam, was that students took "ownership" of his university homework, something that made them feel quite proud. The students used Sam's beta testing problem and independently made the connection with their math learning to solve his problem with the gaming code.

Again, Sam's original objective for involving students was to help them learn social studies. Yet, Sam was not restricted by such preplanned learning goals. Instead, a world with a great degree of freedom was established where students had a chance to explore real-world challenges and deal with situations that required authentic problems to be identified, tested, and solved. With limited teacher interference or direction, students independently explored how the probability learned in math and the social studies contents were presented in the game. According to Sam, he never intended for his students to debug his game design problem. However, while they were engaged in meaningful discourses, students autonomously offered to search for, and solve, the problem. This required students to integrate their learning of different subjects and apply their newly learned knowledge. In the end, they learned a lot more through this experience than they could have by simply reading and regurgitating rules, whether it was mathematics, science, or social studies.

By engaging students in the messy situations inherent in game design, Sam and other teachers observed how such authentic real-life problems inspired their students to apply their knowledge in different contexts. Impacted so much by what they saw and how students in such a learning world created unexpected synergy, Sam and his colleagues started to modify their subsequent teaching practices that better aligned with enactivist principles.

Sam also observed a phenomenon that he called 'cross-pollination of ideas.' That is, the open and explorative nature of the learning world promoted a culture where students and teachers shared thoughts and further were influenced by each other's work in this learning world. For example, students adopted some cards used in Sam's game. Game ideas from one group would inspire and inform other groups and vice versa. In a way, everyone in this learning world became a partial designer of all of the games, because each game embodied ideas of other people in the groups. The cross-pollination phenomenon clearly demonstrated that Sam and his students switched their identities from the traditional teacher-student roles to codesigners of both the games and their learning. The shift of students' roles from passive learners to active codesigners of learning is particularly important because it indicated that students took ownership of their learning.

Such ownership led to more engaged students and their deeper understanding of content knowledge.

To sum up, in this story, Sam integrated his university work of game design, a seemingly simple assignment, into his sixth-grade teaching. The impact of this student involvement was reflected in students' learning of math and social studies, changes of teachers' beliefs about pedagogy, and the cross-pollination of ideas between teachers and students. These changes were not determined ahead of time but rather naturally evolved. This further confirmed the enactivist principle that learners (students) co-emerge with their learning world as well as with others, including teachers, in that world.

In many ways, Sam's story presents a concrete example of an enactivist learning world. As discussed earlier, a possible way to establish an enactivist environment is to integrate digital games and Web 2.0 tools. We can adapt the learning by game building approach where students are immersed in designing and developing digital games for others to use. Students take the identity of a game designer and coauthor of their own learning. In this world, students are immersed in complex problem-solving situations that reflect or mirror real-life situations, capturing and highlighting students' interests. The learning world provides ample spaces for students to freely explore and to interact with the content in an interdisciplinary way. They work collaboratively within and across different social groups. Such social groups can be formed in real life, like in students' courses, school activities, or in virtual worlds, including online game communities like *Sims 3*.

NOTE: In this book, I try to describe the experiences that occurred during our projects using the students' own words whenever possible. However, to provide you with fluid reading, I may or may not use quotation marks. In addition, pseudonyms are used to protect participants' privacy.

• CHAPTER TWO •

Key Elements

Contextualized in the historical studies of learning by game building (e.g., earlier work of using Logo and other programs for learning), this chapter explains the definitions of key concepts including the following: game, rules, learning by game building, and Web 2.0. Then it discusses elements of games (e.g., player, goals, resources, materials) and explores characteristics of good games.

A Brief History of Learning by Game Building

The computer game industry started to grow in the 1980s along with the introduction of educational games. These educational games are often referred to as *edutainment* games because, as the name suggests, they attempt to blend education and entertainment. While many edutainment games developed, only several edutainment games, including *Where in the World Is Carmen San Diego?* and the *Oregon Trail*, were successful. These interactive adventure games became popular because they promote interactive storytelling. These games are contextualized in stories where people play and learn through solving puzzles.

During the same period, learning by game design and building began to gain researchers' attention. In the United States, one of the most famous and probably the earliest research programs in this area was based around the Logo project using Logo developed by Seymour Papert and his team. As I mentioned earlier, the goal of the original Logo project was to create a math land where young children can play with words and sentences. During the play, students learn programming, logical thinking, and mathematics, amongst other topics. The virtual turtles (an onscreen cursor) showing on the screen gives player immediate visual feedback and enable modification. Numerous studies emerged from this work (e.g. diSessa, 2000; Kafai, 1995; Wilensky & Reisman, 2006). Papert's followers have continued exploration of this approach. Their work has demonstrated that students' creative investment during game building directly contributes to their understanding of the content of the games they created. Game building, an effortful and metacognitively guided process, provides meaningful and contextualized learning. Beyond Logo, various game building tools have been developed, including Scratch and StarLogo TNG, along with flurries of research studies exploring the use of such tools (e.g. Klopfer & Begel, 2003; Li, 2010). Some of these studies have looked at how students work as scientists through game building. In one study (Klopfer, Scheintau, Huang, Wendel, & Roque, 2009), students used StarLogo TNG to first create computer models simulating real-world phenomena. They then investigated, evaluated, and critiqued such models. Combining games and simulation with science learning, students had enhanced understanding of the content knowledge. Further, students were highly motivated to learn and be able to exercise their creative muscle.

Games and Squire has provided a good summary of research in this field in their paper (2011) and I borrow some of their discussions in this section to contextualize this discourse. In Europe, several landmark projects have also been conducted (Noss & Hoyles, 2006) to explore the potential and limitations of learning by game design and building. The Playground Project in the United Kingdom used the Toontalk software (Kahn, 1996) to create a digital playground for students, particularly young children, to build and play their own games. Game avatars and objects as well as touch, speech and gesture in virtual reality are all integrated into this digital playground. Students build games by training robots to operate concrete program elements such as cars and houses. Research papers emerged from the project, exploring students' game design and building experiences.

In fact, many software systems with the same focus have developed in both the United States and Europe (Games & Squire, 2011). In the United States, Stagecast Creator (2001) and Agentsheets (Borgman, BAbelson, Dirks, Jahonson, K., Linn, Lynch, Oblinger, Pea, Salen, Smith, & Szalay, 2008) are two examples of game design environments adapting different graphical approaches to foster students' learning by digital game design. More recently, Scratch, software developed at the Massachusetts Institute of Technology, allows novices to easily create digital games, interactive stories, or animations. GameStar Mechanic, another research and development project originally funded by the Macarthur Foundation, provides an online community of game design to help children learn to think and communicate like game designers. In Europe, for example, Game Maker is a game development platform for nonprogrammers, developed in the Netherlands (Habgood & Overmars, 2006). In a nutshell, learning by game design and building has been an active line of research and development since the early 1980s in the field of education and games.

Key Concepts

Increasingly, educators and scholars are noticing the great educational potential of games. The use of games in classrooms can be roughly broken down into three approaches. The first approach is to use standard games, such as *SimCity* and *StarCraft*, in an educational context. For example, games like *Portal* or *Crayon Physics* can teach students physics principles, while *Sims 3* can create an understanding of social systems.

The second approach involves creating educational games that focus on certain instructional objectives. Some games like *Oregon Trail* and *MathBlaster* are examples of educational games. Yet, it is commonly admitted that many of these games are of poor quality, due to various reasons.

The third approach, which is the focus of this book, provides learners opportunities to design and create their own games through which students learn. In this book, the term *game building* is used to include the process of designing and creating games. There are many ways to describe this pedagogical approach of game design and building. Originated from Papert's idea of "learning by making," people use different terms in the field of game-based learning to describe this approach. Such terms as 'learning by game building', 'learning through game building', or 'learning as game building' are essentially describing the same idea. In this book, I use these terms interchangeably.

In the following section, I discuss some key concepts, including game, play, and core game elements. These concepts provide a foundation for game design, and therefore, they deserve our careful consideration.

What Is Game?

In this book focusing on learning through game design and building, a clear definition of game is important. Many definitions exist already. Some definitions put more focus on rules and objectives. For example, Schreiber described game as a "play activity with rules that involves conflict" (2009, p. 10). Clark C. Abt (1970) said the following: "A game is an activity involving player decisions, seeking objectives within a limiting context (i.e. rules)" (p. 9).

Epistemology

Other definitions provide more details that focus on the properties of games. Definitions provided by Roger Callois and Chris Crawford are among these:

> A game has six properties: It is "free" (playing is optional and not obligatory), "separate" (fixed in space and time, in advance), has an uncertain outcome, is "unproductive" (in the sense of creating neither goods nor wealth—note that wagering *transfers* wealth between players but does not create it), is governed by rules, and is "make believe" (accompanied by an awareness that the game is not Real Life, but is some kind of shared separate "reality").
>
> (Caillois, 2001)

> Games have four properties. They are a
>
> - "closed, formal system" (this is a fancy way of saying that they have rules; "formal" in this case means that it can be defined, not that it involves wearing a suit and tie);
> - they involve interaction;
> - they involve conflict; and
>
> they offer safety . . . at least compared to what they represent (for example, American Football is certainly not what one would call perfectly safe—injuries are common—but as a game it is an abstract representation of warfare, and it is certainly more safe than being a soldier in the middle of combat).
>
> (Crawford, 1984, as cited in Schreiber, 2009, p. 9)

Katie Salen and Eric Zimmerman explained that games are a "system in which players engage in an artificial conflict, defined by rules, that results in a quantifiable outcome" (Salen & Zimmerman, 2003, p. 80).

As can be inferred from these definitions, historically, games without explicit or clear objectives, like *SimCity* or *Sims 3*, are not considered games but rather toys. Now, more people are holding a broadened view and admitting that puzzle games, sandbox games, or even *Second Life* are games, although some consider them as virtual worlds. For the purpose of this book, game is defined in a narrow form that constitutes rules, goals, and interactivity, although virtual worlds and other games like the *Sims* provide the perfect platform for game-based learning. This decision of defining game in a narrow form is made based on two considerations: 1) It provides clear and simple language for the discussion of learning by game designing and developing, and 2) learners would most likely build games in the more narrow forms.

Schreiber (2009) compared these seemingly diverse definitions and summarized the following common elements of games:

- Games are an activity.
- Games have rules.
- Games have conflict.
- Games have goals.
- Games involve decision making.
- Games are artificial, they are safe, and they are outside ordinary life. This is sometimes referred to as the players stepping into the "Magic Circle" or sharing an "elusory attitude."
- Games involve no material gain on the part of the players.
- Games are voluntary. If you are held at gunpoint and forced into an activity that would normally be considered a game, some would say that it is no longer a game *for you*. (Something to think about: if you accept this, then an activity that is voluntary for some players and compulsory for others may or may not be a game ... depending on whose point of view you are looking at.)
- Games have an uncertain outcome.
- Games are a representation or simulation of something real, but they are themselves make believe.
- Games are inefficient. The rules impose obstacles that prevent the player from reaching their goal through the most efficient means.
- Games have systems. Usually, it is a closed system, meaning that resources and information do not flow between the game and the outside world.
- Games are a form of art.

(p. 11)

We understand that each definition has its own pros and cons and none of the definitions fits everything. What is important is that such diverse definitions of game allow us to have a broad understanding of what games can entail. Such understanding, in turn, can inform important design considerations when adapting the learning by game design approach.

Play

Play, with its many meanings, is a concept that is obviously closely related to games. In English, the terms *play* and *game* are sometimes used interchangeably. If someone is playing a game, the person is called a player. In some other languages, there are no distinct words for play and game. For example, in Chinese, the term 游戏 (pronounced *YouHsi*) can be used as a verb or a noun. When it is used as a noun, it means game. When used as a verb, it means to play. Playing make-believe, kicking a soccer ball, and

Epistemology

playing chess all are examples of different kinds of play. Schreiber (2009) has discussed the relationship between games and play, indicating that on the one hand, games can be considered as a kind of play. On the other hand, a game includes many elements, such as rules, resources, actions, and stories. We play games, hence, play is one aspect of games. Is this a paradox, then? Can play and games be the same? Well, it depends. For this book, it does not matter. What is important is that play and games are two closely connected ideas. We need to understand them both when adopting the learning by game design approach.

In the earlier chapter introducing Vygotsky's work, I discussed some of his writing related to play to a large extent. Play is a universal concept. Everybody, in every culture, at every stage, plays. While different people developed various categories of play, Piaget described three types of play: practice play, symbolic play, and games with rules (Piaget, 1962). Salen and Zimmerman (2003) proposed three types of play from different angles: game play, ludic activities, and being playful. Game play refers to the formal experience of players interacting with the game system. The second type, ludic activities, includes not only game play activities but also other nongame playing behaviours. The third type is being playful, representing both play activities and the mental state of play embodied in other demeanours. Other definitions state that play is the "activities which are accompanied by a state of comparative pleasure, exhilaration, power, and the feeling of self-initiative" (Gilmore, 1971, p.316). In this book, I adopt the definition provided by Salen and Zimmerman (2003), which describes play as free activities with constraints. This definition includes all three groups of play, and more importantly, it offers valuable information particularly relevant for game design.

We can attain a lot from play, from cognitive benefits to social-emotional gains. For example, brain-based research experiments on rats have discovered that play improves memory and stimulates brain growth (see Pellegrini & Holmes, 2006 for a review). While no such experiments can be conducted on humans due to ethical reasons, it is widely believed that the same principle would apply to people. Existing clinical work has demonstrated that play promotes creative problem solving and helps develop language and mathematics skills. As discussed earlier, Vygotsky has convincingly argued the importance of play, stating that it leads to social, emotional, and cognitive development.

Researchers have explored various kinds of game play and have categorized game into three main aspects in terms of play: game as the play of experience, game as the play of pleasure, and game as the play of meaning (Salen & Zimmerman, 2003). In their book, Salen and Zimmerman (2003) explain that the first of these categories suggests that game playing really is experiencing the game world. Players feel, manipulate, smell, look, examine, hear, taste, and move in the game space. Their experiences in the game world are participatory, allowing them to live through the events of the game and be a part of the game itself.

The second category refers to game as the play of pleasure. Pleasure is a sensation that can be physical, emotional, psychological, or even ideological. We often play games because we believe it will bring fun and pleasure. We know that games are rule bound, and players are expected to follow the rules. By doing so, are players less likely to have fun? Is the experience less pleasurable because of the rules they need to follow? We would say no! Vygotsky's work clearly indicates that a player accepts the game rules to maximize the pleasure of the game play rather than limit it.

The third category, focusing on game as the play of meaning, suggests that players have to make meaning out of the game experience. Game play involves both a game system, which includes the mechanics such as rules and subject, and context, which is the actual game space in which the playing experience occurs. Together, the game system and context, as well as the interplay of the two components, provide the overall meaning of a game (Salen & Zimmerman, 2003).

Game Elements

Opening any game design book, you will find that key elements of a game include players, objectives, rules, resource management, sequence, player interaction, and narratives. These key elements are essential aspects to be focused on when designing a game. Next, I borrow Schreiber's (2009) list and his ways of explanation to describe these key elements of a game.

First, let's consider players since a game would be meaningless if no one plays it. A game can be a single player or multiplayer game, or the player number can be changed within a range. Some games allow players to start and leave the game at any time while others are restricted. One can play against the game system (e.g., *Pac-Man*), or another player (e.g., *Go*), or a team can play against the game system (e.g., *World of Warcraft*).

Epistemology

The second element centers around the goals or objectives of the game. What are the goals of the game? Typical goals are capture, territorial control, race/escape, build, solve, and spatial alignment. In *Chess*, you try to capture and destroy your opponents' pieces. In *Go*, you try to occupy as much land as possible. In *Super Mario*, you try to race as fast as you can. These are the goals that make each game interesting and engaging.

The third essential element is rules, which are sometimes called a game's mechanics. They are vital because they control the whole game play. Well-designed rules contribute to a good game. For example, how do we set up rules that are appropriate and make the best game playing experience? How do we start, end, or progress in the game? How does the game state affect the results? Rules give answers to these questions. People have summarized the essential characteristics of game rules: They provide limits to players' action; they should be clear and explicit; every player agrees and follows the same rules; while rules in each game cannot be changed, they can be repeated.

Although there are different ways to categorize game rules, two types of rules, operational and implied rules, are important to realize. Operational rules are the ones that set up how to start a game, guide what happens during the play, determine when to end the game, and decide the outcomes of the game based on the game state. We often pay close attention to these rules only. Let's consider an example, the simplest version of the *Pac-Man* game (http://en.wikipedia.org/wiki/Pac-Man):

- In this game, you, the player, control the Pac-Man in a maze that contains Pac-dots. Your goal is let Pac-Man to eat as many Pac-dots as possible by touching them.
- After eating all the dots in the maze, you move up a stage.
- In the maze, enemies (e.g., Blinky, Pinky) try to catch Pac-Man. When an enemy touches Pac-Man, Pac-Man is eaten and you lose a life.
- When all lives are lost, you lose and the game ends.

At first glance, these are the operational rules, and it seems they constitute all the rules for the game. But thinking more deeply, we may see some implicit rules. For example, we do not have unlimited time to play, even though theoretically the game allows unlimited playtime. Implied rules, therefore, are not explicitly described, but they are rather unspoken in game play. These rules are either underlying formal structures presented to the players, or they are related to etiquette, good sportsmanship, and other proper game behaviour.

Understanding the differences between operational and implied rules can help us see what makes a game fun in relation to other games. If you want to design a game, especially a good one, you need to carefully consider rules beyond operational rules.

Resource in a game refers to the things that a player can control. Both explicit and implicit resources can be included in a game. Examples of explicit resources include health and equipment in *Starcraft 2*, while time in *Mario Kart* and stickers to be picked up in *Little Big Planet* are examples of implicit resources. Different resources for different purposes are important issues to think about when designing a game.

Another element is called game sequence, meaning the progression of the game play. What is the order of players' action? What is the flow of play? Turn-based, speed-based, and other variations of sequencing of games are commonly observed. In a turn-based game, each player takes turns to act, such as in *Go*. A similar variation is a turn-based game with simultaneous play, where every player takes his or her turn (e.g., write and show their answers) at the same time. There are also different variations like turn order, which is randomized for each turn. Speed-based games require one to take action as fast as possible, like in *Call of Duty*.

In a game, player interaction, the ways in which players interact with each other or with the system, is another important aspect. Do you want the players negotiate or collaborate? Do you like players to experience conflicting and trading, or information sharing? These are some typical player interactions observed in game play. Conflict refers to the interaction in which one player attacks another in order to advance. Negotiation or trading describes the situation where players barter different services or resources. For example, in the game *Animal Crossing*, one can help with the mail service in exchange for resources or other services. Players can also interact through information sharing.

Having storylines in a game can improve the playability of the game. Sometimes narratives are referred to as backstories, settings, or themes. Although not essential, good narratives can link the game to the players so that they are emotionally engaged. Further, appropriate storylines contextualize the rules so that the games become easy to understand and play. It is also a wonderful way to integrate students' learning of language arts and social studies.

Here are some basic yet key elements of games adapted from Schreiber's work (2009). These related and intertwined elements each affect the gameplay in its own way. When designing games, you should carefully consider all of these elements, both individually and holistically.

Essentials for Good Games

What are the essential characteristics for a good game, whether it is a physical game or a digital game? Depending on whom you ask, you may hear a variety of opinions and ideas. Some features, however, are commonly agreed upon and discussed below: the fun principle, the KISS principle, the smooth control principle, the graphics and sound principle, the creativity principle, and the skill development principle (Linda07, 2007). Let me explain these ideas based on the original blog of Linda07 (2007).

The first of these is that the game should be fun and engage its players. This, of course, is not to say that all the existing games are fun. Many games, in fact, are boring. However, I want to argue that having fun should be the number one issue to consider when designing a game, because players will not want to play the game if they do not enjoy it. When playing engaging games, players become emotionally connected to the game and become willing to invest a great deal of their time and effort in it. They enthusiastically participate with positive emotion. They enjoy playing hard, trying their best, and meeting the challenges. A good game can deeply and effortlessly involve players in such a way that they lose awareness of worry and frustration of everyday life.

A second principle is to keep the game simple. People will not play if they get too frustrated while playing. This principle is often described as "Keep It Simple Stupid" or "KISS." This principle is applicable to many fields, but it is particularly true for game design. Offering players clean, straight fun is important because no one likes to be loaded down with complex features with endless loops. A note of caution, however, is that simple should not equate boring. Simple, in this case, refers to the rules. The games should be easy to understand and follow. Additionally, scaffolding is included in a good game design so that tasks can be completed without too much frustration. For example, the use of levels can divide a game into small sections that allow players to progressively accomplish tasks.

The third principle is about smooth controls. The ease of mastering the game controls will determine whether people will play the game. Here, the controls refer to game elements such as the task goals and rules. Does the game have clear task goals so that players know what they need to do? Does the game provide immediate feedback? As well, it is important that players are able to exercise a sense of control over their actions such as mouse movement or keyboard combination. If the game has smooth controls, a seemingly bland game can be fun. On the flip side, no matter how good a game is, people simply will not play it if they struggle with the controls.

The fourth principle relates to graphics and sound, both of which can be determinant factors. We all know that for a job interview, first impression is critical. Most often it determines whether you will receive a job offer. In a similar vein, because players first encounter the visual and audio aspects of the game, you want to design a game that makes a good first impression. Attractive and relevant graphics and sound can greatly enhance the playability of a game as long as they are not overwhelming.

The fifth principle is about creativity and giving players control. If the game gives a lot of latitude and offers various opportunities for players to be creative, a higher level of engagement is more likely, and a greater potential exists for people to want to play.

Finally, a good game can contribute to skill development. That is, players can continue to improve their skills. Many people lose interest in a game that does not allow them to keep advancing their ability. The development of skills can be achieved through the design of a game with appropriate complexity or variation.

These elements present essential characteristics for good games. In short, a good game can get players in "flow" (Csikszentmihalyi, 1997), a term that describes players losing track of time for hours while playing the game. A good game provides an environment that integrates presentation, problem, and control over the system. In such an environment, self disappears during flow, but sense of self is stronger after flow. In a good game, problems are manifested appropriately, although not necessarily elegantly. Problems are rendered in a manner consistent with their meaning, stretching players' abilities to the limits.

This section has discussed key concepts such as games, play, essential game elements, and key characteristics of good games. If you are someone who is interested in learning by game building, it is important for you to have a deep understanding of game design. Although the ultimate goal for you is

Epistemology 45

learning, the fact that this approach is realized through game design and building speaks to the importance of good game design. It is true that sometimes students may design and build a low-quality game but still learn a great deal from the process. However, anyone who cares about and is interested in building a game wants to develop a good one rather than a lousy one. After all, a student-created, engaging game that is loved by players can be the most exciting learning outcome and a very intrinsic motivation factor for the student.

·PART TWO·
Structure

• CHAPTER THREE •

Enactivist Learning World

This chapter focuses on how to create an enactivist learning world, adapting the learning by game building process and Web 2.0. Grounded in instructional design principles, this chapter emphasizes an enactivist learning world that can help students develop skills for the 21st century. The focus then shifts to systems thinking that guides game design and learning through game building. Various types of games are also examined, and a discussion of game design considerations helps to further clarify the principles behind the adaptation of learning by game building.

Skills

To design good games, a designer needs to employ a range of many of skills, such as, programming, creative writing, and logical thinking. Schell (2008), in his book titled *The Art of Game Design*, provides examples of close to 20 careers that present similar skill sets as those needed to design games. Some of these careers focus on such areas as music, history, engineering, business, architecture, anthropology, and economics. His point is that just as a plethora of skills are needed for a variety of jobs, they are also needed in the field of game design.

This is not to say that a good game designer must be an expert architect, a musician, an economist, or an engineer. Rather it points to the idea that designing a game involves a diverse set of skills. So when students design their own games, they have opportunities to exercise all kinds of skills needed to prepare them for a future that may potentially lead to various career paths.

Interestingly, perhaps the skills most needed for successful digital game design and development go far beyond technological skills. Creativity, communication, critical thinking, logic, and problem solving are of particular importance and are constantly practiced during the process of game design and building. Through the process of game design, students have many opportunities to cultivate skills that are vital to the 21st century. When students are immersed in the complex game design and building process, they must continually apply these critical skills, thus preparing them to become active citizens in a participatory culture.

The phrase *21st-century skills* has been a buzzword in the research and educational community for the last several years. The Partnership for the 21st Century Skills (2004) defined the framework of 21st-century skills as the following three broad categories: 1) learning and innovation skills, 2) information, media and technology skills, and 3) life and career skills.

These 21st-century skills are fully discussed in the following sections, considering how the learning by game design approach can facilitate the acquisition and performance of these skills, instantiated with examples. I use Tables 3.1, 3.2, and 3.3 to map these ideas. Note that in each of these tables, the first column lists the skills defined by Partnership for the 21st Century Skills (2004) while the second column describes specific game design elements that support the development of the corresponding 21st-century skills.

Learning and Innovative Skills

The first set of 21st-century skills that we discuss includes creativity and innovation. Mastering these skills will allow one to think creatively, work creatively with others, and be able to implement innovations. Table 3.1 summarizes these skill sets with specific elements in game design that support each.

Creativity and Innovation Skills

Inherently, game design and development is a process that demands strong creativity. With all of the projects we have conducted, creativity has always been the first and foremost trait displayed by students in the learning process. When students learn through game design and building, their creative muscle is constantly exercised. The comments made by a preservice math teacher may say it all: "From nothing I made a game!"

Structure

Table 3.1. Game Design Supporting Learning and Innovation Skills

21st-century Skills	Game Design Elements Support the Skills
Creativity and Innovation • Think creatively • Work creatively with others • Implement innovations	*-Brainstorming game ideas, individually and collectively* *-Evaluating and revising initial game ideas* *-Creatively imbedding educational content into game mechanics* *-Implementing game ideas and developing games*
Critical Thinking and Problem Solving • Reason effectively • Use systems thinking • Make judgments and decisions • Solve problems	*-Analyzing game design and presenting ideas to peers* • Game is a system; designing and building a game requires systems thinking to explore and negotiate relationships between parts of the whole. This also requires ongoing efforts to critically analyze data, effectively assess evidences, and skillfully synthesize information in order to draw appropriate conclusions. • The game designing and building process constantly involves decision making and problem solving. How do I transfer game ideas on paper to a digital format using programming language? This type of question demands continued efforts, in both conventional and novice ways of problem solving.
Communication and Collaboration • Communicate clearly • Collaborate with others	*-Sharing game ideas with groups* *-Writing game design documents* *-Articulating and presenting game design to peers* *-Conducting play tests both with paper prototypes and digital games* *-Working in small and large groups collaboratively to plan, design, refine, and develop games*

I once heard an elementary student comment, "You can let your imagination go wild when designing your game." From my perspective, this really points to the creative power of the game design experience. In the Games in Motion project, elementary students in a summer camp created games to teach others Newton's laws. Data collected from the summer camp experience suggested that students, their parents, and teachers all realized how game design becomes a powerful innovative practice. Here are some of the captured quotes:

- "Making the game is my favourite of this camp. It's really cool that we can make cool stuff with Scratch. It is very exciting because there is not really rules you have to follow. You can just do whatever you want." [student Aaron]
- "[The game making experience] is great! It takes a lot of knowledge and creativity to create any type of game." [student John's mother].

The novelty of this experience was not only fun and engaging for students, but it also pushed the students to be more creative, as exemplified in the following exchange:

- Interviewer: "Do you think the experience teaches you something?"
- Student Frank: "Yes, it improves your imagination and creativity."

Students really liked the game creation activity because it allowed for a great deal of autonomy. They felt a sense of ownership and control of their own learning, which inspired them to work more intently and to broaden their research in order to accomplish their tasks (Li, 2010).

Rick, a sixth-grade student, explained that he enjoyed the experiences of building his own games "because you can have your own cheats . . . you can then beat others." *Cheats* is a term used to describe information that helps players play the game. Typically, this information does not come from the game itself (although in some cases, game companies release cheats after certain periods of time). Cheats, such as unofficial strategy guides or cheat codes, are frequently developed by avid gamers who post them online for others to use. The usage of cheats is often considered a lazy or bamboozling way to manipulate the game. The use of cheats, as the term suggests, usually has a negative connotation and is generally discouraged in learning. Yet by making their own cheats, students demonstrate that they are capable of developing something new that demands a deep understanding of the underlying principles, for example, how force and momentum support a proper understanding of Newton's laws of relativity. Creating cheats, therefore, turns out to be a motivational and fruitful exercise for students to ingeniously learn content knowledge and beyond.

Similar patterns of creativity were noted in teachers who participated in a preservice training during the Call of Math project. These preservice teachers had the freedom to craft their own exploration defined by their own interests and inquiries. To explore creativity, we conducted two surveys, one before (presurvey) and one after (postsurvey) the preservice teachers finished their game design and development. In the presurvey, these teachers described their anticipated challenges about designing and building their own games. A majority of them were concerned about their creative ability to develop a game that would engage students while still being educational. "Creativity can be a challenge for me. I often find it difficult to come up with a good idea from scratch. I need some outside input to work with"; "You can very easily design a game that students find boring, thereby defeating the purpose of using video games in the first place." These were two typical answers found in the presurvey. However, the process of designing and building their own games changed the preservice teachers' perceptions. In the postsurvey, creativity was not mentioned, suggesting that the anticipated lack of creativity was not at all the actual challenge. Rather, many preservice teachers felt they had innovative ideas, yet they were challenged by how to program and translate the design ideas to a digital format. Many felt that they were "limited by what kind of interface we choose for our games—our ideas can be really great and seem simple but are hard to put into action." Such challenges pushed the teachers to become creative problem solvers because the game making was a continued process of uncovering and overcoming barriers (Li, et al, 2013).

Their creativity was also reflected in both the aesthetic and logistic choices of their games. Many of the games developed by these teachers demonstrated their attempts at innovative pedagogy, which suggest that these preservice teachers recognize the value of adapting nontraditional approaches to teaching mathematics. For example, Marilyn created a game to introduce the Fibonacci sequence through a diorama based on a fictitious classroom. She explained, "I wanted to get really creative, stepping outside of the norm of teaching and my comfort zone."

The experiences of the students at the summer camp and of the preservice teachers both demonstrate how the enactivist learning approach can cultivate creativity in and out of classrooms. The process of game creation builds up students' innovative abilities. The associated complex tasks demand students to think divergently and involve both fluency and freedom. That is, students not only need to spontaneously generate new and rich sets of ideas, often in a free-flowing manner, but they also are required to fluidly shift their views among various perspectives. Such divergent thinking transforms and facilitates creativity (Csikszentmihalyi, 1996).

I have a particular recollection of Tom's story during our Do It Yourself project, where practicing teachers enrolled in a graduate course focusing on game-based learning. This course required students to complete a "Gamer Profile" assignment. The assignment was simple: Each teacher needed to develop a case study of gamers, and describe the gamer's habits, gaming experiences, preferences, and reflections. The teachers would identify and interview their gamers to uncover why and what these gamers played. Other than asking the practicing teachers to use creative forms (i.e., NOT a paper or PowerPoint presentation) to deliver their work, I gave no limitation. During our in-class sharing time, many teachers used video, online interactive photo essay, and other forms to showcase their gamers. The work of Tom, however, caught everybody's eyes. Tom interviewed seven gamers, ranging from an elementary student to a university biology student to a teacher. He then built the case study of these seven gamers by creating a board game titled "Profile That Gamer!" The gamers and their profiles became game mechanics that were organically embedded into this board game. The game contained decks of cards and sets of rules. Below is Tom's description of the game rules:

Profile That Gamer!
Number of Players: 3–7
Basic Premise:
"*Profile That Gamer!*" is an ode to the classic board game "Pit." There are 7 different gamer profiles with 7 cards in each set. In addition, there are 3 wildcards, which could be used as a substitute for any missing profile cards. The objective of the game is to collect all 7 profile cards for one gamer. Once this has been achieved, the player calls out the gamer's name and the round is over. At the end of each round, the winning player shares 3 tidbits about his or her chosen player and then the score is tabulated. The winning player receives points based on which gamer he or she chose.

- *Expert gamers* (Nick and Kelly)–20 points

Structure

- *Average gamers* (Peter and Bobby)–15 points
- *Casual gamers* (Jan, Jen, and George)–10 points

At the end of the round, any player caught holding any of the wildcards will be penalized. Each wildcard represents a loss of 5 points.
The first player to reach 61 points is declared the winner.

Starting the Game:
The number of cards required will depend on the number of players. In general the number of gamer profiles should match the number of players in the game. Three profile cards are removed randomly and the 3 wildcards are inserted in their place. The deck is shuffled and each player is dealt 7 cards. Each player looks at his or her 7 cards secretly and decides which gamer he or she wants to collect in each cycle; a maximum of three cards can be traded between players. A player indicates how many cards he or she wishes to trade by yelling "One" or "Two" or "Three." After cards are swapped, each player examines his or her new hand and decides how many cards he or she wishes to swap next. This continues until a player has all 7 profile cards for one gamer.

Figure 3.1 shows some sample cards from Tom's game. As you can see, each player's profile is cleverly meshed into different parts of the game. During the class, when the teachers were presenting their gamers, six of them played this *Profile That Gamer!* game while others watched. There was plenty of laughing, screaming with excitement, groaning in frustration, and cheering for winning. Everyone was engrossed! The playing process vividly painted a picture of all the gamers Tom wanted to show us. Tom's innovative way of presenting his gamers wowed us. It became the best testimonial to showcase how such an enactivist approach can facilitate learners' creative thinking. When learners, like Tom, are situated in authentic experiences that encourage embodiment and are given the freedom to explore the relationships between themselves and the world around them through acting in and with the world, their creative muscle is practiced and developed.

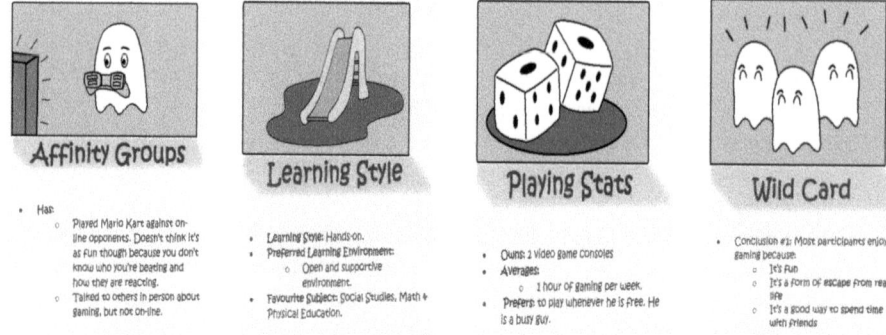

Figure 3.1. Sample Cards from the *Profile That Gamer!* Game

Problem Solving and Critical Thinking

The second set of learning and innovation skills directly corresponds to problem solving and critical thinking, which are routinely exercised during the game design and building process. In fact, game designing and building is a journey of problem solving itself. How do you convert your mental vision into the finished game that can be played on the screen? What needs to be included? How do you present the content covered? Questions like these are endless and can be found at every step while designing a game, regardless of the time or resources available.

Critical thinking and analytical skills are also essential in the game building process, although they may not be immediately visible when playing your game. When collectively brainstorming ideas, you listen to, evaluate, and build on the presented, ever evolving thoughts in order to form your own ideas. From the myriad of ideas initially generated in the brainstorming step of this process, you need to analyze each of them in searching for the best and most appropriate. Whether using existing pictures or creating a new setting, you must constantly review and critically evaluate the materials that best represent your points of view. When play testing, you have the opportunity to articulate the strengths and weaknesses of the game, as well as judge players' actions against your intentions.

Students in the Games in Motion project, for example, worked tirelessly on building, testing, and refining their games, thus problem solving was a predominant course of action. Unlike other conventional learning activities, failure became the norm. Students started to accept the idea that they could learn from failures instead of feeling defeated by them. While working with

Structure

Newton's laws, students willingly and persistently wrestled with problems, and through this experience, they developed identities as expert problem solvers. Jason, the camp teacher, commented on the students' experience:

> The best thing was how students solve the problems on their own. I've seen some students come over and say let's try this and not only they fix the problem but also take other students to different directions. What surprised me was just how students were willing to wrestle with the problems so they could fix them.

Students welcomed the challenges because these were authentic problems that needed to be solved through their design process. They not only learned to identify and solve problems, but they also became the owners of the process, finding solutions and figuring out how to make those solutions work.

These problems, whether in math, science, or programming, were intrinsically connected to the real world. Solving problems to accomplish the goals became a fun and engaging process, therefore transforming students into passionate learners. The following conversation, which I had with Andy, a fifth-grade student, exemplifies this:

Me: Why is the game design and building process exciting?

Andy: Because it's pretty hard to design a game. I like to try hard things and to take challenges and figure out.

Me: Anything surprised you?

Andy: It's waaaaaay more difficult to make the games than I thought about. But I am very, very happy about the outcome. It is very fun!

Problem solving often demands that students become more persistent and determined. "Pleasantly struggling" became the norm in this process of finding ways to work out a solution. Because the students were often at the outer edge while at the same time within the regime of their competence, even if they failed, they could still see the progress they were making. Jack, a fifth-grade student, commented on his game building experience: "I keep trying like scripts, in this case, see what happens, and then if doesn't turn out what I like, I switch the script, so it fits into the thing I want it to be."

Throughout every game design project, we noted that students were receptive to inventing unique ways of solving problems instead of fixating on a single idea. When one approach did not work, they tried another. For example, Tony, a second grader, created a game involving a spaceship that shot aliens. He wanted to have many aliens appear on the screen at once so as to increase the difficulty level of his game. Initially, he thought of using the "random" command in Scratch so that aliens would randomly pop up everywhere. When he failed at this, he discovered the bouncing command and instead decided to build a myriad of aliens bouncing around. This approach essentially created the same effect for his game, thus solving the problem. Tony told me, "You can't expect things to work the first time. It doesn't work the first time, 'cause sometimes it might not be the thing that you need. You have to change it like combine more than one program to get what you need" (Li, 2010).

Communication Skills and Collaboration

Good communication skills go hand-in-hand with collaboration. In order to collaborate, you need to be able to clearly communicate and interact with people. Similarly, game design and building goes hand-in-hand with continued communication, whether you are creating the game scenarios and rules, or brainstorming game concepts with group members, or play testing your prototype. For example, the Kodu games, like *Shellshocked 2* and *Fraction Town*, developed by preservice teachers in the Call of Math project, began with clear and concise instructions of what the players needed to do and what keys needed to be pressed in order to make the avatar move around. Such writing required the preservice teachers to work collaboratively, taking several iterations of drafting, sharing, and revising. The quality of the end result demonstrated that the preservice teachers had indeed enhanced their communication skills.

Collaboration is also an integral part of game building, and it can take many forms. In a sense, there is a continuum of corporation ranging from the typical partnership between you and your best friend, to group work in a class, to situations that allow an online acquaintance to use your art pieces for her game. In some cases, my students chose to work in small groups to complete their game design projects. In other cases, some preferred individually working on their game design, yet the process inevitably involved collaborative efforts.

For instance, in the Call of Math project, although preservice teachers had the option to work individually or in small groups to create their games, almost all of them collaborated in one way or another. Even for those who worked individually, their game design started in a small group setting and their prototypes were tested and discussed during the class, where peers provided valuable feedback for the refinement of the games. For those who chose to work in groups, collaboration was ongoing throughout the entire process, from the initial birth of the game idea to the finished product. Katie described her experience collaborating with Lisa in the development of their Kodu game, exemplifying such collaboration:

> Lisa and I worked both collaboratively and parallel on the game. Initially we discussed our game vision and ideas to make that happen, then we each played with *Kodu* separately to see what was possible. We reconvened and decided what would work and how we would implement it. We would pass the game back and forth between our computers to each try and problem solve/debug separately and discuss the optimal/most effective solution. At certain points we would stop and discuss if what we were designing met the math objectives.

Collaboration was also demonstrated beyond small group work, focusing on building one particular game. Since all of the preservice teachers were learning a new skill (i.e., how to use a game interface), oftentimes they helped each other even if they weren't in the same group. For instance, during one class, the preservice teachers were given time to work on their digital games. Those who were using Kodu were struggling on how to get started. Martin had already worked past this point, and he gave the class an impromptu lesson on Kodu. Many of the teachers stayed past the end of the class to work with each other to improve their games.

Information, Media, and Technology Skills

We live in an era characterised by information abundance, constant and rapid changing of technology, as well as the unprecedented ability to connect with others. In response, the second set of 21st-century skills is focused on information, media, and technology. Table 3.2 details this set of skills as defined by the Partnership for the 21st Century Skills (2004), along with the description of how the learning by game design approach supports the development of these skills.

According to the Partnership for the 21st Century Skills (2004), information literacy refers to our ability to access, evaluate, use, and manage information. Ethical and legal issues surrounding access and use of materials and data are also an important part of information literacy. Media literacy involves media analyzing and creation, while information, communications, and technology (ICT) literacy deals with how we can effectively apply technological tools. When immersed in learning by game design, you become naturally involved in the process whereby you can achieve information literacy. From getting game ideas to programming to play testing, you inevitably need to search for information, discern what is useful and important, and select what is most appropriate to help you achieve your goals. When you design and develop games, you are creating media products using technological tools to express and interpret the world around you.

Table 3.2. Game Design Supporting Information, Media, and Technology Skills

21st-century Skills	Game Design Elements Support the Skills
Information Literacy • Access and evaluate information • Use and manage information	• *Searching for useful information for both game ideas and the educational content to be integrated; selecting most meaningful and applicable information to be used* • *Discussing ethical and legal issues so as to correctly use materials*
Media Literacy • Analyze media • Create media products	• *Analyzing existing games to see how they can be used for educational purposes* • *Creating games for instructional or other purposes*
ICT Literacy • Apply technology effectively	• *Using various software and hardware (e.g., game console, handheld devices) to create digital games*

One good way to practice media literacy skills is to integrate media analysis into game design. For example, before letting students think about designing their own game, let them spend time playing existing games. These games can be commercial, off-the-shelf entertainment games or free, online educational games. Encourage students to critically examine the games, seeking answers to essential questions such as these: What are the media messages? How are they constructed and from whose point of view? How can they be used in classrooms? Answering guiding questions like these, as well as opening the discussion to a larger learning community, can help students gain significant understanding of media literacy. In summary, the process of game design and building organically enmeshes activities practicing information literacy, media literacy, and technology literacy.

While analyzing data from the Call of Math project, my research assistants and I were pleasantly surprised at the extent to which the information, media, and technology skills were applied in game building, because it was not obvious to us at the outset that those skills would be necessary. For example, Bill, a preservice teacher, described how he solved a programming problem by researching and adapting previously completed games: "I had to go to the Scratch website and find other creations that did what I wanted to do. Then I had to search for the right thing in the code that did what I wanted to do." Here, Bill used information literacy skills by finding, assessing, managing, and finally using previously developed Scratch games. Many of the preservice teachers noted the use of tutorials and Internet searches as methods for learning how to program in their chosen game interface (Li, et al. 2013). Not only did everyone in the project create a functional game, but some of the preservice teachers actually developed additional media products, such as movie trailers, to promote their games.

Life and Career Skills

The final set of 21st-century skills is based upon our lifelong and career experiences. To live and work as a 21st-century citizen, flexibility and adaptability to different roles and responsibilities are a necessity. The learning as game design process inherently invites flexibility. Effective lifelong learning and working, both independently and with others, are aspects that contribute to successful citizenship. Management of time, goals, and projects, as well as leadership, is also required for one to function well in society. Game design and building is a messy and complicated endeavour. In order to create a functional game, you need to learn with others and also independently. It is also crucial that you understand how to properly manage resources. Table 3.3 lists detailed descriptions of this set of skills by the Partnership for the 21st Century Skills (2004), along with the educational elements in the learning by game design approach to support the development of these skills.

Table 3.3. Elements in Game Design Support Life and Career Skills

21st-century Skills	Game Design Elements Support the Skills
Life and Career Skills • Be flexible and adaptable • Manage goals and time • Work independently • Be self-directed learners • Interact effectively with others • Work effectively in diverse teams • Manage projects • Produce results • Guide and lead others • Be responsible to others	• *Working in small groups, each student adopts different roles (e.g., manager, graphic designer, programmer, teacher).* • *Students need to work both independently and collaboratively to complete the design and building tasks. This demands that students manage their projects, take leadership, and be responsible for others. They need to understand different viewpoints and come up with workable ways to solve problems.* • *Game design inherently is messy and complex. Students need to work effectively in this learning world. They need to be flexible and be able to solve problems in ambiguous situations.* • *Each student needs to go beyond what teachers have taught in class, searching for, evaluating, and using new ideas for games, along with new knowledge for content learning and new programming skills for building games.*

In the Call of Math project, preservice teachers demonstrated flexibility and adaptability skills when designing and building their games. In the post-survey, many preservice teachers noted that their biggest challenge was getting the program to do what they wanted. As such, they had to adapt their original plan to fit the programming platform they chose. The experience of Erin's team creating their game *Awesome Adventure* using the game *Little Big Planet 2* exemplified their exercise of flexibility and adaptability. Originally, the game idea of presenting the math problem was that players would select and drop what they thought were equivalent fraction blocks (wooden blocks or hay stacks with written fractions) down a hole. If the answer was right, the hole would fill up a bit until the players could cross it. If the answers were wrong, the block would fly out of the hole. Unfortunately, Erin's team could not figure out how to program this in *Little*

Big Planet 2, so they had to consider alternative ways to implement their math problem. At the end, instead of using blocks that filled up a space, the team decided to use triggers that could only be flipped if the right answer was given. For example, in one situation, the players had to find three fractions that were equivalent to different representations of fractions (decimal, percentage, visual). If the player got all three answers right by putting the correct blocks in the right space, this caused an "and" switch to be triggered, which resulted in the appearance of a bumblebee. The bumblebee could help the player fly to the next level. This new approach not only created similar affects that Erin's team wanted but also increased the fun level of the game, as it is much more interesting to fly on a bumblebee than to simply walk over a set of blocks (Li, et al., 2013).

Perseverance

Though not a specific skill as outlined by the Partnership for 21st Century Skills, perseverance is another important skill for us to embrace in order to thrive in this participatory culture. Game building, from designing to programming, keeps you in a constant state of problem solving that requires a great deal of determination. Our work with a wide range of learners, from elementary summer camp students to adult, practicing teachers, demonstrates that students have to persistently pursue their goals when they are immersed in game building. Earlier in this chapter I discussed the story of Erin's team building a math game. This group of preservice teachers was confronted with a very difficult problem: how to design questions in *Little Big Planet 2* so that players knew when they were correct and when they would be unable to continue on until they got the correct answers. Team members tried many different approaches until they found a solution. I once asked them what the most important lesson was that they took from this experience. Erin answered as follows:

> Perseverance! Perseverance! Perseverance! We worked so hard. We had to be creative to find different ways to solve problems! Sometimes we were really frustrated, but we did not quit. We did not give up and as a result, we were able to find an even better solution to our problem! I think many of our students in schools are lacking this very important skill. They are very impatient problem solvers and this will hurt them in the long run.

Mary, a practicing teacher in the Do It Yourself project, also expressed how perseverance was necessary throughout her experience: "I have learned to persevere. I had a lot of difficulty at the beginning, but kept at it and finally got a great game."

For some learners, programming can be frustrating and difficult, yet when a game is finished, the reward of a job well done is worth all the hard work. The overall benefit of perseverance is supported by our survey data from both the Games in Motion project (with elementary summer camp students) and the Run for Math project (with high school math students). We surveyed theses two groups of students about their emotions in different stages of their game building process. When asked about their feelings after their games were finished, every single high school student expressed happiness and pride in their accomplishment. No one revealed any negative emotion about the process. The elementary students' answers demonstrated a similar pattern, with a vast majority of the students feeling excited, proud, and happy, while only one or two students felt frustrated or annoyed (Li, 2010; Li, et al., 2013).

Solving problems during game design is quite different from solving textbook problems. For one, textbook problems are almost always well-structured, while problems revealed during the game design process are often ill-structured. In a textbook, problems are neatly organized and carefully divided into small chunks that fit nicely into predetermined sections and can be solved by recently learned formulas. Problems appearing during game creation are typically emergent dilemmas that are not constrained by the content domains being studied in the classrooms, and their solutions are not predictable or convergent. Problem solving in game design, therefore, is intellectually demanding and engages learners in higher order thinking skills. Different from solving textbook problems, game design naturally provides challenges that push students to use their problem-solving skills, and students take the ownership of these problems. Elaine, a preservice math teacher, told me the following:

> Programming, for me, has this amazing ability to push me to seek solutions. I am not satisfied with a non-working program. Maybe it's that there is this amazing feedback present where it smacks you in the face: "this does not work," "there is a huge bug in the program that may be hilarious/frustrating but not acceptable to function." So you push yourself. So you persevere until you get to that moment of completion. Then of course, you can add bells and whistles and go on forever. But at

Structure

that moment of completion, where you have something that works, that does what you want, and you KNOW that it does what you want, there is this euphoria.

Systems Thinking

Enactivism, as discussed earlier, is also informed by systems thinking. While different sources may define systems in their own specific ways, it is generally agreed upon that systems are biological, natural, mechanical, and social. Perhaps the most commonly accepted and widely used definition of system is one that highlights a collection of related elements to produce a bigger arrangement, different from any individual parts. Systems thinking, a field of study to explore systems, is developed to help us better understand our world.

I did a Google search of the term *system*, and the results yielded a quite extensive list. One link that appeared was The Free Dictionary. According to that site (http://www.thefreedictionary.com/system), the definitions of "system" are as follows:

1. A group of interacting, interrelated, or interdependent elements forming a complex whole.
2. A functionally related group of elements, especially:
    a. The human body regarded as a functional physiological unit.
    b. An organism as a whole, especially with regard to its vital processes or functions.
    c. A group of physiologically or anatomically complementary organs or parts: the nervous system; the skeletal system.
    d. A group of interacting mechanical or electrical components.
    e. A network of structures and channels, as for communication, travel, or distribution.
    f. A network of related computer software, hardware, and data transmission devices.
3. An organized set of interrelated ideas or principles.
4. A social, economic, or political organizational form.
5. A naturally occurring group of objects or phenomena: the solar system.
6. A set of objects or phenomena grouped together for classification or analysis.
7. A condition of harmonious, orderly interaction.
8. An organized and coordinated method; a procedure. See Synonyms at method.
9. The prevailing social order; the establishment. Used with *the*: You can't beat the system.

Wikipedia (http://en.wikipedia.org/wiki/System) used a similar, but slightly different, definition: "A system is a set of elements/components and relationships which are different from relationships of the set or its elements to other elements or sets."

Wikipedia also discusses how most systems have three important elements: structure, behaviour, and interconnectivity. Structure is determined by the system components, while behaviour refers to input, process, and outputs. Interconnectivity describes the relationships amongst different components.

These definitions, though different, are essentially comparable. The concepts of components, part and whole, and the relationships amongst different components, form the foundation of systems thinking and closely tie to the enactivist view. Three key principles of enactivism are derived from complex system theories. First, the whole is much bigger and more complex than the sum of its elements. Second, the individual organism and its world are coupled in a relationship in which they shape each other simultaneously, rather than one determining the other. Third, we cannot understand a complex system by simply analyzing its elements and the ways those elements are assembled (Davis, Sumara, & Luce-Kapler, 2008).

A way to apply this idea of systems is through game design. Games are complex systems. Here, game is defined to include both the game mechanism (e.g., the rules, the game pieces) and the people involved (e.g., players, designers). Applying the aforementioned three principles to games, we see the following: A game is much greater than the consolidation of the game rules and the mechanics or individual players. Game mechanics and rules are played and shaped by players; at the same time, the players condition the elements of the game like rules and mechanics, and a simple set of rules can result in complex possibilities, some of which may be unpredictable. Our thorough understanding about the nature of, and relationships among, elements alone is not enough for us to understand the whole game system.

Under this view, game playing is equal to the exploration of possibilities a game provides. Meaningful, engaging play means that the game offers a large and flexible space of possibilities for players to inhabit. A good game motivates both novice and expert players to repeatedly engage the game, because it offers surprising experiences every time. Designing a good game, therefore, should focus on furnishing players unlimited, new experiences through their interaction with the game (Schreiber, 2009).

A game designed by Sam, one of my graduate students, during The Driven project, illustrates a good design of a complex game system that

Structure

potentially creates endless new play possibilities. As described earlier, The Driven project involves graduate students designing games to teach people road rules. At the time, Sam worked with another graduate student to design a digital game that would teach drivers rules based on the provincial government's driver's handbook. Starting from the beginning, Sam wanted to create a game that allowed players to learn the rules of the road through experience, rather than having the rules explicitly taught through direct instruction, as if the learners were in a lecture or listening to a tutorial. Sam's team designed a game titled *Splat!* where players had to come up with their own rules and use them for roads. The following descriptions of the game are based on the design documents created by Sam.

> The basic idea of *Splat!* is like this: Splatland is a beautiful place occupied by Splatters in this game world. Splatter, the main avatar of the game, is a fluid filled snail kind of creature. They move around in the Splat Travelling System which is very simple to start with: the system is reminiscent of roads. But you may not easily see them as roads because they do not have orange and white lines. In addition, no rules or traffic signs or anything like that exists. Splatters travel frequently and travel fast. But since there are no rules to follow, Splatters can get out of control and splaccidents can occur frequently. That is, when Splatters bump into each other while they are moving: Splat! they pop into watery gooey splashes. It often takes the disoriented Splatters a few seconds before they can reconstitute. Remember that Splatters do not like being turned into Splats! The goal of the game, of course, is for players to design and establish an efficient and functional Splat Travelling System with appropriate rules to reduce the occurrence of Splats or splaccidents.
>
> (design document)

Sam further describes the game in his design documents:

The Splatland has a total of six types of Splatters traveling around: the happy Splatters, the frustrated Splatters, the mad Splatters, the bad Splatters, the emergency Splatters, and the courteous Splatters. The Splatters can change their appearance, which provides information about the problems that are happening in the Splat Travelling System. The happy Splatters, the frustrated Splatters, and the mad Splatters can transform from one to another depending on their travelling experiences. Each Splatter is color-coded:

- The Happy Splatters are green. They follow the rules and signs because they are happy. But a Happy Splatter can become a Frustrated Splatter—a purple Splatter, if other splatters cut them off or do not follow the rules, or if following the rules means that a Splatter cannot get to where it wants to go.

- The purple frustrated Splatters try to follow the rules, but also are willing to break the rules if it is taking too long to move to where they want to go. The conditions of the Splat Travelling System may cause a happy splat to become purple, but it might also be purple just because it had a bad day.
- Mad Splatters are red; they are also a menace. Mad Splatters can become very dangerous and will recklessly move in ways without realizing that they can cause Splaccidents.
- Bad Splatters are black and they simply do not care about being safe.
- Emergency Splatters are blue and their job is to look for bad splatters. They also help calm splatters after a Splaccident.
- Courteous Splatters are yellow and if they receive a friendly wave, they can help reduce the frustration level of a purple Splatter or a mad Splatter.

(design document)

With the six types of Splatters, the team developed a set of operational rules for the *Splat!* game, which included the following:

1. Although the road rules, signs and pathway markings are at the player's disposal, the entire set of road rules and signs are not available from the start. The player needs to master the use of one before he/she can move on to the second.
2. When 90% of the Splatters reach their destination, the player has successfully mastered the current level and he/she can move on to the next one.
3. A player's solution to a problem is dependent on the cost of solving the problem. That means, the player does not have unlimited resources. So even if the player wants/needs the pedestrian light, he/she probably cannot afford it. Crosswalks may be the only choice.
4. A player needs to make sure his/her rules help all splatters. When splatters wait too long in the traffic, for instance, they will turn into Mad Splatters and not follow the rules anyway.
5. Just because a player mastered the driving on the right side of the road problem in level 1, doesn't mean that he/she won't need this information as part of his/her solution to level 5. Once he/she has used a rule seven times, he/she should be able to toggle it so as to show it is always available.
6. Sometimes a problem does not have a solution. The "should this be a playground zone or a school zone" problem, for instance, doesn't have one logical solution. Playground zones often start after school starts and school zones often end right about the time kids start playing in the park. A possible solution is to have hybrid school/playground zones, or to change the start times for playground zones.
7. There is a construction kit in the game that can be used for players to design their own levels or puzzles.

(Design document)

Given this set of basic rules, we can see that the game *Splat!* is a very complex system. We often observe that frustrated drivers make mistakes, and road rage is common in our daily life. Designing the Splatters with an inherent, central quality of frustration, the game reflects real life and provides opportunities for varied outcomes. In the game, complex possibilities arise from two levels: the local context of interaction between game elements and the higher level of player actions. At the local level, for example, installing a traffic light versus a roundabout in this intersection can affect the player's decision on the next intersection or road. The rules, therefore, change according to the context for which they are placed.

At the player level, complexity also occurs. One possibility is that some players will behave in completely different ways: They may want to increase rather than decrease the occurrence of splaccidents. Creating a chaotic Splatland may amuse these players. So instead of developing rules for splats to travel efficiently and safely, they may design rules so that they can drive all of the Splatters into mad Splatters. The effect of such behaviour could not only result in an upsurge of Splaccidents, which may ripple outward, but it could potentially impact the larger fabric of the overall play.

Sam's choices in the design of the game *Splat!* created a fun and compelling virtual space that encourages players to understand and apply the various rules of the road. The game offers endless possibilities for players to interact with the elements of the game and therefore offers a very compelling game for players to learn road rules in an engaging way.

Types of Games and Design Considerations

Different Types of Games

Adapting learning by game building means that you have to understand games and game design. This section briefly describes different types of games and discusses basic game design considerations. If you are a game player or a game designer, you probably have seen many different types of games and sometimes are even confused by the categorizations. You may have heard players say that they like shooter games but hate puzzle games. These loosely defined terms are useful in helping you understand different genres of games, because they provide a common language. Game developers, researchers, and educators use different taxonomies for games. For the purpose of this book, I use Gros's (2007) seven categories:

1. Action/platform games: reaction based games such as *Mario* or *Sonic the Hedgehog*.
2. Adventure games: these games set a virtual world for players to explore and along the ways they solve problems to advance.
3. Fighting games: in these games, a player fights against others, either computer-generated avatars or people controlled characters like shooting games.
4. Role-playing games: players assume roles of people or creatures in these types of games.
5. Simulations: players explore recreation of an environment or situation to achieving certain goals.
6. Sports games: games based on sports like *Madden NFL* simulating real NFL games.
7. Strategy games: games involve players to apply strategies in historical or fictional environments.

(p. 30)

These categories may not be mutually exclusive, meaning it is possible that one game belongs to more than one category. But it is a way for us to discuss types of games and understand how different types of games can inform our practice. Our experience with learners suggests that students can design any type of game, regardless of the specific curricular topics they are focusing on or the software platforms they are using. This being said, the most popular game types learners tend to adopt are adventure games, simulations, and strategy games. Table 3.4 details the characteristics of the practicing teacher-designed educational games during our Do It Yourself project. This example demonstrates that these teachers have targeted a wide range of students (from Grade 1 to adult learners to English as a Second Language [ESL] students), focused on content knowledge (from math to traffic rules), and utilized divergent tools (from Scratch to Flash). The adventure game, nonetheless, is the game type that is most frequently chosen by the teachers to implement their ideas.

Of course, sometimes one game may even include a variety of minigames of different genres. Take Allen's *The Driven* game, for example, which is a traffic game developed in The Driven project. It is a strategy game with a dark, gritty detective story. Allen integrated action and fighting minigames into the larger game context.

Structure

Table 3.4. Characteristics of Teacher-Designed Games

Game	Curricular Objectives (link to the game)	Subject	Target Audience	Genre/ Taxonomy	Platform*
Eggcellent Math	Order of operations and computations	Mathematics	Grade 4	Adventure: Question and Answer (Q & A)	Scratch
Blizzard Zone	Cartesian grid	Mathematics	Grade 6	Strategy	Adobe Captivate
Find It	Identify 3-D objects/2-D shapes	Mathematics	Grade 1	Adventure	Scratch
Goblin Mountain	Create storyline and text	Language Arts	Grade 7	Role-Playing Game (RPG)	Scratch
Keeping Up with the Joneses	Balance chemical equations/reactions	Science: Chemistry	Grades 6–7/Science	Adventure: Puzzle	Flash
Little Cashier	Count money	Mathematics	Grades 4–7	Adventure: Puzzle	Flash
Mathematia	Order of operations and computations	Mathematics	Ages 6–9	Adventure: Q & A	Scratch
Myth-Givings	Ancient Greek culture	Social Studies	Grade 6	Turn-Based Strategy/ RPG	Scratch

Title	Description	Subject	Audience	Genre	Platform
SimFant	Childcare-giving (http://scratch.mit.edu/projects/dweebly/987971)	Life Skills	Grades 7–9	Simulation	Scratch
The Vault	Historical figures (Newton, Cleopatra, etc)	Social Studies	Grades 4–6	Adventure: Story-Driven	Flash
Biome Survival	Biome eco-systems	Science: Biology	Grade 7 Science	Adventure	Scratch
Aquaria Life	Aquatic eco-systems	Science: Biology	Ages 7–12	Simulation	Scratch
Brian's Return	Novel study and application	Language Arts	Grade 6	Adventure: Story-Based	Scratch
Drive for Life	Driver's handbook	Life Skills	New Drivers	Simulation	Kodu
Elena's Dragon	Body parts	Science: Biology	English as a Second Language	Adventure	Scratch
Fortress	Test generation	Teacher Training	College Instructors	Action: Mystery	Adobe Captivate
Get Crack'n	Order of operations and computations	Mathematics	Grades 1–6	Adventure: Q & A	Scratch
Guitar Theory	Identify musical notes	Music	Grades 1–6/Music	Action: Skill and Drill	Scratch
Invention Convention	Novel study and application	Language Arts	Grade 3	Adventure: Story-Driven	Scratch

Structure

Little Sprout	Plant eco-systems	Science: Biology	Ages 5–9	Simulation	StarLogo TNG
Periodic Table	Chemical elements	Science: Chemistry	Middle School/Science	Fighting	Scratch
Samsara	East Indian culture	Social Studies	Grade 3 Social Studies	Turn-Based Adventure	Flash
So You Think You're Canadian, Eh?	Canadian history, culture and geography	Social Studies	ESL/New Immigrants	Adventure: Q & A	Scratch
Quadratic Commander	Cartesian grid (http://www.youtube.com/watch?v=J_1tXsYgd0Y)	Mathematics	High School Math	Strategy	GeoGebra
You Auto Know	Traffic rules	Life Skills	New Drivers	Adventure: Q & A	Kodu
Next Gen	Canadian history, culture and First Nations (http://goo.gl/VKO4L)	Social Studies	Ages 12–16	Adventure: Q & A	Kodu

*Scratch, StarLogo TNG, and Kodu are free programming development environments. Flash is a multimedia and software platform used for authoring graphics, games, and animations. Adobe Captivate is authoring software for developing interactive content. GeoGebra is open source, interactive software, allowing users to dynamically play with mathematical ideas and concepts.

Design Considerations

Since the focus of this book is on learning by game building rather than game design itself, I am introducing just the basic game design principles, mostly through the lens of action. From the enactivist point of view, at the heart of a game, it is what players can DO or act in that game that counts the most. Whether "game" is considered as *the play of experience, the play of pleasure, or the play of meaning* (Salen & Zimmerman, 2003), it is nothing until someone plays it. In other words, a game is just an object, an artifact, a program of codes, but nothing else unless someone interacts with it and gives it a life. This is also the core characteristic that separates a game from other media products like movies. You hear people say, "This is not a game. It is just an animation or a story." When asked why, they would often answer, "Because the audience or player cannot do anything, or what he or she does cannot affect the results of the thing." Unlike movies or TV shows that require little interaction, games demand participation. The players' participation is most likely realized by their actions. When designing a game, therefore, we need to carefully consider the actions involved in the game play.

Because action is so central to designing a good game, we need to focus on augmenting interesting game actions. The following list of four tips, adapted from Schreiber's work (2009), provide some starting points to think about good designs for actions in a game:

1. The first logical idea to consider is to integrate more actions so that players can act differently and more opportunities to perform. A direct benefit of such increased choices of action is that it can increase player interactions, therefore may heighten the fun level of game play. When you play a game that allows you to run, shoot, build, push, collide, destroy, and fortify, you potentially have more fun than if you can only run and push. Of course, do not expect careless addition of endless action choices will guarantee an engaging game. Rather, the essential idea is that you have to precisely craft the design so that these actions best interact with each other.
2. The second idea is to design an object that has multiple functions rather than a singular one. For example, if you design a game in which a carrot can only be eaten, the game is probably too simple to be played. If the same carrot, however, can be eaten, played with, used as a light, as a

sword to fight, a gun to shoot, a horse to ride on, a pen to write, and so forth, you are opening a wide range of possibilities. You still have the carrot object, but by adding the plausible ways the carrot can be used instead of just the "being eaten" function, the number of meaningful actions can increase, hence improving the engagement value of the game.

3. Another thing to consider is to create different paths to achieve the goals of the game. Imaging this: you have many different ways to act in the game, yet you only have one way to reach the goal. The replayability (i.e. the likelihood that you will replay) of this game is low because you already know what will happen. For example, if the goal of this game is to occupy the Mountain Black, and the one way to get there is to climb to the top on the existing trail, the player will do just that. But if a player can reach the top by hiking on the trail, or riding the elevator inside the mountain, or using parachutes to land, or sitting on the gondola, the game will be way more dynamic and rich. Let me provide one word of caution here: You need to make sure to provide equitable options so that no one approach is significantly easier than the other.

4. A useful tip to keep in mind is to create different subjects. Adding more subjects appropriately can increase the number of meaningful actions in a game and can enhance interactions amongst game elements. Consider a simplified version of *Tetris* that contains only two kinds of pieces, say a rectangular shape and a square shape, it will become a boring game. By adding different shapes, or subjects, in this simple game makes it more interesting to play.

(adapted from Schreiber, 2009)

Although the tips discussed here suggest different ways to design a game that affords players more exciting and interesting possibilities for game play, it is absolutely essential to balance the different elements in the game. While generally increasing the number of subjects or functions of an object or passages to achieve the goals can increase possibilities in a game, you also need to consider what is manageable and feasible. Remember, when carefully designed, it is possible to achieve seemingly endless possibilities with limited subjects, characteristics of the subjects, and paths.

When designing the game *Splat!*, Sam's original idea was that players would have complete freedom in terms of designing the travel system. They could draw a sidewalk anywhere and in any format; they could design a stop sign in any shape or in any colour. The ideas were initially very interesting and the total freedom would have indeed provided players unlimited possibilities to explore the game space. However, when the team started prototyping the freestyle game Sam desired and explored possible software choices, they realized that it would be too difficult for the team, especially with the limited time, money, and technical skills they had. As they shared their dilemma with me, I invited other teams to join the discussion about the constraints, and together we brainstormed possible ways to solve the problem. Finally, we came up with an idea: We would design the game with limited sets of choices of objects, functions, and other game mechanics. A stop sign, for instance, can only be chosen from 20 different shapes and colors.

This change from freestyle design (with unlimited possibilities) to a design with limited possibilities significantly decreases the options a player has in the game. Yet, when the number of choices of each game element (e.g., stop sign, speed sign, line shape, line color) is relatively large enough (e.g., 20 choices per element), and the number of elements is large enough (say 100 elements), then the players will have seemingly endless choices because playing the game is experiencing the interaction of all the game elements. We therefore have good reason to believe that this change of design would not compromise the game play. If it did, the compromise would be minimal at best and insignificant compared to the amount of time and resources saved.

The obvious benefit of this change, needless to say, is that the process of game building becomes much more achievable and manageable. After making the necessary changes, the team was able to create limited sets of game elements, signs, for example, and assemble them to a complete game. Thinking deeply, though, another benefit of this approach is the possibility to integrate the targeted content knowledge. Again, consider the case of a stop sign. Since this is a game intended to teach the road rules described in the government driver's handbook, it is necessary to have players remember what a stop sign looks like in real life. If we had the freestyle design, a player may well discover that he or she needs a stop sign through the play and therefore create his or her own stop sign, which could be a giant, glittery, blue cubic blob kind of object. This blue cubical stop sign may function perfectly in the Splatland, yet this player may still have trouble driving on North American roads because he or she does not know what an authentic stop sign looks like. The player may have seen it in real life but fails to make the connection. When we change the design to the style with limited choices offered, we can easily include the stop sign in the real world as one of the possibilities provided. The player would then have a much easier time linking the correct sign with his or her daily living experience and consequently have a better understanding of the rules.

Although students can learn from designing any kind of game, a frequently adopted approach for learning by game-building is for learners to design educational games. This is particularly beneficial if the learners, in this case also the designers, are preservice or practicing teachers. When designing educational games, some design considerations need to be carefully thought out, especially pertaining to the educational focus. In addition to keeping good game design principles in mind, one must focus on the educational aspect. These pedagogical design considerations are critical. What are the learning goals? Where do we desire the learning to occur? What kinds of learning would we like to occur? How do we want it to happen? How do we know whether the learning has occurred? To what extent has the learning occurred? These are the sorts of questions we need to ask ourselves. The pedagogical design considerations can be roughly grouped into three main areas: learning content, process, and assessment.

The learning content must be the first consideration when designing an educational game or adapting a game design approach. Here, you can see parallels with the concept of backward design, an instructional design approach familiar to many teachers. What are the main learning goals of this project? What subject matter knowledge is the main focus? What are other semiotic domains that can be integrated to provide situated, authentic learning? What knowledge is considered essential while others are only nice to know?

The learning process is the next area that needs to be carefully crafted when implementing learning by game design. We need to always keep in mind the learning goals. How do we provide learners with ample opportunities to practice so that they can achieve the goals? How can we set up the learning world to encourage active and critical rather than passive learning? How can we promote ongoing learning so that learners are achieving at higher and higher levels through cycles of new understanding, comprehension, challenged mastery, and then new modified understanding (Gee, 2008)?

Assessment is last but of critical importance to adapting learning by game design. After all, "what gets tested is what gets learned." We need to thoroughly think about what, when, and how to assess learning. Do we want to assess learning in the game? Do we want to assess it outside the game? Do we exclusively use students' games for assessment purposes? Or do we allow them to have other companion components? How can we assess the games created? What should we focus on, the learning or the game design?

Allen's design of his *The Driven* game provides a good example of practical real-life application of these three major domains of pedagogical considerations, namely content, process, and assessment. Overall, Allen wants his game to treat the "learning" part as a secondary benefit. That is, it is important for the content to be seamlessly integrated into the game and for learning to occur naturally through fun play, so that most of the time, players do not even realize they are learning. To him, educational games that are strictly "Let's Do Some FUN Math Problems with Graphics Quest Game" are considered "Chocolate Covered Broccoli" games—a term describing poorly designed educational games. Sugar coating boring schoolwork will not help. Most of the following discussion of Allen's design process is extracted from his blog posts.

To design his game, Allen first considered the content and how much of it he should try to convey to the player in the game. This determined the game concepts he generated. He believed that certain types of games would be better suited for teaching certain knowledge. Content that is text heavy, like historical facts, is better couched in a game that is designed to deliver a text-heavy presentation such as adventure games or role-playing games that have a significant storyline component. Teaching mathematical equations, on the other hand, would fit better with quick and action-oriented games, such as a car race game that teaches long division. These types of games can get the players quickly involved rather than focusing too much on reading or other less-relevant ideas.

Allen started planning by identifying all the content from the handbook that he felt needed to be included. Prioritizing is also important because it is impossible to include every idea into a game. The first level of *The Driven* game is about teaching traffic signs. Allen realized, during the design process, that no realistic way exists to include every single traffic sign from the handbook in the game. To determine what should be included, he rank ordered all the signs in the handbook based on their importance. First, he asked himself this: What are the most serious traffic situations a driver would encounter? Drivers need to understand what a school bus stop sign looks like, what a merge sign means, and what they should do when they encounter a sharp turn sign. Such signs can play a part in life or death situations in real life, and they definitely needed to be included.

Structure

The second criterion Allen considered focused on what signs he personally encounters frequently. Drawing on his personal experience as a motorist for 15 years, he was able to pick the ones that are used in our daily life. Based on these two criteria, Allen developed a list of signs. He then realized that some signs are similar, therefore teaching one sign would be enough. For example, could a player learn about a "double left turn" sign just by studying a "double right turn" sign? Most likely, yes. This, therefore, eliminated another subset of signs to be included in the game. Last, Allen weeded out signs that are not imperative. This included the "Parks Canada Road" sign: Knowing about it might be nice, but drivers do not need to know about it in order to be safe drivers.

This prioritized content knowledge gave Allen a knowledge domain that is limited and manageable in a game, which also helped him determine his storyline. Where does it start? Where does it end? The storyline and the key learning goals should be aligned and well mapped out. For his game, he had a high-level framework for each stage as well as for the whole game. Details such as conversation scripts, plot points for the story, and characters encountered could then be easily and purposefully choreographed.

He then contemplated about how to cleverly "hide the learning" inside the game so that it was not too overt to players. He also wanted to make assessments discreet in order to creatively evaluate learners. Throughout the design process, Allen considered both content and assessment simultaneously by looking at what the game player will do in each level. He approached this through considerations of two categories of events in each chapter: the *imparting events* and the *testing events*. Imparting events are the components of the level that impart knowledge to the gamer. He used diary pages, computer screens, character statement, and other means to give out information. The testing events are the checkpoints where he used minigames or challenges to test the knowledge he wanted the players to retain. Specialized combination locks, puzzle boxes, challenges with other characters, or even fighting scenes are some of the examples of the testing events he designed to assess learning.

When considering these imparting and testing events, Allen used a formulated approach to maintain a structure and simplify the design process. He listed two to four imparting events and another two to four testing events in each stage of the game. They were mapped with each other and to the whole game. This way, he made sure that the same types of knowledge would be imparted (i.e., learned) and tested (i.e., evaluated), although every single event is different. He carefully crafted each game event to avoid building a series of slight variations of the same thing. The uniqueness of each game event made players excited because they were constantly facing new challenges.

·CHAPTER FOUR·

Core Principles

This chapter covers specific instructional tactics for establishing the enactivist learning world focusing on learning through game building. The chapter starts with an overview of the game building process, delineating phases of conceptualizing, prototyping, implementing, and evaluating games. Next, it discusses idea generation and how to place learners at the center of the process. The focus then shifts to ways to create fun and facilitate the development of intelligence. This chapter concludes with specific strategies to encourage students to explore, play, test, and revise.

The Process of Learning by Game Building

There are many models that describe the game design and building process. Schreiber's (2009) iterative game design with rapid prototyping model is a rather simple yet effective model that is adapted widely by professional game designers. The idea is that you start designing, and then create a paper prototype, followed by an evaluation of sorts, and then return to the beginning design phase. You will continue this cyclical process as long as possible until you are happy with the outcome. Next you implement the design by digitally developing the game. Once you have a digital game to play, it is important to find players who can participate in play testing sessions. Results from the play testing sessions should inform your evaluation of the game, subsequently leading you to modify the implementation of the game, which goes back to the starting point of this cycle.

Learning by game building, of course, is different from game design itself, for it focuses on learning instead of the final game product. Here, I propose the Learner Design Educational Game (LDEG) model (see Figure. 4.1), based on Schreiber's model (2009). The LDEG model provides a relevant and detailed framework to guide learner game design and the development for educational purposes. Before describing this model in detail, substantiated with sample instructional activities, I reiterate that a useful approach is to ask learners to design educational games aiming to teach others content knowledge. This approach can be applied for both school students and adult learners. An advantage of this approach is that educational content can be easily and organically integrated into the task. For example, if the targeted content learning is addition of fractions, the task can be designing educational games to teach others about adding fractions.

The LDEG model starts with an "introduction" to various games through activities such as playing and evaluating free online games and Commercial-Off-the-Shelf (COTS) games. Since some of you may be nongamers, such activities enable you to become familiar with this media. For those who are gamers, this exercise gives you an opportunity to reexamine digital games through the eyes of teachers and or designers, focusing on educational values rather than just the entertainment value of the games. When you are relatively familiar with different games, brainstorming sessions, both in large and small groups, are organized to help you identify learner needs, which provide the basis for you to determine your game ideas.

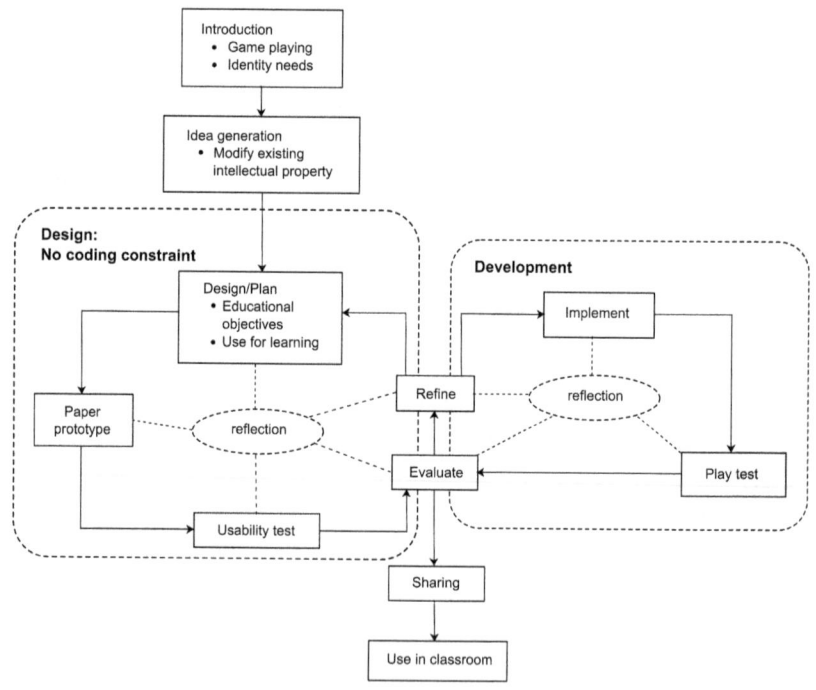

Figure 4.1. Learner Design Education Game (LDEG) Model

Structure 83

After identifying the needs of learners, you move to the "idea generation" phase. For teachers who are new to the field of game design, this is challenging, because they either struggle to generate game ideas or hold naïve beliefs that any idea will do. Therefore, specific tasks are designed to scaffold this process. One example is to ask learners to adapt an existing intellectual property (e.g., a movie) and modify it into a game idea. Such tasks not only can inspire learners to brainstorm game ideas but also enable them to realize that the quality of ideas is important as well. Another possibility is to use various games that already provide existing game mechanics and can be easily modified to get students familiar with games and game design ideas. Games such as *Gamestar Mechanics* or *Little Big Planet 2* fit in here.

Once you have a good game idea, the "Design" phase is next. This is where you design, prototype, test, and refine your games. As represented in the left dotted rectangle in Figure 4.1, this phase reflects an interactive process that includes the stages of design, paper prototype, usability test, evaluate, and refine. During this phase, you need to free yourself from thinking about the codes and concentrate on the strengths, weaknesses, and possibilities of games. Pretending that the development job would be contracted out to a professional programmer, you can create design documents describing your criteria of the production of your games. To maximize learning, the design documents should include basic elements such as the name, goals of the games, the audience for your games, estimated length of game playing, and game rules. If you are a teacher designing instructional games, you should articulate your design considerations, such as rationales for your design, educational objectives of your games, how your games can be mapped to curriculum, design constraints, and the ways your games can be used for learning.

Your next step is to create a paper prototype based on your design documents. This is where games are materialized in a paper version. This process involves creating rough, even hand-sketched drawings of an interface to use as models of your design. It not only helps you to generate more design ideas, but more importantly, it serves as the first round of usability testing for your game. During the usability test, you develop questions for play testers and test your game with colleagues, friends, or students, for example. Feedback collected from this process allows you to detect problems, identify possible solutions, and discover important issues that cannot be identified otherwise. Such an iterative process enables the games to be polished and improved with a minimal amount of time and resources.

Once satisfied with your paper version of the game, you move to the "development" phase, as represented in the right dotted square of Figure 4.1. In this phase, you use development software such as Scratch or Adobe Flash to actually create the digital game you proposed and paper prototyped. In the Chapter 8 of this book, some game design platform options (e.g., Scratch) are discussed in detail.

This development phase again is an iterative process where you develop, play test, evaluate, and refine your game. In this stage, you can narrow down the feature set in the original design to what is feasible and useful. After the paper model is implemented in digital format, you share and evaluate your game with peers and/or potential users. This process can inspire more ideas for potential use of the game and serve as another usability test (the first is conducted during the paper prototype phase) to see how well your game has been designed. The game does not have to stand alone, but rather you can develop supporting materials for users. Writing background information, explaining how the game would work, and providing supporting documentation and materials gives you opportunities to consider design and development coherently.

For example, Devin created his game titled *Quadratic Commander* using GeoGebra (an open source mathematics software) during the Do It Yourself project. In the game, players took the role of a soldier defending the earth from alien invaders. The player needed to launch a projectile from an anti-aircraft cannon to strike invading alien spacecraft. The projectile would move in a parabolic path determined by the player-defined quadratic function. Devin posted his digital draft versions of the game on a website and invited his colleagues to provide feedback. One classmate commented: "It was entertaining to figure out how the discharge unit (i.e., large gun) could be moved to nail the targets. Reminds me a bit of skeet shooting. There was an information sheet at the start. I am wondering if it would be helpful to show a graphic along with the html info sheet to give players an idea of what they are looking for?" Devin thus created a video demonstration of the game play and added it to the main game page along with supporting instructional documentation. Another colleague added this: "I realize the option for students to enter the game at multiple levels. This certainly would keep up a high enough level of challenges to keep students interested in continuing to work in the game. Is it possible that the challenge may be too great for some students or do you feel that the changes in entry levels would keep any anxiety in check?" Devin considered the feedback and added a "cheat mode" to the game that enabled players to view the parabola they were creating. This function provided students with an opportunity to learn how their changes of the numbers impact the function, but no points were awarded for the use of this feature. During the play testing session of the game with high school students, one student commented: "The alien needs to be in the sky!" So Devin added a sky background to the game. The left-hand picture in Figure 4.2 shows the initial game board design of *Quadratic Commander*, while the image on the right-hand side is a screenshot of the revised game board.

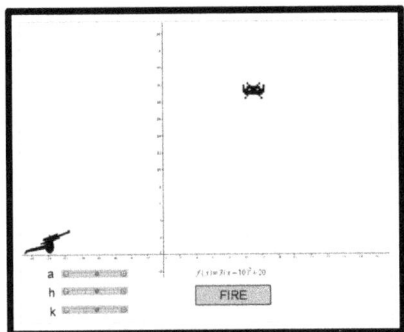 

Figure 4.2. Before and After Versions of the *Quadratic Commander* Game Boards

It is important to note that "reflection" is central to both the design and development phases. As represented by the dotted lines, reflection is an ongoing exercise that occurs in every stage. Reflective process can be structured or unstructured. For example, at the end, you look back at your design and building process, revealing specific assumptions you made and how the games could be used in real-life contexts. Reflection can be shared through written assignments as well as online blogs where you can discuss successes and frustrations, as well as critically consider your beliefs, actions, and experiences.

After the final revision, it is time for you to share your digital game. Such sharing should not be limited to your colleagues in class. The entire learning community, for instance, those found on the official Scratch website, can also benefit from the work you are doing. In the Do It Yourself project, some teachers presented their work at local conferences and others published their games online for general public use. Showcasing their self-created games to colleagues and beyond bolstered these teachers' interest in building and further refining their games. The last phase of the LDEG model is the "use in classroom" stage, when learner-created games are put into real use in educational settings.

As you can see from the LDEG model, iterative design is an important aspect that is often autonomously implemented in every stage of the process. This is exemplified in the students' experience during The Driven project. While designing traffic games, these graduate students constantly revisited and altered design considerations that were made earlier. From the very beginning, they realized that the nature of game design involved cycles of design and development. Frank remarked in a pre-interview at the start of the project: "As you plan, there are a lot of things you won't foresee in the program, so you'll have to kind of look ahead and see what problems you might face and be able to look at them and see what you would do if some things came up."

Yoshi, another graduate student who participated in The Driven project, described her team's efforts in an interview:

> During different stages of design, we are working together and going back and forth. First, we update different components of design during our discussion or during our work. We would call on different people to have valuable inputs, making it a better story. Second, there is more sophistication especially with the scenarios. The multi-agent and artificially intelligent scenarios are to be implemented. Once again, it does not only include the story level of the operational phase coverage of the traffic but also the construction for the traffic planning phase. The players have to face the scarcity of all these resources to solve problems. It's quite a sophisticated design in the script phase and we are doing trial and error between the script phase and design and implementation of the structural phase of that part.

Allen's diagram shared on his blog post, shown in Figure 4.3 (Li, Tay, & Louis, 2012), provided another example that visually demonstrates the iterative design process he experienced. Because The Driven project had a prescribed goal—to teach people road rules based on the government drivers' handbook—Allen started with the idea generation phase, exploring initial concepts, issues, and specific goals, among others. Allen's blog revealed that he jotted down everything that came to his mind in the brainstorming stage. When revisiting and analyzing these initial thoughts, he selected one or two

Structure

good ideas for further development. According to Allen, usually ideas stood out automatically. By then, he had a rough outline of the entire game and began to add general details into the plan. Once the rough outline was refined and determined, he would revisit each component to add more specific details. At this point, he was ready to begin sketching out parts of the game, including characters, scenes, storyboards, minigame ideas . . . whatever he had in mind.

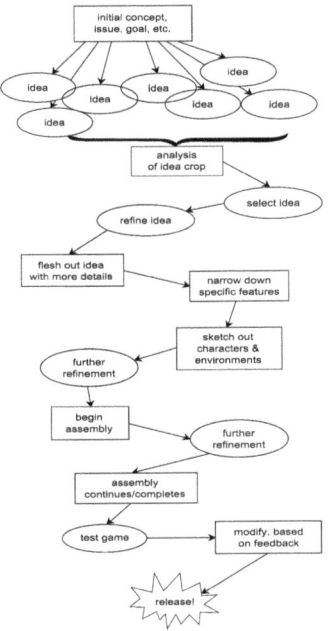

Figure 4.3. Allen's Design: Diagram (originally published in Li, et al., 2012)

Once he had some sketches and diagrams, Allen began to see where further refinement was necessary and where his ideas were very specific. He was also able to think through what his players would be doing in his game. A quick paper prototype helped him further work out the game logistics. He then started his initial assembly of the first part (e.g., first level) of the game. This assembly process allowed him to discover the realistic logistics: What was possible? What might not be possible? How could he overcome this difficulty? These sorts of questions forced him to further refine the game design, and he continued this assembly process until at least one level or stage was functioning properly. At this point, he conducted his play testing sessions where volunteers played this initial game. These tests provided feedback to inform his subsequent refinements and further design. Allen confessed that by doing this each time, for each level or stage of the game, he could feel secure and confident about his final product.

Idea Generation and Student Choice

A good game idea is half a good game done. Idea generation, therefore, is absolutely essential for digital game design. It is also a critical first step of learning by game building. It is important to realize, however, that not every idea is a good game idea. Learners, particularly those new to game design, need help generating quality game ideas.

As described in the earlier discussion of the LDEG model, idea generation is the initial stage of game design where designers explore various possibilities and search for diverse concepts. In this process, you not only retrieve information from memory but also generate new ideas through knowledge assembly, adaptation, and transformation. Previous research (Liikkanen & Perttula, 2010; Nijstad & Stroebe, 2006) suggests three effective strategies to facilitate idea generation: 1) to provide different search cues; 2) to ask proper questions; and 3) to collectively brainstorm ideas.

According to these researchers (Liikkanen & Perttula, 2010; Nijstad & Stroebe, 2006), the first strategy is to offer different search cues to learners—the game designers in this case—as suggested by previous work. This can inspire designers to search for information from a wide range of sources. Previous work in psychology demonstrates that people tend to work with the least cognitive effort possible. When generating game ideas, students may likely get a set of slightly changed instances of existing ideas if no cautious effort is made. Intentionally giving different semantic groups of cues proves to be an effective approach to enhance creativity. The frequent shift between different stimuli allows a flexible idea generation process. These semantic categories of cues include, but are not limited to, verbs (describes actions or functions), nouns (references to objects to perform an action), images, and questions. Using verbs as a stimulus can help students recall actions and abstract functions in different games, while providing carefully selected nouns allows them to make explicit references to certain objects. Providing images to students can remind them of details and features of specific objects, contexts, or environments. The second strategy to help idea generation is by asking appropriate questions (Liikkanen & Perttula, 2010). These questions should be strategically structured to inspire learners to think about critical issues in relation to their games, such as who (e.g., people), what (e.g., facts), why (e.g., rationale), how (e.g., approaches), where (e.g., spatial), and when (e.g., temporal).

The third strategy is to brainstorming an idea collectively. When students work together to consider different ideas and are exposed to others' thoughts, they can gain insights and get new inspirations. The variety of perspectives presented can stimulate further associations (Liikkanen & Perttula, 2010). Needless to say, diverse thoughts enlarge the breadth of idea generation. Discussing homogenous ideas, on the other hand, helps deepen and refine the ideas suggested. Such collaborative work of exploitation can result in a rich pool of creative ideas that can set the successful stage of the game design experience both face-to-face and online.

What is the best way to conduct such brainstorming work? One easy and frequently used approach is to have students, in small or large groups, discuss and verbally share their thoughts. This has its advantage, because one student's comments may inspire and trigger other students' ideas and imagination. Potentially, a rough idea can generate well-polished thoughts, which may flourish into an interesting brainchild. Face-to-face verbal sharing, while useful, has some drawbacks. Some researchers (Nijstad & Stroebe, 2006) have cautioned possible issues with this approach. For example, the nature of verbally sharing ideas in a group means it is a sequential process, because people have to wait for their turn. Inherently, this limits the breadth of ideas generated, because people tend to follow their peers' ideas. You probably have experienced or heard of the "free riding" problem, where some students become dependent on others' efforts rather than exploring their own ideas. Furthermore, students may forget their ideas while listening to others' thoughts, or they may even fear others' criticisms, which may cause them to refrain from open sharing.

To avoid these pitfalls, a possible way (Nijstad & Stroebe, 2006) to execute successful brainstorming sessions is to start with individual students using different coloured sticky notes to list their initial ideas. The benefit of this is fourfold. First, it promotes equity because it allows each student an equal chance to share his or her ideas without waiting for the floor time to talk or worrying about the ideas being suppressed by others. Second, it increases the accountability of individual students and provides opportunities for each student to shine. Third, it encourages diversity for it diversifies the ideas generated, potentially increasing the breadth and depth of the ideas. Fourth, it helps assessment since the coloured post-it notes record the students' exploration process, enabling easy assessment of individual student progress and becoming an intermediate and constantly evolving representation of the ideas.

After students finish writing their initial thoughts, all the proposed ideas are then discussed, summarized, and evaluated. This may iterate several times until a rich set of good game ideas are generated. This may inspire further ideas or correct misconceptions that emerge through the process. It also ensures that important and creative ideas are highlighted.

Sometimes students, especially those new to game design, do not even know how to start thinking about game ideas and the design process. Careful scaffolding, therefore, plays an important role for adapting learning by game building. A useful activity to model the game design process is to modify an existing intellectual property. For example, we can ask students to convert a movie to a game. First, ask them to generate a list of movies that they really like and would like to focus on for this activity. Then have them create a list of themes that reflect the core ideas of the movie. After careful examination of these themes, students should extract the representative verbs of each theme. Based on these verbs, students then try to brainstorm ideas for games.

Remember the *Splat!* game? Have you ever wondered how Sam came up with such wonderful and creative game ideas? Let's look at the process that Sam used to develop the *Splat!* game. The following descriptions of this process are based on Sam's blog.

> When Sam and his team started to brainstorm ideas for the game to teach road rules, they had a clear idea that the game should be grounded in problem solving rather than traditional tutoring. They considered the road rules from two perspectives: drivers and traffic engineers. As a driver, you may think that the road rules are randomly defined and difficult to remember. The engineers created these byzantine rules that interfere with driving. From the perspective of the designer of roads, however, the road rules are carefully crafted to solve real life problems on the road to ensure safe and efficient travel. Guided by this thought, their game idea was to let players experience what traffic engineers experience: develop road signs, regulations, and signals for safe driving. From this lens, road rules should not be understood from explicit, direct instruction, but from a problem-solving process.
>
> Inspired by the movie *The Karate Kid*, Sam envisioned a Karate Kid effect in the *Splat!* game: while the initial hard work of the Karate Kid (e.g. waxing cars,

Structure

painting fences) seemed random and unconnected with learning karate, all these efforts eventually morphed to karate moves, enabling the Karate Kid to reach his final goal of mastering karate. Applying this method to the *Splat!* game design, Sam had a wonderful concept for the game. That is, all the play in the game should turn into learning the road rules. Similar to games like *Social City*, Sam designed the initial *Splat!* game land with no rules, only roads and traveling vehicles on them. Players have the power and the tools to design their own rules if needed. At the beginning of the game, everyone can drive however they want. Soon, players may observe wild car crashes that cause traffic jam and injury. To solve this type of car-crashing problem, the players may realize that they have to develop their own traffic regulations.

But Sam had a design dilemma. On the one hand, he believed that experiencing car crashes could teach people a great deal since it simulated many young drivers' behaviour. On the other hand, he understood that teaching road rules and logically appropriate driving behaviours was the ultimate goal of the game. Designing a game where cars constantly crashing into each other might be counter-productive. Sam came up with a brilliant idea to address this dilemma by replacing the car with a splatter: a fluid-filled grape kind of creature who loves travel at high speeds. Splatters come with different sizes and varied colors. If they bump into each other while they are moving, they get into crashing splaccidents. The goal of the game demands that the player thinks about ways to reduce the occurrence of splaccidents. The creation of the splatters not only preserved the idea of teaching through car-crashing incidents, but it also avoided exacerbating bad driving behaviour.

(modified from Sam's blog)

Remember Allen? He was another graduate student who worked alone to design and build his traffic game in The Driven project. Allen's story provides another example of how game ideas can be generated. In Allen's blog, he talked about how he came up with an appropriate game idea. He first considered the goal of the project. Since teaching people road rules via games was the purpose, Allen wanted to use an interesting and engaging story as the driving force for the knowledge transfer. He brainstormed the concept by jotting down anything and everything that came to his mind. The following bulleted points extracted from his blog reflect his thinking process, which is kind of like an exercise of his free-flowing consciousness:

"DMV Quest Game"
- Fantasy-themed mystery game (Like Folklore for PS3)

- Futuristic Robot Game (build a robot)
- Zombies? (Dmv employee zombies)

Fantasy-themed mystery…
- Search for clues (in the drivers' handbook)
- The Movie, "Identity"
- Gumshoe detective story
- The game "Clue"
- Solve clues to the mystery by assembling handbook pages/excerpts

What about…?
- GTA-Like game?
- Fighting Game?
- Puzzle game? (this would fit for a detective game)
- 15/16 year olds don't want silly.
- Persona 3, card battle style?
- solve auto-related crime mystery using regulations provided by the Drivers' Handbook
- "sleuth" trying to solve a series of car-related accidents/crimes using handbook facts?

2 Strangers…. United by One Mystery……………
- "Jones": a broken down ex-cop turned P.I.
- "Jessica": a spiritual law college dropout; brave
- What is the mystery?
    - mysterious phone call?
    - mysterious crashes with missing persons?
- but what does this have to do with the drivers' handbook?
- analyzing crime scenes with drivers' handbook.

(Allen's blog)

From these ideas, Allen came up with the initial outline of his story, and it read something like this: "Jessica and Jones are the two main characters of the game. Jessica's mother died from a complicated car accident. Jessica wants to solve the mysterious death of her mother and therefore hires Jones, a detective, to help. They each find clues containing information in the drivers' handbook. The player needs to master information in the drivers' handbook in order to solve the puzzles, interact with the characters, and of course solve the crime. Jones's story is a gritty detective noir crime story, while Jessica takes a more supernatural approach to finding out what happened to her mother. While the pivotal catalyst car accident was horrific, no body was discovered at the scene. Thus, the plot thickens" (Allen's design document).

After ruminating on these initial thoughts, Allen revisited them. At that point, one or two ideas were dominant in his mind. He chose one and started fleshing out the details. The idea generation was a cyclic process where Allen constantly absorbed new ideas from existing games, movies, or other resources. Allen also bounced ideas off of other people, although not as regularly or to the extent as those who were working in collaborative groups.

As a novice to game design, you may belong to the group that thinks that game ideas are easy to come up with. You may also think that any game idea can be a good one. Or, it is quite possible that you consider yourself not creative enough to propagate game ideas. No matter which camp you belong to, help is needed to guide you through the initial phases of game design and also during the processes of learning by game building. In this section, I have discussed the importance of idea generation and some strategies to facilitate creativity through the process of game idea development. As suggested by the divergent stories of Sam and Allen, a common theme clearly emerged in both stories. Sam and Allen continuously absorb nutrition from a wide variety of sources, from movies, to comics, from video games, to real-life scenarios, which precipitated the conception of a great game idea.

Creating Fun

When asking someone why he or she plays a game, fun is probably the most popular response. Fun, of course, is intrinsically related to learning, and if we want students to learn, it might be in our best interest to offer some fun along the way. When learners are provided opportunities where they experience elusive fun, deep learning occurs. Brain-based research (see Willis, 2006 for details) shows that fun not only benefits student learning but is also required for long-term memory.

We have fun all the time. When playing Jeopardy with a competitor, we have fun. When reading a good novel, we have fun. When spending a night with good friends socializing, we have fun. Although these are all fun activities, many questions arise. You probably have realized that the fun we have with reading a good book is different from the kinds of fun we have while playing a baseball game. So, what are some possible types of fun? What makes one have this type rather than the other type of fun? How can we systematically create a particularly type of fun? The concept of fun, therefore, has attracted researchers' interest. LeBlanc and colleagues

(Hunicke, LeBanc, & Zubek, 2004) have identified eight different categories of fun specifically related to digital games: sensation, fantasy, narrative, challenge, fellowship, discovery, expression, and submission. Below, I discuss their definitions adapted from Schreiber (2009), along with examples to instantiate each type of fun:

- Sensation: The first category refers to the fun giving us direct sensory pleasure. Some examples of this type of fun include the music involved in *Guitar Hero* and the visuals of *My Little Big Planet*.
- Fantasy: The second category is about the fantasy a game world creates, enabling one to escape from the real world. When playing *Starcraft*, a player can be immersed in that fantasy world, mentally removing himself or herself from the reality temporarily.
- Narrative: Game storylines and contexts can give us another type of fun, the fun brought by narratives. Whether it is the prescript storylines embedded in the game or the stories emerged through game playing process, such narratives can bring us great pleasure.
- Challenge: Meeting and being able to overcome challenges also give us enormous pleasure, which is the fourth category of fun. When playing a car race game in *Super Mario Kart* and trying to beat playmates, we enjoy the thrill of competition.
- Fellowship: The social aspect associated with game playing gives us the fifth type of fun, the fun of fellowship. When playing a game, for instance, *World of War Craft*, we interact with different people, such as people in our guild. Such opportunities for collaboration and communication bring us a great sense of pleasure.
- Discovery: When we delve into an uncharted space, we enjoy the experience of exploring the unknown. The fun of discovering is the sixth kind of fun, and it often occurs in adventure and role playing games such as *Myst*.
- Expression: We are all interested in ourselves. So the opportunity for us to express ourselves via games brings us another sense of fun, the fun of expression. *Second Life*, for example, offers a wonderful digital world in which you can live and express yourself.
- Submission: Pastime or submission is the eighth kind of fun related to games. Submission suggests that players engage in games as an ongoing hobby rather than as isolated events. Many avid gamers play

regularly.

This taxonomy, although far from exclusive, helps us understand the kinds of fun people enjoy. It can provide a valuable lens to consider how to systematically integrate fun elements, whether you are an educator who is adopting learning by game building or a learner who is designing games for others to use. While using this framework, you need to remember two important things: First, any game, good or bad, can contain some kind of fun in different combinations. Second, having more types of fun in a game cannot guarantee a higher quality game. In other words, whether someone enjoys a game or not depends on both the game and the player. Some players may enjoy a certain combination of types of fun more than another group. There is no Holy Grail game that everyone enjoys, no matter how many kinds of fun it contains.

Table 4.1. Game Design Elements to Facilitate Fun and Intelligence

Fun	Multiple Intelligence	Possible Game Design Elements
Sensation	Musical, spatial	Using sound effects, visualization, art
Fantasy	All	Creating imaginary scenarios with rich narratives and great visuals
Narrative	Linguistic	Writing complex storylines or narrative background
Challenge	Logical, mathematical	Introducing calculations, logic, classification, critical thinking
Fellowship	Interpersonal	Finding opportunities for sharing, collaborating, large group simulating
Discover	Bodily-kinaesthetic	Involving the whole body or hands-on experience
Expression	Intrapersonal	Inspiring personal memories or evoking emotional feelings
Submission	All	Engaging players emotionally, encouraging communication, multilayered challenging to continually interest players

If we compare the kinds of fun with the idea of multiple intelligences (Gardner & Hatch, 1989), we see parallels. Table 4.1 provides a comparison of the kinds of fun and multiple intelligences involved. It also offers some examples of possible game design elements that link certain types of fun and multiple intelligences. For example, some people are audio, visual, or kinaesthetic learners. People in this group are more inclined to find fun in games that include these characteristics. Those who like fellowship fun may pose interpersonal intelligence, while narrative fun may link to linguist intelligence. When adopting learning by game building, you can intentionally promote certain kinds of fun based on students' intelligence. For example, for students who have linguist intelligence, we can scaffold learning to integrate narrative fun in the game design by letting them write rich storylines and/or create narrative background information. Another way to promote deep learning is to focus on a particular set of fun in student game design based on the learning you want to emphasize. If you want to foster students' creativity, you may ask them to design games that are heavily invested in fantasy fun or discovery fun. If you are targeting students' mathematical or analytical skills, you may encourage them to design games that focus on challenging fun.

Next, I describe several games created by teachers or k-12 students in our research projects. These are all demonstrations of how intelligences can be linked to different kinds of fun in game design. Figure 4.4 contains screenshots of three of these games.

 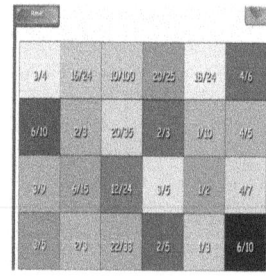 

Figure 4.4. Screenshots of Games: *Shellshocked 2* (left), *Faction Mahjong* (middle), and *Square Up* (right).

During the Call of Math project, the preservice teachers worked on developing digital games for secondary math students. Naturally, logical-mathematical intelligence was the main focus. A close examination of the

Structure

games created by these teachers revealed that many games explored the fun of challenging. The Kudo game *Shellshocked 2*, developed by Jack and Mark, for instance, exemplified a game promoting the challenging fun. Essentially, *Shellshocked 2* is a sandbox game where players decide between two storylines. They can either help Turtle Montana destroy the oil refinery that is making people sick, or they can help Kloud King by rescuing his kidnapped son. The game starts with this narration: "Welcome to Coduu, a world in chaos. Two factions, the Klouds and the Turtles, are at war and you have decided to become a mercenary for one side."

The players, regardless of which side they choose, have to collect a certain number of fire crystals and water crystals. To do this, they need to spend time in the fire area to gain fire crystals and in the water area to obtain water crystals. The catch is while in the fire area, players not only acquire fire crystals but also lose water crystals. There is a similar catch in the water area. So players have to carefully balance the time they spend in each area. The amount of time spent in each area is not apparent from the outset and needs to be worked out by setting up and solving a system of linear equations. At no point in the game are players told how to do this. They have to work out the problems and solutions on their own.

In this game, rich problems are provided so that the players always feel challenged at the peak of their ability. For instance, after finishing one level, the players are prompted: "Thank goodness you are here! The Turtles and Klouds do not know what to do! Mr. Irrationality has locked up some of their friends! You need things to be EXACTLY the same on both sides of the war. Rescue either turtles or cyclists and bring them to the side of the war that needs them." In this level, players need to master additional skills and solve different math problems in order to progress.

Fraction Mahjong, another game created by preservice math teachers, is a modified *Mahjong* game. Instead of finding identical tiles, the players need to find tiles with equivalent fractions. Like *Mahjong*, the objective of the game is to decide which tiles to choose, and open up blocked tiles in such a way that all tiles can be removed. Many cognitive strategies are used here, including planning, hypothesizing, organizing, and testing to solve the game, with an emphasis on challenging fun to engage players.

Brian's Coming Back is an adventure game created by two practicing teachers aimed at elementary students learning language arts. Based on the novel *Hatchet*, Brian, a survivor of a plane crash, is the main character in the game. He has to survive in the wilderness until he can repair the airplane and get home. The game has organically integrated various activities for classroom use. For example, students need to read the novel, discuss narrative elements in the novel (e.g., setting, tone), create a script for role-playing, and add narrations on a comic strip in order to ultimately complete the game. This, therefore, is a game that creates a great sense of narrative fun and facilitates linguistic intelligence.

The *Square Up* game is a geometry game developed by two high school students. In the game, players have to keep critters away from a break dancer by pushing or pulling certain objects into correct positions. Using geometry principles, players need to decide which objects to move to a particular space. When the objects are moved to a correct place, the critters are pushed back. If the answer is incorrect, the critters continue to advance. As the game progresses, the critters begin to advance more quickly. In this game, players with more bodily-kinaesthetic intelligence enjoy the hands-on experiences while exercising their logical mathematical skills.

The game *DDD*, created by Tim, an ESL teacher, is a game that represents fantasy fun. This game was adapted from an existing board game called *Dungeons & Dragons*. The DDD game sets a scene in Goblin Mountain within the Thunder Mountains. In this imaginary world, players need to venture through Goblin Mountain in order to rescue Lady D'Mis's brother, Lord Thomas. In some places, players are given a map to guide them through different levels and spaces. In other parts of the game, no existing maps are available. Players have to venture through the land themselves and develop their own maps. In this game, diverse intelligences are involved. For example, linguistic intelligence is exercised because rich and complicated narratives offer the context of the game. Spatial intelligence is also explored when the players manoeuvre through different areas and levels in the Thunder Mountains. Interpersonal intelligence is practiced when there are multiple players.

These sample games, all created by learners, demonstrate how we can focus on particular types of fun and at the same time promote deep learning that caters to different intelligences.

Prototyping and Play Testing

As described in the LDEG model discussed earlier, learning by game building involves two critical steps: prototyping and play testing. In the paper prototyping phase, you can easily revise and rebuild parts or even the entire game. Identifying and solving as many problems as possible in the paper prototyping phase, therefore, allows you to polish your game with much less effort and resources than it does in the digital game building phase. When we ask students to learn through building their own games, it is important to give them time to do paper prototyping and testing. Often we, as teachers, are confined by the limited time we have to cover seemingly unlimited content. It is important to understand that providing opportunities for students to paper prototype, test, and refine their games can save time in the long run. In addition, discovering and addressing potential issues with minimal effort in the paper prototyping phase can remedy possible student challenges or frustrations.

How to Paper Prototype?

Most professional game designers, if not all of them, will agree that maximizing the iteration cycles of your game design can result in an optimal final product. In fact, this rule applies to the design of almost anything, from a game, to a machine, to a lesson. Therefore, after forming your core game idea, you should put it into a playable form in the most efficient and economic way so that it can be easily revised. That is why paper prototyping, one of the cheapest and fastest ways, becomes such a valuable practice.

The essential idea of paper prototyping is to transfer the vision inside the designer's mind into a tangible, shareable work for people to manipulate and test. This process of transferring abstract ideas into concrete models helps students learn how to visually express their visions to others. In today's world of global inhabitants, visual literacy becomes increasingly important because graphic information is everywhere. We communicate with each other using visual materials in addition to text and auditoria information. Acquiring visual literacy helps our students become full participants in the digital society (Jenkins, 2007). Paper prototyping provides excellent opportunities for learners to practice the visual communication skills that are powerful and meaningful.

Knowing the importance of paper prototyping, your next question may be this: "What material do I need to paper prototype my game?" The answer is that you can use pretty much anything available to you or your students; no fancy materials are needed (Schreiber, 2009). When students are ready to make a paper prototype for their games, we often bring the following items (list adapted from Schreiber, 2009):

- Coloured paper. We always bring different colored sheets that can be used to take notes and to make game boards or surfaces.
- Coloured pens/pencils/crayons. Students often use these for color coding, drawing pictures and images, or annotating their game elements.
- Paperclips and binder clips: The coloured clips are the best. These items have purposes other than just holding papers together. We have seen them used to represent avatars, to make spinners, and to become tokens, among other things.
- Coloured sticky notes. These can be used for note taking or helping students visualize ideas by putting ideas on the notes and then arranging them on a large sheet of paper. They can also be put on the game elements (e.g., trails) to mark or customize them.
- Coloured beads, different patterned buttons, or similar small items. These can be used for markers, playing pieces, or counters.
- Rulers or meter sticks. Students can use them to draw grids, game boards, among other things.
- Different patterned paper cups. We have seen students using these to build castles, forts, or other structures.
- Toothpicks. These can be used for different constructions.
- Index cards. Students can use these to create and customize their own cards.
- Scissors and glue sticks or tape. Students may use them to cut out shapes and put them together to make different structures like buildings.
- Dice or spinners. I often bring different sorts (e.g., 4-, 5-, 6-, or 20-sided dice). These items can easily provide random variables that are independent rather than dependent (e.g., drawing a card).
- Larger sheet of paper or cardboard. I often bring a small stack of larger sheets of paper (sometimes even the flipchart sheets). They can be used as a game board, and they are often useful for storyboarding the game ideas.

Some optional items are pieces from other games, coloured sticky dots, or low value coins such as pennies. Remember, paper prototyping focuses on the game mechanics rather than the aesthetics or the technology. The appeal of artwork, the quality of the audio, or the friendliness of the user interface is not something that can be easily tested from paper prototyping. Instead, the main goal of paper prototyping is to test the game in its most raw state to examine what works and what doesn't (Schreiber, 2009).

Play Testing

Play testing is a critical step for any game design, whether for a commercial entertainment company or a student building game meant for learning fractions. Play testing can help you identify problems, find loopholes, and improve the playability of the game you are creating. Ideally, play testing should be a continuous task, meaning that a game should be play tested at multiple points and by different groups of play testers.

In our work with learners, play testing has played a significant role in their game design. For example, in the Do It Yourself project, Sam created the *MythGiving* game that focused on elementary students' acquiring social studies concepts. It is a game similar to the board game *War* but involves players calling upon God or Goddess and possibly getting gifts to build their own Greek city or state; this is modelled either on the democratic government of Athens or the militaristic oligarchy of Sparta. After he created the game board and pieces, Sam gave his sixth-grade students an opportunity to play the card version of the game. He closely observed students' interaction with the paper version of the game and each other. He further gave a survey asking students to rate the game on a scale of 1–10, where 10 means the students absolutely love it. His game achieved a mean score of 8.2, telling him that the players were generally quite positive. However, he also identified some issues from this testing stage. One observation he made was that the students took slightly longer than he expected to get to the building round. He therefore decided to reduce the number of resources needed to start building so that players could get to a place to buy resources faster.

Another teacher, Seetha, created the game *Blizzard Zone* to introduce players to the Cartesian system of coordinates. It was originally designed to help sixth-grade students understand the idea of navigating in a space through provided coordinates, which in turn translated to directions. Players are placed in a confined game space in an Arctic plane, reflecting the four-quadrant concept of the Cartesian system, where four "safe" stations are located at the four corners of the space. At the center of the game space is the danger zone, namely, the "blizzard zone." Players have to move their squad members by navigating in a coordinate system, from the center of the blizzard zone to the safe stations at the outer corners of the plane. The following narrative introduces the game:

> You are the commander of a special science squad, made up of 4 scientists, deployed to the North Pole on a mission to study climate change. However, your scientists have been stranded at the center of a blizzard zone in the Arctic plane. Unless you can guide them to safety, they will die. Use the Escape Guides provided to guide them to safety.

In the game, Seetha used a reward system called Joints (like tokens) where players can get them when they have correctly guided people to move from different zones. After the paper prototype was developed, a 45-minute play testing session was conducted. Because Seetha had no access to sixth-grade students at the time, she did the play testing with adults. Yet she found that these adult testers were very much engaged in the game play, which led her to extend her targeted audience from Grade 6 to a broader population. During this play testing session, Seetha identified several problems. For example, some of her rules were not clear. In one instance, when a scientist was close to a safe station, it was not specified in the game which side of the safe station he or she should land in order to enter it. In the situation demonstrated in Figure 4.5, the scientist is currently located in the red "O" position. Because no rules specified how a player could move into the Safe station located at the bottom right-hand corner, the player could have many choices. For example, a player could move one step down and then move one step right, or a player could move one step right and one step down, or a player could move one step up, then two steps down, and one step right. This list can go on and on. Identifying this issue allowed Seetha to modify her game rules and be very specific about every aspect of the game.

Another observation Seetha made was that players were confused about the portion of the rules that explained when to use the Joints. When a Joint is released, should the player have another turn to throw the dice? Or should the player give his or her turn to the next player? Some play testers said that they did not mind the lack of stringent rules because, for them, it provided more flexibility. Others, however, felt frustrated by the ambiguity. Seetha decided to revise her design to incorporate different possibilities to different modes of the game. This way, players would not be confused while the game would still maintain the same level of elasticity. Seetha listed about 10 issues identified in this play testing session and discussed how she had addressed them in the subsequent iteration of the game.

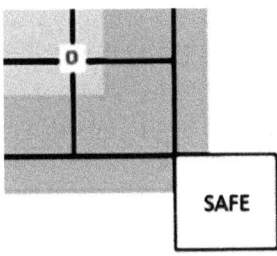

Figure 4.5. Blizzard Zone Field

Examples like these show how a simple, quick play testing session can reveal many problems associated with the game design. Even if you cannot find testers from your targeted population, letting anyone play the game would still give you great insight into how the game is functioning or not functioning. Such user feedback provides rich information for you to make decisions on how to address problems in the actual games.

Having said this, you may find that some problems simply cannot be uncovered in the paper prototype stage. For example, you can only identify programming issues when you actually code the game. Let's look at the case of three practicing teachers, Iso, Libby, and Janet, who created a math game when they participated in the Do It Yourself project. In this game, players have to solve randomly generated multiplication problems. Initially, designers decided to give each player two minutes to solve each problem posed by a farmer, and if the timer reached zero, the game would be over and the player would need to restart the level of the game. When they play tested the paper prototype of the game with third-grade students, this rule worked out fine. However, after coding that first version of the game, they play tested it again, realizing that the time between the farmer posing the problem and the answer bar popping up for the player to answer was far too long. Initially, 10 seconds after the farmer asked a question, the answer bar would show. This turned out to be excruciatingly long considering the fact that after the answer bar appeared, the gamer was given yet another two minutes to answer. So the extra 10 seconds was needless, especially if the player knew the answer almost instantly. Consequently, they changed the time from 10 seconds to 1 second, which also eliminated the potential problem of players accidentally inputting the answer and hitting the "enter" button before the answer bar popped up, thereby reducing the likelihood of the game resetting in these instances.

They also found a glitch during play testing: If a player could not answer a question before the timer was over, the game waited at 0.00 for an answer from the player before resetting itself. Because the farmer "asked" the question and was expecting an answer, if no answer was provided by the time the clock reached zero, the game stagnated. The solution was to let the player know that the game was over but that he or she must input something to essentially "wake up" the game play and consequently reset the game. They used a "Game Over" sprite (a programming command in Scratch) to solve the problem.

When adopting the learning by game building approach in a classroom, we are often limited by time and availability of play testers. The easiest solution is to get students to play test each other's games. There are, however, other levels of play testing that can offer tremendous motivation for the students' game design.

Sam, the elementary teacher we met in Chapter 1, is a big believer in game-based learning and has worked in several projects involving students building their own games. Whenever he works with elementary students on these types of projects, he establishes his gamer credentials from the very beginning by telling students: "I play *Madden 12*, *Bioshock 2*, *Angry Birds*, *Call of Duty MW2* . . . " Students usually are thrilled to hear such introductions because he is treated as someone who gets "it." Sometimes students even test him: "Well what was your favourite attack to use on a Big Daddy?" (Sam's blog).

In one particular project, Sam worked as an expert gamer and game designer with a teacher who taught fourth- and fifth-grade students. These students built maze games that supported learning math concepts. During the process, students realized that some of their self-built games were extremely challenging and others were incredibly fun to play. With guidance from the teachers, students developed a reward system that largely promoted their game design. In Sam's blog, he described the reward system that worked like this:

- "Level one: When a student finished his or her game, he or she could request other students to play it.

- Level two: If the players agreed that the game had great merit, they could ask their school principal or their teacher to play.
- Level three: The highest level of all was a game that was worthy of this cry: "Mr. Sam, please come and beat my game!" This meant that the polished levels had already challenged many players including their peers and their homeroom teachers and/or the school principal."

As Sam depicted in his blog, watching Sam got stuck on a problem in a game, as far as the students considered, would be as exciting as watching a man landing on the moon! If Sam could easily beat a game, students would quickly develop a plan to improve the game and eagerly share it with him. Whatever comment Sam makes, students listen carefully, whether it is "tricky" or "fun" or "a nice easy first level" or "wow, are there more levels coming?" They value the feedback because the feedback reflects expert's honest critiques (Sam's blog).

The lesson learned here is that finding a gamer to play test students' games can be an extremely useful strategy. It not only allows for a new aspect of feedback from an expert's serious analytical review, but it can also drive students' interest to a much higher level.

I have discussed several examples demonstrating the importance of the prototyping, play testing, and revising process. When play testing, you need to focus on both the usability aspect and the playability aspect of your game. The usability aspect is concerned with how easy or difficult it is to play the game and how clear or confusing the rules are. When considering playability, although connected with usability, you mainly emphasize the questions surrounding how much fun a game is and whether the players enjoy the game. It is important to note that play testing can be conducted with any number of players and from any population. You can conduct a good play testing session and get great results from one or more players. As a designer, your job in a play testing session is to be a good observer rather than an instructor. You need to refrain from attempting to tell the players how the game works or what the best strategies are for playing the game. Although you can certainly discuss and brainstorm with them after the play testing session, your focus during the session is to learn about your game design by watching the players interact with each other and your game. If you implement learning by game design in your class, play testing with peers not only gives each student feedback on his or her own game but also promotes peer collaboration, which ultimately enhances student learning.

A caveat is that revising and refining process can be tedious and therefore create frustrations. Learners are often excited about generating their game ideas and developing their own games. But after they receive feedback from the play testing of their games, they need to revise those games in order for them to be fully functional.

In several of our research projects, working with a range of learners, from elementary science students, to high school math students, to graduate students in education, we have conducted surveys looking at students' emotional states. These include happiness, excitement, pride, confusion, frustration, boredom, and annoyance. During each phase of game development (building the game, testing the game, modifying the game, and finishing the game), it is quite possible to experience each emotional state. Regardless of the age level of the student population, "bored" or "annoyed" are the least frequent emotions students expressed. Yet, modifying is the stage where some students feel frustrated or bored even though the overall feeling about the game design process is overwhelmingly positive. Students' narratives show that those who felt bored said that it was because of the tedious tasks required for modifications in the game. One narrative read as follows: "I feel bored because modification was really repetitive." Another student wrote the following: "I was frustrated because of the obstacles and tedious work stopping me from completing my goal."

It is important to take such comments into consideration when building an enactivist learning world. As students learn from game design and building, we need to pay particular attention to their emotional states through all stages of the process, especially when they modify games. They should be challenged, which may cause confusion and frustration; yet, such confusion and frustration should not be allowed to hinder their commitment to the task. In other words, we need to provide appropriate scaffolding that will enable students to experience a "pleasantly frustrated state." Essentially, the frustration should be a "sweet spot" that encourages students to gain inspiration from their moments of confusions and to struggle through the challenges, which will ultimately lead to deeper learning and engagement. Finding that sweet spot is the key!

PART THREE
Culture

•CHAPTER FIVE•

Enactivist Learning World and Culture

This chapter explores the enactivist learning world through a culture lens. Contextualized in the emergence of a participatory culture, this chapter argues that such a new context requires a new way of thinking about learning and therefore presents new challenges. The case is made establishing the enactivist learning world as a necessary agent in meeting the challenges of allowing students to learn by doing the things that people do in real life, participating in authentic recreations of the way people in the real world learn to innovate. The chapter concludes with a delineation of the related concepts of collaborative learning and community building.

Culture and Participatory Culture

Culture

What is culture? Like many key terms we have discussed in this book, culture has multiple meanings and has yet to be assigned a universally accepted definition. The term describes a complicated phenomenon that allows for many open-ended ideas. We can describe culture from the topical perspective, the historical perspective, the behavioural perspective, the normative perspective, or the structural perspective. According to Salen and Zimmerman (2003), culture really contains three main aspects: the way people think, how people behave, and what people have produced. Culture, in regard to games and gaming, refers to the environment or the context where games are played. Any game, therefore, reflects and is situated in a certain culture.

Why is it important to consider culture when we talk about games and learning by game design? As discussed before, a game is a dead object until players have given life to it through their play. As soon as people interact with a game, a culture is created. Culture, therefore, is a critical concept when considering learning by game design. When designing games, we need to contemplate on what kinds of cultural structure the players will engage in during the game play. A game can directly reflect different cultures and consequently can be used to expose players to different cultural ideas. What is the winning condition of a game? Is it through defeating your opponent or helping people? By destroying buildings or establishing a community? How are valuables, such as precious coins or ironsmith skills, collected in a game? Each of these design decisions can suggest particular values and beliefs, hence cultivating a specific culture. The process of game design provides an excellent opportunity to discuss culture.

Mike, a third-grade teacher in Western Canada, was a participant of the Do It Yourself project. Mike's students were expected to learn about Indian culture per the third-grade curriculum. Mike, a Caucasian who grew up in Western Canada, had never been to India, and his knowledge of India came from readings. Even after having taught the unit several times, Mike admitted that he constantly found holes in his knowledge, especially concerning the religious aspects of Indian culture. As a way to learn more about this area, he chose to design the game *Samsara*. This, he believed, would excite his students about Indian culture, and at the same time, enhance his own understanding of this culture.

Mike's game, *Samsara*, is a single-player digital game designed to introduce learners to various aspects of Indian life, culture, history, religion, and geography. Directly addressing specific learning outcomes from the curriculum, *Samsara* aims to foster students' curiosity about Indian culture.

In his design document, Mike details how the game works, which provides the base of the following discussion about his game. In Samsara, players follow a cycle of the following basic stages: arriving in a city, earning money, becoming involved in dharmic activities, and then travelling on the road. The final goal of the game is that players visit all the cities on the map, safely travel to the Karni Mata temple, and win enough karma to become a Brahmin priest.

> At the beginning of the game, the players are foreigners who are at the lowest level of the caste system. In a city, they engage in dharmic activities by taking quizzes to demonstrate their knowledge of India. Their involvement in these dharmic activities allows them to earn rupees, buy food, and acquire karma points. When players are on the road, they have limited food and receive some chance events (e.g., an event that gives you karma points by chance). All these stages contribute toward the main objective of the game: collecting karma so that players can advance through the levels of the Indian caste system.
>
> In the game, players need to make strategic decisions and deal with chance

situations. Progressing through the game, players must fulfill personal obligations, callings, and duties by working, learning, visiting temples, and helping others. This reflects Hinduism's principle that everyone needs to fulfill his or her dharma. Decisions players make would affect the number of karma points they receive. When the players get 50 karma points, they are reborn in a higher level of the caste. Although collecting karma points is the ultimate goal of the game, players need to work to earn money (rupees) to buy food so that they can survive.

Mike added a chance factor through random events during the game play, allowing either positive or negative events to occur. Adding this chance factor largely increased the playability of the game, making it more exciting. For example, players might encounter criminals or poachers, child marriage, taxi scams, or police corruption. Other possible negative events include the contraction of a disease like dengue fever or malaria or natural disasters like an earthquake. Positive events can also happen, such as meeting and training with a Yogi master or celebrating an Indian holiday like Diwali, Holi, or Gandhi's Birthday.

(modified from Mike's design document)

It is obvious from the description of *Samsara*, both delineated in his design document and embodied in his final game, that the Indian culture is interwoven into every aspect of the game, including the story, game rules, chance events, and goals. Both the main goal of becoming a Brahmin priest and the minor goals like acquiring money, improving life quality, or surviving the perils of travel, parallel the goals for actual inhabitants of India.

Mike's design document articulates how the factual and conceptual information are organically integrated into the game. For instance, each time a character is introduced, detailed information about his or her role in religion or society is described. The main game screen is an accurate map of India. Indian jobs, Hindu deities, Indian food, and Indian landmarks are introduced through various dharmic activities, while chance events convey knowledge related to climate, holidays and celebrations, geography, human rights, health, and poverty. The game embodies the essential Indian ideology of the endless cycle of life from birth to death, a prominent facet of Hinduism. A historical perspective of Indian culture is also reflected in the game. For instance, the caste system, although outlawed in 1950, its influence still exists in India today. Blending the caste system into the game, therefore, introduces players to this historical concept. In the game, players have to make decisions on various issues related to poverty, natural disasters, and other situations, which send key messages about social justice and human rights to the players (Mike's design document).

For third-grade children in North America, playing the game and assuming character roles in India allow them an opportunity to experience the challenges and successes associated with Indian culture at a personal level. Consequently, the process helps students internalize the sociocultural principles in a very safe environment. Immersion into such environments not only increases students' curiosity about the culture but also helps them develop a better understanding and appreciation of how social and cultural factors affect the quality of life in India.

In his design document, Mike indicated that the *Samsara* game is meant to send key messages about equity, social justice, and ethics to students through game play. Such ideas embody current values, beliefs and ideology, that is, the current culture. As demonstrated by Mike's game, creating a game is about creating a culture. In Mike's case, his game not only teaches students Indian values and beliefs, but it instills in them Western views and principles that Mike believes to be critical.

When considering learning by game design, it is important to consider what kinds of cultural structure the game designers, and learners in this case, will be engaged in during the design process. How can we create a world that cultivates a culture that nurtures learning in order to achieve the desired outcomes? Such learning worlds reflect our beliefs and values about learning, about students, and about knowledge. For example, when students create their own games, will collaboration be allowed? Even encouraged? Will small group work be enabled for students to design and build their games? Will interaction amongst students be constantly promoted? Will flexibility be provided and endorsed? Will the outcome be shared and cherished, and with whom? Your decisions on these issues will cultivate the culture of your students. This culture, and the modern-day culture that has been shaped by the web, is one that may need further exploration. This, then, leads to a relevant discussion about the emergent participatory culture.

Participatory Culture

A participatory culture has emerged in recent years, largely driven by the development of Web 2.0. Web 2.0 is a continued transition of the web from static websites created by few experts to well-developed platforms serving web applications for everyone. It is commonly agreed that Web 2.0 is more of a conceptual change than a technological change; this means that we are moving from passive consumption to active creation (Dede, 2008). The spectrum of Web 2.0 tools is wide, ranging from social networking (e.g., Facebook, blogs), to media sharing (e.g., Flickr, YouTube), to collaborative knowledge generating (e.g., Wikipedia, Harry Potter fan fiction), to game building (e.g., Scratch).

We have observed how such development is fundamentally changing our society, especially in the ways in which we communicate, socialize, and play. For example, our increased use of tools like YouTube and Flickr forever change the television and movie industries. News stories are no longer only being covered by television channels. Rather, we receive instant coverage from news feed via the internet or tweets through twitter. As early as 2007, already about 64% of the net generations (i.e., those between the age of 12 and 32) created and shared digital content online, an increase from 57% in 2006 (Tapscott, 2009). No doubt that this number is much higher today. This phenomenon of civic engagement in culture, brought about mainly by Web 2.0, leads to the emergence of a participatory culture – i.e., "a culture with relatively low barriers to artistic expression and civic engagement, strong support for creating and sharing one's creations, as well as some type of informal mentorship whereby what is known by the most experiences is passed along to novices" (Jenkins, Clinton, Purushotma, Robison, & Weigel, 2006, p. 3).

The emerging participatory culture challenges our conventional views about knowledge, experts, and learning. For example, Dede (2008) pointed to the differences between traditional definitions of knowledge and what is suggested by Web 2.0: Traditionally, knowledge

> consists of accurate interrelationships among facts, based on unbiased research . . . there is only one correct, unambiguous interpretation of factual interrelationships . . . the content and skills that experts feel every person should know are presented as factual "truth" compiled in curriculum standards and assessed with high-stakes tests . . . Epistemologically, a single-right-answer is believed to underlie each phenomenon, even though experts may not yet have developed a full understanding of the systemic causes that provide an accurate interpretation of some situations. In contrast, the [participatory culture] definition of "knowledge" is collective agreement about a description that may combine facts with other dimensions of human experience, such as opinions, values, and spiritual beliefs. (p. 80)

This fundamental shift of views about knowledge, expertise, and learning calls for reconsideration and redesign of our formal educational system and the pedagogical approaches currently being employed (Dede, 2008). It underscores the importance of how, in a participatory culture, students learn, teachers teach, and everyone plays a role in education. In order to work, learn, and live in a participatory culture, we need to know and become familiar with its rhetoric. Nowadays, plunk any question into Google, and we can instantly acquire the needed information with details. Consequently, what used to be considered as core knowledge for students needs to be reconsidered. Since in a participatory culture, knowledge is based on findings of a consensus articulation, remembering accurate facts is no longer important. Rather, because of the possibility of information overload, the focus of learning should be more on helping students develop critical, analytical, and creative skills so that they can differentiate facts, opinions, and values, as well as appreciate the complex relationship amongst them in order to create meaning.

The emergent participatory culture thus demands us to think carefully about what we want out of education in this new context, in particular, how the digital world can help our students learn. As discussed earlier, the web is a tool that provides information, platforms to express creativity, as well as opportunities for communication and collaboration. Grounded in enactivism, learning by game design and building with the support of web tools can foster the establishment of participatory communities. For example, game-based websites such as the Scratch websites provide places for students to learn and communicate, inside and outside of their schools. They offer space for students to form new identities, to develop expertise, to make connections, to exercise leadership, and ultimately to participate in real-life practice.

As we design enactivist learning worlds that adopt learning by game design, a critical issue to contemplate is how to create a culture that prepares learners for the emergent participatory culture. To establish an enactivist world for 21st-century learning, the following pedagogical ideas need to be considered:

- *Collaboration principle*: In an enactivist learning world, collaboration is highly valued and always encouraged. For instance, students can work in small groups for designing and developing their games. During the game design and building process, from

brainstorming game ideas, to paper prototyping, to revising games, students are always given opportunities to collaborate, both in small groups and in larger communities such as their classes.
- *Freedom principle*: Freedom, as discussed in the previous section, is a critical aspect from an enactivist viewpoint. In a classroom, freedom can be realized through flexibility that provides space and conditions for students to freely explore the learning world. For instance, if students possess different technical backgrounds and have different goals in mind, we can give them choices of using specific software for the creation of their games. Giving students the option of working in teams or individually in their game design project adds another layer of flexibility. In addition, flexibility can be implemented by allowing students to decide on their products: what games they want to create, to what extent they develop a fully functioning game, what supporting material they create, and so on.
- *Scaffolding principle*: Scaffolding is another important principle to consider, whether it is about students' learning the content knowledge or how to program the games. For example, the freedom principle discussed earlier suggests that we can provide students choices of employing game development software. We cannot simply throw them into the sea of programming without coaching or helping (unless the students are seasoned programmers). Instead, we need to provide appropriate scaffolding so that students can achieve their goals yet are always on the verge of challenge. But the dilemma is that we, as the teachers (except for maybe programming professors), do not necessarily master all the game development software that students choose. It is either not desirable to do so, or it is too difficult, if not impossible, to master them in a timely fashion. What we need to do is select one or two easily accessible (this usually means online, free, downloadable), user-friendly, powerful enough, flexible game development software programs and use them as the primary game building tools for students' programming. These tools can become the programming platform for the majority of the students for which we provide training and scaffolding. For those who choose to use other software tools, the expectation is that they will be responsible for learning and mastering the specific software on their own.

- *Sharing principle*: Consistent with the idea of participatory culture, sharing is highly regarded in an enactivist learning world. Students' learning should go beyond producing tangible outcomes only for teachers to grade. Rather, their creations contribute to the distributed cognitive knowledge base. Their work, therefore, is always shared and showcased within the learning community and beyond. In some cases, students and teachers work together to create fun gaming classes where they can play each other's games. In the Games in Motion project with elementary students, for example, we arranged a family night, inviting the parents as well as students in other classes to come play the games created. Such sharing, showcasing, and celebrating significantly stimulated students' motivation to further refine their games.

  Sharing is not limited to students' final product. Rather, students' thoughts, working processes, and draft ideas are all encouraged to be presented, in structured or unstructured ways, so that others can get feedback for improvements. For example, I often intentionally set aside instruction time for students to play test their prototypes. I urge students to play test their ideas with other people, like their students, parents, and friends. I also offer multiple ways to promote such sharing. This includes using in-class time for presentations, creating online forums for discussion, and helping students publish their games through social media or related websites.

- *Reflection principle*: Sharing is closely linked to reflection and provides an excellent way to promote reflection. When students share their thoughts, games, or prototypes with each other, they observe and listen to others' reactions. Giving students opportunities to reflect on their own and others' ideas, on the building process, and on ways of solving the problems that arise can greatly enhance their learning and understanding. Sometimes, the reflection can be a large class discussion guided by teachers' intentional questions. Other times, it can be a written reflection by individual learners.

These principles provide useful guidance for teachers to establish an enactivist learning world adopting learning by game design. Yet, the successful building of such a learning world depends, to a large extent, on the teachers' understanding and abilities to take full advantage of this approach. It is ideal to give teachers a chance to design and build their own games, therefore gaining firsthand experience of this approach in order to facilitate student learning. Teachers have the potential to produce games that best align educational goals and students' need because of their expertise and experience with the curriculum, their students, and educational contexts.

Teacher Design Games

The emergence of participatory cultures demands our reconsideration of teaching and learning. As discussed earlier, letting teachers design games for their students offers an excellent opportunity to prepare them to teach in this new era. But, to what extent do teacher-designed games embody pedagogical principles? When teachers are immersed in game design, what are their perceived affordances of such experience? Let's look at our Do It Yourself project.

During the Do It Yourself project, 32 practicing teachers designed and built a total of 27 digital games for educational purposes. These included 15 adventure games, 3 strategy games, 3 action/fighting games, 5 simulations, and 1 role-playing game. For each game, teachers developed a written design document before actually building their game. Were teachers able to incorporate different pedagogical components into the design and building of the games? We created a rubric (a detailed discussion of the rubric is included in Section 4 of this book) to evaluate their design considerations on the following 11 categories: problem solving, active learning, exploration and reasoning, connections, collaboration, scaffolding, assessment, engagement/motivation, participation, strategy, and user friendly/ease of play. For each of their design documents, we assessed how the game design integrated these ideas by checking whether the design minimally, fairly, or extensively represented these 11 pedagogical components.

Table 5.1 presents the frequency of our evaluation of the teacher design documents. For example, "problem solving" was extensively represented in 21 of the game designs and was fairly represented in the other 6 documents. "Active learning," however, showed an opposite trend: It was only minimally represented in 13 designs, fairly represented in 10 designs, and extensively represented in only 4 design documents. Looking from a general lens, we could see that in every category except "strategy," more than half of the games achieved standard or above standard levels. In other words, out of the 11 pedagogical categories, 10 were represented either fairly or extensively in the games. This suggests that practicing teachers as designers were fairly successful at integrating educational components into the planning stages of the design process. They could address the necessary pedagogical considerations and propose a design to integrate the learning goals into a digital game. Successful integration of content and curriculum objectives into a digital format creates the possibility of presenting relevant learning opportunities in the students' preferred format for today's technologically savvy "digital natives."

Table 5.1. Frequency of Rubric Ranking of Design Documents

Category	Minimal representation	Fair representation	Extensive representation
Problem solving	0	6	21
Active learning	13	10	4
Exploration and reasoning	10	9	8
Connections	0	1	26
Strategy	14	6	7
Participation	0	5	22
Engagement/motivation	0	9	18
User friendly/ease of play	0	7	20
Collaboration	7	11	9
Scaffolding	4	15	8
Assessment	1	19	7

We also used the rubric to assess the actual digital games teachers created and found that almost every digital game *fairly* or *extensively* represented the rubric categories regardless of whether the corresponding design document fairly or extensively represented the same rubric categories. These results demonstrate that these teachers were not only able to plan, but they could also implement good pedagogical considerations into game design and building.

An interesting pattern emerged when we compared teachers' design documents with their actual games. The four categories "active learning," "exploration and reasoning," "strategy," and "assessment" scored higher in the games than in the design documents. Since active learning, exploration and reasoning, and assessment are critical pedagogical considerations for learning, the improvements in these categories from the planning stage to the developed games suggest that the nature of digital games has the potential to promote positive learning in these aspects. The category "exploration and reasoning," defined as complex and challenging problems through students' exploration to discover the concepts inherent within, provides a more reactive and cerebral exercise. The games here provided a perfect platform for teachers to naturally create and embed complicated and rich problems, which in turn promoted active and engaging learning experiences.

An additional benefit of teacher game design stemmed from the types of assessments that games can provide. The improvements of ranking scores from planning documents to the actual games in these highly regarded pedagogical considerations suggested that teachers could successfully create a plethora of problems in game environments to stimulate, motivate, and strategize for active learning. Traditionally, definitive assessments that are administered in a classroom are met with apprehension and risk avoidance. This behavior can potentially lead to poor performance and trepidation toward test taking. Using digital games, teachers can weave in assessments in a more fluid and contextualized way, thus promoting engagement and personal achievement.

Through our work with practicing teachers, we have explored teacher perceived affordances of their own game design process. A significant discovery of this exploration is that the design experience afforded opportunities for teachers to reconceptualize pedagogy and enhance their creativity based on students' input and feedback. When considering game design for learning, the teachers tended to adapt a more holistic approach to the curriculum by integrating students' learning of different subjects, skills, and knowledge. Regardless of the primary subject area, all the teachers incorporated elements and objectives from other subject areas in their game design. That is, all of the teacher-created games integrated different subjects rather than focusing on any single discipline. In a traditional classroom, teachers often focus on one or few curricular objectives at a time, whether it is the format of the lesson presented, the layout of the textbook that is used, or the pedagogical beliefs of the teacher, curriculum, or school. Yet, when considering game-based approaches, these teachers opted to adapt multidisciplinary approaches instead of focusing on one curricular objective at a time. This suggests that during the design process, teachers have the potential and the inclination to connect from and integrate with different subject areas.

Our work suggests that teachers benefit from the experience of designing and building their own games. First, the experience allows teachers to understand that a gaming platform is not linear and game building requires multidimensional design considerations. Many games work on a sensory level as well as on a cerebral one. Strategy and problem solving are almost always present in some capacity in such games. Games also give students the chance to assess and evaluate themselves. Such deepened understanding can provoke teachers to incorporate games in classrooms for better retention of concepts learned.

Secondly, digital games have the potential to include many events to contextualize learning with aesthetic and sensory stimulation as well as multilevel access to numerous subject areas. Letting teachers design their own games may result in the need for teachers to change their pedagogical beliefs, pushing them to consider and reconsider an interdisciplinary approach in the future, with or without games. The building of digital games can compel practicing teachers to learn more about their students' academic lives (provided their students are the probable players). By doing so, the teacher can integrate other topics currently being learned or planned by teachers in other subject areas to create a more comprehensive and connected digital environment in which their students can learn.

Finally, game building has the potential to allow multiple teachers opportunities to provide expert input from their subject areas, to encourage collaboration of many teachers surrounding the academic welfare of their shared students, and to offer a much needed global context for individual subjects to shine through. This, in turn, can foster a more socially and academically conscious group of students and teachers.

In short, teachers play an important role in helping children learn and grow in participatory culture. Game design offers opportunities for learning, creative expression, civic engagement, and political empowerment; all are important for the participatory culture. Letting teachers experience game design themselves enables them to practice skills, acquire knowledge, contemplate ethical frameworks, and build confidence so that they can help their students become full participants in contemporary culture.

Culture

Collaborative Learning

As alluded to in the previous section, creating a culture that promotes learning for 21st-century skills calls for collaborative learning. Collaborative learning is not a new concept. While many teachers may utilize this strategy in their classrooms, it does not mean simply putting students into groups. The term *collaboration* suggests that people 1) cooperate by acting purposefully toward a communal goal, 2) coordinate with synchronized efforts and shared resources, and 3) cocreate novel outcomes (Klopfer, 2008). Unlike other collective efforts, collaboration is about joining forces to achieve common goals AND creating something new together.

Most likely you have had the experience of benefitting from collaboration. In fact, there could be times when working with others may prove more helpful than working alone. Sometimes we use the term *synergy* to describe such situations. The results of being able to learn in a community and the social interaction that takes place can be surprising. The following story of Rosie, an elementary student, exemplifies this.

Rosie's Story

Rosie's story was shared in the blog written by Sam, a teacher we met in Chapter one who participated in the Why Read If I Can Build project. In this project, Sam taught a sixth-grade class where he integrated game design for math. It was the week before spring break and students had been working on Scratch programming for weeks in small groups. Sam acknowledged that overall he was contented with the students' work. While noticing the struggling of a couple of groups, Sam was not worried because those groups were programming some fairly difficult games.

> One morning, I opened an unexpected e-mail from Rosie's mom who was really worried. Rosie was a great student in class who loved school and loved being in my class. In the e-mail, the mom explained that Rosie was agonizing with her Scratch project because she was confused with Scratch programming. Rosie's partner in school was on vacation, leaving Rosie to work on the programming alone. At home, nobody could help her, since her parents and older brother did not know anything about Scratch or programming. Rosie cried a lot at home, even showed reluctance to attend school on the days that the Scratch project was scheduled.
>
> I was devastated. "How had I missed someone struggling so much? And what could have caused this frustration?," I asked myself. I always believe that struggling and frustration are natural and even inevitable in the processes of problem solving and

debugging. Euphoria occurs when one eventually figures things out or finds a new solution to the problem, providing a rush of excitement. My teaching practice has been focusing on fostering deep learning by allowing students to internalize concepts, especially through such a struggling process. This approach, however, often requires students to persevere. Well-timed scaffolding as well as social interaction and teamwork can help students persist.

With this in mind, I e-mailed back and arranged a lunch meeting with Rosie and one of her friends. During the lunch meeting, Rosie demonstrated her program to me, with her friend sitting by her side. Rosie's game idea was to convert a board puzzle game titled Buggy Jump (http://www.mathfair.com/puzzles.html) to a computer game. Buggy Jump is a game involving three red ladybugs and three white ladybugs. These ladybugs are sitting on lily pads as illustrated in Rosie's drawing (Figure 5.1). The ladybugs become bored and want to play a game. At the end of the game, the positions of the red bugs are exchanged with the positions of the white bugs. These ladybugs need to follow these rules in the game:

1. A ladybug can move from its current lily pad along a line to an empty lily pad if it does not pass over another ladybug.
2. When a ladybug is in a corner lily pad, it can jump over another ladybug of a different colour as long as it jumps in a straight line and lands in an empty lily pad.
3. A ladybug is not allowed to jump over another ladybug of the same colour.

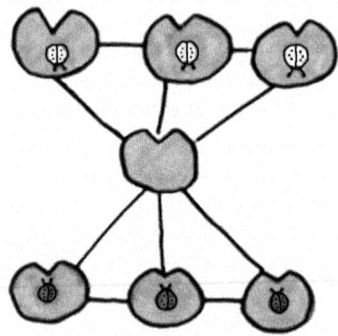

Figure 5.1. Rosie's Drawing of *Buggy Jump*

Rosie's team tried to convert this board game to its digital version. She wanted to program the game so that when a player clicked on a ladybug, it would jump to the empty lily pad if it could, or else it would stay still. Rosie had already coded variables, with a number of conditional statements (e.g., if... then). But she forgot that she needed to modify the code for a lily pad from "empty" to "full" after a ladybug jumped. Watching her describing the process, I confirmed that Rosie was frustrated and had low confidence for problem solving at this point. I decided to work with Rosie on the program for one ladybug, and let Rosie talk through her variables. Along the way, I praised her and together we made some quick coding decisions. Through this playing, programming and talking, Rosie soon realized that she had already done all of the key programming parts. She only missed several "broadcasts" commands to inform her "lily pads" if they were empty or occupied. Rosie became thrilled because she immediately realized the solution. After she spent all lunch hour working on the game with her friend, Rosie completed the coding. Noticing what Rosie had accomplished, other students treated her as the new Scratch expert. Rosie became the newly selected best programmer in the room. Even the boys who considered themselves "Scratch experts" admired her scripts and asked her for assistance. Her confidence level was soaring.

That night, I was happy because my teacher mission was accomplished: confidence rebuilt, problem fixed, and students back on track. "Oh, no!" was my reaction when I received another email from Rosie's mom titled: "Another Scratch Problem." I said to myself, "not again!" I clicked the message and started reading: "I don't know what you did today, but you are a miracle worker. My daughter is so excited and happy about her Scratch project and she is constantly showing it off. I have another problem with Scratch though. Now she is working on her project so intently, I can't get her off the computer and into bed!" I was pleasantly surprised and happy to solve this new problem!

(Sam's blog).

True Collaborative Learning

Rosie's story illustrates the importance of social interaction and collaboration in the process of learning, yet simply putting people together cannot guarantee the best results. Successful collaboration depends on the following five elements: positive interdependence, interaction, individual accountability, interpersonal and small group skills, and group processing (Johnson & Johnson, 1989). Johnson and Johnson (1989) describes these five key elements for collaborative learning:

1. *Positive interdependence*: Team members believe that everyone's efforts benefit the whole team, or in other words, they "sink or swim together."

2. ***Interaction:*** Significant cognitive development occurs when group members support each other and have positive interpersonal dynamics.
3. ***Individual accountability***: Each member is accountable and his or her performance is evaluated individually to assure no "free rides."
4. ***Interpersonal and small group skills***: Students learn interpersonal and teamwork skills in addition to learning content knowledge.
5. ***Group processing***: Students reflect on how well the group works together, aiming to improve subsequent teamwork.

The nature of learning by game-design supports collaborative learning because it requires students to cocreate digital games, that is, novel outcomes. When designing an enactivist learning world, adapting learning by game design with appropriate educational components can stimulate true collaboration.

If we examine specific educational components of learning by game design, we can clearly see how they overlap with collaborative learning. When students design games, this is often a joint endeavour involving team efforts. Everyone on the team has to contribute in order to successfully build a game, which conforms to the *positive interdependence* of collaboration. During the game design process, each member of the team focuses on one aspect of the game but needs to communicate, to discuss, to compromise, to negotiate, in short to work together for a coherent game. This is where promotive *interactions* come into play. When we assign each member a role and request everyone to evaluate each other's performance during the game building process, we can ensure the *individual accountability* of the collaboration. While students interact with, accommodate, and listen to each other, they develop *interpersonal and small group skills* that are vital for 21st-century citizens. As delineated in Chapter 4, continued reflection is necessary during game design in order to improve the group dynamics, which complies with the *group processing* principle of collaborative learning. In summary, various opportunities can be organically integrated into an enactivist learning world that can facilitate collaboration.

Our experiences tell us that when developing instructional activities, we must consider the age and background of our students, as well as how we plan to deliver or implement these activities in order to maximize student learning. On the one hand, for adult learners, such as preservice teachers or graduate students, choices of working in small groups or individually can be solely their decisions. This flexibility is particularly important when the delivery mode of learning is exclusively online. On the other hand, when working with younger students, especially elementary students, we ask students to work in small groups of two or three and often arrange them to have complementary skill sets. A team works well when at least one member has good technical skills and another with good writing skills and/or organizational skills. In the team, everyone is assigned a role and specific descriptions of the roles are provided. The example given here is what teachers have used in the Do It Yourself project.

Group Roles

Group members are asked to take one of the following roles: **project manager, designer,** or **programmer.**

While every group member must actively participate and contribute throughout the game design and building process, the **project manager** needs to coordinate the project, keep teammates organized and on target, and communicate with the teachers. The manager ensures that the finished game is representative of the ideas and discussions held by the group. The manager also makes sure submitting the finished game by the assigned deadline to the project website and other related places (e.g., Scratch website).

The **designer's** responsibility is to organize and coordinate the design of the games. In this role, you review and decide upon design options with appropriate technologies as well as instructional and assessment strategies. All group members have input, but the designer is responsible for the initial plan and follows through with the design process.

Although everyone in the group needs to contribute to the game development, the **programmer** is the primary person to code the game and to assemble the program pieces. The programmer is also responsible for arranging play testing and revising the game.

In conjunction with the roles assigned to each group member, we always integrate peer assessments in an effort to hold students accountable for their performance with the team. This peer assessment is always submitted to the teacher(s) privately to avoid potential tension among group members. Table 5.2 provides an example of the peer assessment we use for classes.

During The Driven project (Li, et al, 2012), graduate students worked together to create games that would teach road rules. Collaboration played a significant role in their game design process, occurring through both structured and unstructured interactions. Graduate students collaborated in three different ways: 1) small team, 2) large group, and 3) online interaction. Some graduate students chose to work in small teams. By doing so, they realized how team members' skills complemented one another to help them accomplish tasks effectively. Some of these students enthusiastically explained that the highlight of the experience was the opportunity to work in teams and practice collaboration skills. Frank's comment best demonstrates this:

> A highlight [of the process] is TEAMWORK! I would say collaborative skills! It wasn't a one person job and it was fun, but we had different ideas to where we wanted to go . . . so we compromised or we used both ideas . . . I love collaborative imagination, collaborative problem solving!

Table 5.2. Peer Assessment Form

Name and Role on Project	Your Name Here	Partner #1 Name Here	Partner #2 Name Here
*Actively contributing ideas**			
Willingness to participate			
Always on task			
Completed assigned role			
Comments			

* Rating scale: Excellent, Satisfactory, Not Satisfactory

In addition to structured small group work, large group meetings were held regularly to enhance collaboration. Such meetings provided a common ground for teamwork and a platform to present and view peers' ideas. During the meetings, graduate students not only shared games but also thoughts, feelings, and strategies. Everyone involved in the project was engaged and had input to improve and refine the games. These students, including the one who chose to work individually on his game design, highlighted that distributed cognition expertise helped them solve problems. For example, some students had artistic skills while others were musically inclined. Exchanging artistic works with musical pieces or helping each other on different aspects of games became a common practice. In this project, Alan drew art pieces for Mosa, and Mosa made musical pieces for Alan and

Lawrence. When they encountered technical difficulties, some asked colleagues for help while others sought assistance from different online communities. Lawrence, a student from India, said, "I actually had to contact people in India to help with the programming part of this game."

Peer interaction through online communication such as blog sharing also facilitated collaboration. We intentionally created a common repository online for all students to access and contribute information. In this repository, web links provided access to resources like tutorials for Flash and other action scripts as well as road rules practice tests, all of which benefited the students. Blogs by individual students provided up-to-date status reports on their projects and allowed peers to exchange comments and feedback. Their asynchronous interaction on blogs provided the means to stay connected and brought about a sense of togetherness on the project. Some unexpected collaboration also occurred through such interaction. For example, Alan came up with the name of his game, *The Driven*, from Sally, as explained by their online dialogue:

> Alan: I have been working on my design but am finding it difficult to come up with a name for my game. Sally I like your blog name with which you write your posts.
> Sally: Glad you like my blog name! Why don't you use the name for your game? 'The Driven' has a nice ring to it?
> Alan: Actually yes, that would really sound good for the game. Are you sure I can use it for my game?
> Sally: Absolutely!

In short, during The Driven project, we were able to cultivate a culture that promoted distributed cognition and encouraged systemic collaboration not only among peers but also to the broader communities at large. The following list specifies the educational components we integrated in the project to promote collaboration based on the five key elements of collaborative learning (Johnson & Johnson, 1989):

1. **Positive interdependence:** Team members have complementary skills, working together toward building a functional game. For example, graduate students in education were paired with graduate students from computer science. Distributed cognition in the learning communities is evident, breaking the geographic barrier.

2. **Interaction:** Regular small group and large group meetings encourage sharing and discussion. Online discussions and blogs provide another venue for students to interact.
3. **Individual accountability:** Each team fills out a form to indicate who focuses on what parts of the project. Each member evaluates other members' performance.
4. **Interpersonal and small group skills:** Group members need to learn how to discuss, communicate, and compromise to solve problems.
5. **Group processing:** Reflection is an ongoing process that takes place at each stage of the design and examines how the group is functioning.

Our work in The Driven project is simply one example of how collaborative learning can be established in a game building situation. Although beneficial, collaborative learning situations are not necessarily easy to set up. When students need to work together on tackling game design tasks, conflicts can happen, and they prevent learning. We need to not only properly structure the learning environment but also to teach students social skills to work with others and resolve inevitable conflicts. The following strategies are useful tips to consider when designing collaborative learning:

1. Identify and resolve small group conflicts as early as possible.
2. Create and share clearly defined rubrics at the beginning of the project and use them for guiding the learning process and assessment of the final work. Collaboration should also be a vital component of the rubric.
3. Group formation should be carefully considered. For adult learners in face-to-face situations, it is best to give them the freedom to choose their own groups. For younger learners or when students are learning in an inclusive online world, teacher-designated groups provide a more effective approach. Making sure to coordinate people with complementary skills (e.g., programming vs. writing skills) in a group is optimal.
4. Creating a safe and relaxed atmosphere can make problem solving easy, and consequently, make collaborative learning fun and engaging.

The following section focuses on one particular type of collaboration, small group learning, and discusses its manifestation in game design and building projects.

Small Group Learning

Allowing students to work in small groups can be extremely beneficial, regardless of their ages. When designing games, for example, students with strong technical skills working with students who have stronger writing skills may find an enhanced learning experience, since the skill sets can be shared. As a result of these shared skill sets, students may experience lowered anxiety levels, thus allowing their confidence to soar. Additionally, the social exchanges that take place in small group settings can foster the development of communication and negotiation skills. Overall, the learning that can occur within a small group may far exceed the content expectations. Equally as valuable of small group learning is the potential that it can bring self-directed, natural learning (Armstrong, 1979).

There are many ways to organize small group learning, ranging from teacher-assigned small groups based on students' abilities to freestyle groups that allow students to choose their own group members. Depending on the particular student population as well as the scope and nature of the game building projects, teachers can choose the most appropriate ways to structure small group learning. Usually, the younger the students, the more likely they will need detailed directions.

Let's peek at a classroom in our Run for Math project, where high school students learned mathematics through game building. The students were asked to create games for others to use, focusing on the math content they were currently learning. It was the third week into the project, and Flourish, the teacher, introduced the game development software Kudo to the class. Diane, a student with very low confidence in math as well as anything that is technical, freaked out. Without even trying the programming tutorial recommended to her, Diane exclaimed the following:

"This is impossible!"

"We do not have enough time!"

"There is no way we could possibly brainstorm and program a game, no, not even with help!"

Flourish was deeply concerned about such attitudes, as reflected in her blog: "Now, I don't disagree that the task of programming a game can be a bit intimidating and daunting. But, I take issue with freaking out when someone hasn't even tried. You can't tell me something is too hard if you have put no effort towards it yet."

Attempting to calm her students, Flourish asked Diane to team up with her friend who had a strong technical background. Flourish guided the team to brainstorm interesting game ideas while exploring the potentials of the software tool. The next several days went by quietly, until one morning, Diane rushed to Flourish's office with great enthusiasm. She told Flourish the exciting news: Her team had not only come up with wonderful game ideas, but they also built a new game called *Logarithmath* based on one of the ideas generated. They were elated with the project and with themselves while Diane was proudly showing the game to Flourish. Noticing such excitement and pride, Flourish encouraged Diane to demonstrate *Logarithmath* to other teachers. Diane, along with her friend, admitted that the experience was not nearly as bad as they thought it would be. Contrary to their original thoughts, the team found that making the game was actually quite fun. Team members could not help but acknowledge that creating a game as a way to assess their learning was much more challenging yet at the same time way more interesting than taking a test. Flourish reflected in her blog: "It was a good game and something worthy to be proud of! Would Diane ever have done that with a test? Probably not."

In this case, working with a partner allowed Diane to ease her anxiety toward programming. It also enabled her to share and test ideas with a friend who had the same goals. The outcome of the small group collaboration was optimal: a student-designed game that boosted students' confidence and interest in both the math content and game design.

The benefit of small group collaborative work can extend beyond the individuals within the group. For example, students who work in different game design projects can inform and help each other by sharing their ideas. Consider the case of David and Bill, two high school students who created a mathematical gameland in our Run for Math project. This mathematical land contained numerous apples, and in each apple, a math concept was hidden. Picking up an apple would then reveal the particular math question to be answered or the math problem to be solved. When playing the game, players would compete with each other or the nonplayer characters to pick up as many apples as possible and correctly answer the questions embedded in the apples as fast as they could. While developing the game using Kodu, David and Bill had trouble programming polynomial graphs within the terrain of the game. They turned to the teacher, Flourish, for help. Flourish was very honest with them, "hmmm…I do not know how to program it. Can you find a way to graph it? You can then teach me how to do it." David and Bill worked together earnestly to explore online resources. Knowing that they were searching for solutions to a problem for which even the teacher did not know the answer was extra motivational. Several days later, the team discovered a solution to overcome this challenge by changing the colors of different areas in the land. It worked like this: They developed a green background with a blue grid as the basic coordinate plane. On the plane, two perpendicular lines were coloured gold to represent the x-axis and the y-axis. Red apples that players needed to collect were strategically placed at certain points on the grid. When all the "useful" apples were picked up and the associated problems were solved, the graph of $y = x^2$ appeared in the "land." This graph was illustrated by drawing the form of x^2 with burgundy terrain over the top of the green background. From a bird's-eye view, it looked like the graph of x^2 in the first and second quadrants.

Very excited about this discovery, David and Bill shared the approach with other students in their class. This knowledge was then communicated with teachers and students in other classes. As a result, several teams created games using the same technique, showing graphs in terrains. One team used the same strategy to create a very cool Venn diagram.

Stories like this demonstrate the value of small group learning and how such collaboration can foster deeper understanding. Students need the flexibility and encouragement that small group learning provides. Working with others through the struggles of the messy design process and the creative building experience strengthens confidence and collaboration skills. While game building can certainly be done individually, the process, as a whole, becomes more authentic and fun when working with others.

As we understand the significance of collaborative small group learning, logistic issues must be considered before implementing such an approach. How should we determine the composition of a small group? Should the teacher decide or let the students choose? What is the optimal number of people for group work? How do we actually compose a small collaborative group? We, as teachers, need to carefully think about questions like these before we give students the task of working in small groups. Generally speaking, younger students, particularly elementary students, need more structure to form groups than older ones. However, when students work in an exclusive online environment, teacher-assigned groups work the best. This is because online communication, particularly asynchronous communication makes it more difficult and time consuming for learners to select their own groups.

Let me bring you to an elementary school where we conducted the Why Read If I Can Build project. During the project, three teachers worked with three Grade 6 classes, focusing on math and science learning. Students worked in small groups to design and build a digital game based on mathematics puzzles or problems. Because students in these three classes had limited cross-class interactions before this project, one question arose was, "How do we best create programming teams mixed across the three classes?" At the beginning of the project, students worked on small tasks. At this stage, the teachers did not give specific instructions about how to make groups. Students often rushed to pair off with their friends. In pairing off, students automatically grouped themselves homogenously based on gender: girls with girls and boys with boys. In addition, several students seemed to have difficulty finding a partner and lingered in the classroom until the teachers intervened and grouped them.

This process of openly exploring partnership worked well at this beginning stage, giving students the freedom to discover game design and software templates. Before long, the teachers realized the need to adopt a different approach when students worked on their final project. The teachers believed that it was important to not only delegate more formally structured small groups but also to enhance students' understanding of the necessity of such collaborative work. The teachers decided to implement the process of collaborative work with a sort of introductory explanation of how a game is developed.

One of the teachers, Mr. Sam, held a forum with the entire group of 80 students, where he gave an introduction on how to properly form a team for game design and development.

He began by posing a question: *"What are some of the things I would look for if I were the boss? Who would I hire?"*

A boy shouted, *"Ah . . . maybe like an animator . . . ."*

Mr. Sam agreed, *" . . . so I'd want somebody who can do animation . . . . I'd probably want to hire somebody like that on my team . . . especially if I'm doing something that uses animation."*

A girl said excitedly, *" . . . an organizer . . . ."*

Mr. Sam reiterated, "... *so did you hear that? I'd probably want an organizer.... I'd want somebody I know who can be a project leader ... somebody to help to figure out where resources go....*"

Another boy added, *"A programmer?"*

Mr. Sam responded, *"I'd probably want somebody who could program ... somebody who has a good understanding of the idea of how to make these things work...."*

A third boy cried, *"..... somebody who could make sounds...."*

Mr. Sam continued, *"I might want somebody who could make sounds ... put music to a game. That might be something that's special...."*

He prompted students to think of another important expertise: *"We miss out on one of the big ones for a gamer or game design. How many of you tried to play a game and you couldn't figure out what was going on?"*

Some of the students raised their hands. Mr. Sam continued, *"If you ever tried to play a game and you couldn't figure out what was going on ... has anyone heard of the solution RTM?"*

The students looked puzzled. He continued, *"... Read The Manual?"* The students all spoke amongst themselves indicating that they should have known that.

Mr. Sam then called the students' attention and continued, *"If you're really stuck ... you're depending on somebody with really good writing skills ... you need somebody who can write ... not just write instructions ... but if you have a storyline, you need somebody who can write story, that can write good dialogue for the characters to say. All of those elements need to come together."*

Mr. Sam then summarized the number and types of expertise that would be needed in a game design project while the students watched and listened intently. Applying the list of expertise to how students should organize their own groups for their game project, Mr. Sam continued, *"Out of five jobs in making a good game, one job is actually programming ... 20%. If I were to hire people out of this group to make the game, would I hire you and your best friend?"*

Some of the students replied, *"No!"*

Trying to further reason with them on the formation of effective gaming groups, Mr. Sam continued, *"If they have the right skills maybe ... but if they don't have the right skills, if that's not a really good partnership, then that's probably not the people we should put together. You don't need to be good friends to work on a team. You need to have complementary skills...."*

When we make groups we seek out groups that can work together. The idea in a group is that everybody in the group is better together than they would be able to do something on their own."

He then introduced the learning style survey (see Example 5.1) to the students and explained that the objective of this survey was to obtain information on their learning styles in order to group them for the final game project. "We're going to take your answers from the survey and we're going to try to make really strong groups . . . we want to make sure there's somebody in the group that can do each of the tasks that we need for the game to be done."

Example 5.1. Elementary Student Learning Style Survey

When we work alone on a project, we depend on our personal skills to complete the project. Imagine Fred has to make a research display board. It doesn't look very pretty, because he is not the best at making visual display boards. He is really good at doing research though and finds it easy to search out and understand information.

Another project, created by Samuel, has an amazing display board. Samuel loves to draw and has an outstanding knack for using colour and arranging things on the display board in a logical manner. His research skills are not the best though; he would rather spend time making his display board perfect. These two students would make good partners because each partner brings skills from which the other can benefit.

Answer the following questions to help your teachers match you with just the right people for your final project. By knowing your strengths and weaknesses, we will be able to make SUPER groups that have the right people for making an amazing project.

For the sentences below, choose a number from 1–5. 1 means that it is not really like you, while 5 means that it describes you perfectly!

1. *I like to draw, paint and create artwork.*
2. *I like to think things through, like when we solve math problems.*
3. *I like to read and write stories.*
4. *I am musical. I love to sing and to play music.*
5. *I do well when I work in a group. People like to work with me because I am a good group member.*
6. *I like to build models. I need to see how things work.*
7. *I like to work by myself and have time alone to reflect and journal.*

8. *I like to do things with the outdoors and nature. I understand how things in the environment work together.*
9. *I am very organized.*
10. *I am not afraid of being wrong. I will just keep trying things until something works.*
11. *I want a group to work well together. It is important to me that everyone in a group is happy.*
12. *I love to think through problems step by step. I love to try to find out what makes something work.*
13. *Scratch is fun to use. I have enjoyed solving the Scratch challenges.*
14. *Programming in Scratch is easy for me.*
15. *I play video games.*

Using the information from the survey, these teachers were able to put together well-balanced teams, with each team gaining a student who enjoyed the programming aspect, one with good creative artwork, and another with good program management and organizational skills. Our observation also showed that the process was helpful to students in supporting their understanding of the ways they were grouped together with complementary skills, which resulted in better collaboration.

Learning Communities

Enactivism stresses that our mind is inseparable from our body and the surrounding environment. Our cognition co-evolves with our action and our learning world. Therefore, the promotion of deep learning should not be limited to any individual or school boundary. Building learning communities, both within classrooms and beyond, can foster such deep learning, the type of learning we, as teachers, want from our students.

For example, during the Games in Motion project (Li, 2010), the original task for these camp students was to develop games that would teach others Newton's laws. Without any prompting, students autonomously started to involve people around them in what they, the students, were doing. At home, these students taught their parents and siblings not only Newton's laws but also how to use Scratch, the software they used to build their games. In fact, about one third of the students taught others Scratch. Billy, an 8-year-old boy in the camp, had a twin sister Sally, who was not enrolled in our summer camp. The first day Scratch was introduced, Billy excitedly went home and downloaded the game on his computer. While doing this, Sally watched and asked what he was doing. Billy patiently told her that he just learned this "cool program" and could not wait to show off his game building skills. Sally was intrigued and wanted to do the same. Billy taught her the basic skills, and the two of them started to have a competition of creating and playing their own games. A week later, I watched Billy upload his new game to the Scratch website by himself. He told me that he and Sally each created three games in four days. While he was proudly demonstrating some of their games to me, he identified a few problems in one of Sally's games. He said, "Oh, I have to tell her this problem and she needs to change it."

It was at this point that I decided to invite parents and siblings to look at Scratch and Newton's laws, not so much to work on it but rather to simply enjoy exploring it all together. I started interviewing and surveying teachers, parents, and siblings. This was certainly not something that I planned to do at the outset. While I did intend on having students design games to teach others, I had not anticipated extending this work into the community. It was this "hap" (Weinsheimer, 1985) event, an unplanned and unplannable occurrence, that inspired me to extend my research boundaries into the community. This decision actually proved to be a very fruitful one, allowing intriguing phenomena to surface and rich data to be collected. Following are a few anecdotes that I would like to share.

Diana's dad was a software engineer. When Diana had difficulties programming her game at home, she would approach her dad and ask for help. While Diana's dad enjoyed teaching Diana basic programming skills and realized the huge benefit for her to acquire such skills, he admitted that even he got some new, creative ideas from working with Diana.

Leon, a seven-year-old boy in the summer camp, had the last name Newton and took great pride in that. He also took great pride in the work he did with the games. In an interview that took place at the end of the 2-week camp, Leon's mother told me, "Leon talked about his games non-stop for a few days. He loved it and talked about it to anyone who would listen . . . . He also talked about other [things] he learned and as a result, I am very well versed in Newton's Laws now!"

These examples demonstrate how learning, when done in the right setting, can become a daily action involving community members, rather than isolated and meaningless "school work." Students who become deeply engaged in learning also become deeply engaged in the action and discussion that takes place around their learning, and ultimately, this is what leads to strong habits of mind.

Teaching others demands a deep understanding of the content, and the case of the Games in Motion project was no exception. Whether students were teaching Newton's laws or the Scratch commands to others, previously perceived dry facts or boring principles became meaningful information for solving local problems. These facts and principles were applied, used, manipulated, and explored, thus becoming part of students' daily living and dialogue. These students were engaged, thoughtful, and motivated. Learning had gone beyond school boundaries and affected people in the learning environment outside of the school. Parents, siblings, and friends all became part of their learning world. This is what enactivism embodies. Enactivism views that our body, mind, and the surrounding world are co-evolving, and by intentionally helping students build learning communities, we are ultimately helping them build an understanding of lifelong learning.

• CHAPTER SIX •

Important Aspects

This chapter investigates strategies to promote interaction, collaboration, and community building that support the establishment of an enactivist learning world. It starts with a discussion of game dynamics from a design point of view, followed by a discourse of narratives and storytelling in the game building process. Such discussion includes practical guidelines appropriate for implementation for different learners (e.g., children vs. adults, online vs. face-to-face learners) in different settings (K-12 classrooms, afterschool programs, and higher education courses).

Game Dynamics

While this section is about game dynamics, I would like to start the discussion with rules. We know how rules are essential in any game. But what are some different kinds of rules in games? What makes a good rule, and what makes a bad one? How do game rules affect or impact players' experiences? And how are rules decided upon from the beginning? Much of the following discussion in this section about game dynamics and its relationship with different kinds of fun are based on the work of Schreiber (2009).

If we look at the more technical side of gaming and game design, the concept of game mechanics refers to the "rules" of the game, the constraints established to enable the game to operate. These rules determine how to start and end a game, what actions a player can take, and what actions are not allowed. They also help in deciding what constitutes a win and a loss in the game. In short, game mechanic sets up all the boundaries that a player must follow (Schreiber, 2009).

Game dynamics, on the other hand, define the PLAY of the game when the rules are in action. What strategies emerged from the rules? How do players interact with the game mechanics and with each other? Different dynamics are created when the same game is played by different players because the interactions are different. While game mechanics provide potential game dynamics, yet, ultimately it is the game dynamics that determine a player's experience.

Most, if not all, game designers strive for creating fun and engaging games. Yet, we all know that some games are not fun at all. As a game designer, you can only develop game mechanics like the rules and goals, hoping that the desired behaviour will emerge from these game mechanics. That is, you can only design game mechanics (or rules) but not game dynamics (or play). While you do not have complete control of players' experience, there are certain strategies you can adapt in designing the game mechanics so that particular game playing dynamics are more likely to occur. One of these strategies is to consider both the designer's and player's perspectives; this can lead to your observation of how even a tiny tweak in one design aspect can greatly affect game play (Schreiber, 2009).

In Chapter 4, I introduced different kinds of fun, such as the fun of challenge, the fun of expression, and the fun of fellowship. You need to remember that different game rules bring about different dynamics in the game. These dynamics impact how players think about a game's fun factor. For instance, using time pressure or competition through opponent play creates a challenging sort of fun. Rules encouraging information sharing amongst team members and/or including winning conditions that are difficult to achieve alone often enable players to enjoy the social sort of fun along with the challenge. If your game mechanics allow and even promote players to personalize their game world (e.g., players can customize their avatar), players are likely to have fun from the self-expression and self-discovery. Many games now allow players to design their own appearances and other traits. You can create a system for buying, building, or earning game items and equipment or ways for players to design, change levels or contexts, or customize personal, unique characters. When you incorporate game rules that build tension, players will most likely experience the fun of dramatic tension.

In general, increasing game objects and/or the ways for objects to interact can produce a more complex game dynamic, which often leads to more interest and enthusiasm on the part of the player. However, games that are not so complex can also result in successful game playing (Schreiber, 2009). *Pac-Man*, for example, is a simple but fun and addicting game. The mechanics in the Asian game *Go* are very simple, yet the game has proven its success by attracting countless number of players for hundreds or even thousands of years.

Can learners, instead of professional game designers, also create simple, yet fun games when they are engaged in the process of learning by game building? Let's look at a student-created game during the Why Read If I Can Build project. In that project, over 80 sixth-grade students developed dozens of casual games, just for fun. These games were in addition to their major math and science game projects. The games were uploaded online to allow broader audiences to play. Students were also encouraged to rate the games. One activity was to let students rate which games they considered to be the most fun. The top-rated game was called *Catch It!* and was created by Sarah and Elaine. This was a surprise to me because at a first glance, the game seemed really mundane with a plain background, simple rules, and few game objects (a fish and a shark). The fish swims in the water and the player controls the shark, trying to eat the fish. Every time the shark touches the fish, the fish shrinks. The smaller the fish, the faster it moves. This continues until the fish becomes too small and disappears, indicating that the fish has been eaten piece by piece. The trick is that at a certain point, the fish becomes so tiny that it is difficult to see it on the screen. The player needs to find where the fish is, not so much by watching the fish itself (because it is too small), but rather by observing and guessing what is going on in the water (e.g., seaweed moves when the fish swims close by). To be honest, I was unable to understand why this was a top-rated game until I actually watched how students played. Players had to interact with the game in meaningful ways and often make strategic decisions quickly. They were challenged and engrossed in the game play. In one instance, a player was screaming with excitement or frustration, while others stood near him, watching and shouting out strategies. Instances like this exhibit the possible enjoyment interesting game play dynamics can produce.

According to Schreiber (2009), game dynamics can also be created by *feedback loops*, which comprise both positive and negative loops. Positive feedback is the positive amplifier, reinforcing what has happened. In games, this means that a player's current performance is magnified, making rich people richer and poor people poorer. For example, when players successfully beat the game, they get access to an extra game play mode or promote to a higher level. So the players' high scores in a game are positively reinforced, leading to more powerful game play so that they can achieve even higher scores. Similarly, a poor game play could result in less power and consequently lower scores. Both cases are considered positive feedback, even if the feedback is not good news for the player.

Negative feedback, on the other hand, acts as a negative multiplier, pushing the player toward the middle ground. Therefore, if a player has good performance, the game becomes more challenging so that he or she does not feel that the game is too easy. Similarly, struggling players get a boost with their performance so that they don't hit a dead end.

When the feedback becomes a loop, it positively or negatively multiplies a player's performance again and again. When used appropriately, both feedback loops can be wonderful tools in game design. If you do not want a prolonged game to bore your players, you want to integrate positive feedback loops because it speeds up the game play. You probably have already realized that positive feedback loops can end the game faster; destabilize the game, leading a player to one extreme; and make early game playing more important because the effect of the decision magnifies over time (Schreiber, 2009). In the Do It Yourself project, Adam, a high school music teacher, created a game called *The Quest for Elvis's Guitar* to increase student engagement with learning music theory. The game is a quest for finding Elvis's guitar, which serves as an allegory for the player to be a better musician and gain a deeper appreciation of music. As the players' journey progresses, they explore the virtual world and learn skills by answering questions. Correctly answered questions can lead to awarded points and players are given additional clues. As the players proceed through the game, questions become progressively harder, but the correct answers are rewarded with more points so that they can advance to new levels. Here, Adam integrated a positive feedback loop to create interesting game dynamics so that students are constantly challenged to learn and explore.

Unlike positive feedback loops, negative feedback loops prevent a lead by limiting the lead or giving advantages to the losing players. Incorporating negative feedback loops in a game, therefore, often makes the game end slower; stabilizes the game, leading a player to the middle; and makes early game playing less important. Although both positive and negative feedback loops can create powerful game play, they can also be devastating tools if not used properly. What is important is that feedback loops are used to design games that create players' perceived notion of "fair" play (Schreiber, 2009). More broadly, when designing game mechanics, you should strive to make the most exciting aspects of the game occur.

Narratives and Storytelling

Writing is an essential skill for most jobs. More importantly, it is an essential life skill. Often, it is the primary basis upon which others judge our work, learning, and intellect. Whether we are in college, the workplace, or in the community, our writing skills matter. When examining different educational reform movements like the No Child Left Behind Act, Common Core Standards, and the Race to the Top initiatives, we can easily identify that amongst all the subjects, writing grabs the most attention in our school curriculum.

What is the most important goal of writing? To communicate, you answer. Logically then, a vital educational goal of writing is to help students communicate effectively. Traditionally, writing education almost exclusively focused on syntax rules and other mechanical aspects. Yet, current focus of writing education on learning effective communication skills often call for authentic and situated learning experiences. Years ago, Gee (2007) provided a persuasive argument about these skills and experiences: Language is learned in context, and games offer an ideal environment for such learning. In an enactivist learning world, where learners are immersed in the game design and building process, rich opportunities are provided for learners to practice, interact, explore, and communicate, whereby they develop effective communication skills in different media forms.

For instance, when considering a game design, we know that adding narratives and background information can enhance the game's playability. By asking students to create games with rich narratives and/or storylines, we are encouraging better writing as well as potentially a more interesting game design.

But what are some strategies for writing good narratives for games? Schreiber (2009) discussed various approaches to good writing for games. He indicated that the first thing to consider about game narratives is the emotions writing can bring about. Just like well-written stories can have a powerful emotional impact, the same is true for well-written games. One way to write narratives into games, in order to elicit that emotional impact, is to consider the techniques good authors use in traditional storytelling. These techniques include focusing on a theme, developing a meaningful plot, including detailed images (through words, pictures, or others), deeply developing characters, and offering audience-appropriate drama. All these principles are applicable in game design.

Culture

After you have carefully thought about the emotional aspect of your story, you now consider how your narrative can be organically integrated into your game. Many commercial games use a linear design, meaning that each small part of a story is connected to its corresponding segment of the game. Completing one part of the game allows the player to move to the next level following the story (Schreiber, 2009). Some good games have strong narratives embedded in them, while others do not.

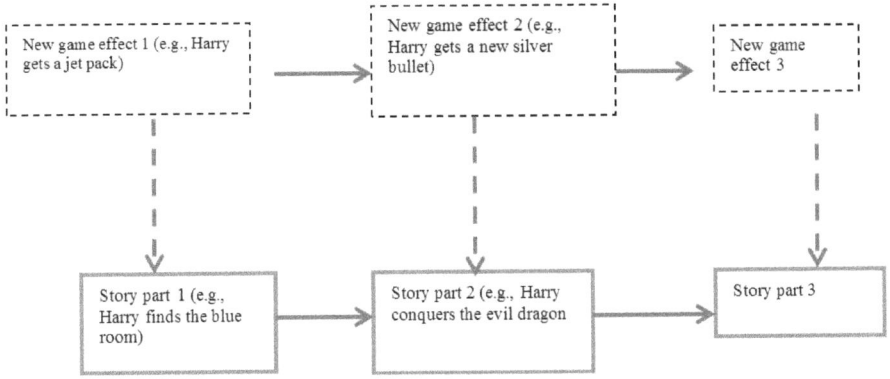

Figure 6.1. Linear Storytelling

Specifically, after the game's storyline is developed, you divide the story into small sections with embedded game play elements. Figure 6.1, adapted from Schreiber (2009), gives a visual presentation of this linear storytelling technique in a game. For example, when a story element happens (e.g., when Harry uncovers the secret blue room), new game play effects become available (e.g., Harry finds a jet pack that offers him a new powerful way to travel).

According to Schreiber (2009), while this linear way of story telling in a game is simple and easy, it has a major drawback: with only one story hence one thread, the player actions cannot affect the outcome of the game play, making the game not very exciting. To avoid this, you can create multiple threads of a story or different branches of the story that can be reached through different decisions during game play. In this case, the player would start the story, and then at a certain point the story would stop. The players must make a decision, and based on their decision, the game would go to one branch of the story or another. For example, in a game, Harry finds the blue room. After he walks into the blue room, he notices that he needs to choose a path, either through the oval door or through the pentagon-shaped door. If he chooses the oval door, he walks into a forest with beautiful flowers and birds, as well as poisonous mushrooms and vicious wild cats. If he takes the pentagon-shaped door, he dives deep into an ocean filled with colourful fish and pretty sea plants, as well as ferocious sharks. Figure 6.2, adapted from Schreiber (2009), visually presents a possible multithread storyline that can be used in a game.

As mentioned earlier, game design can offer many opportunities for writing. It is very common to start a game with a narrative that describes the context. Remember Sam and his *Splat!* game discussed in Chapter 3? It provides an example of how narrative writing is integrated in a game to set up the scene.

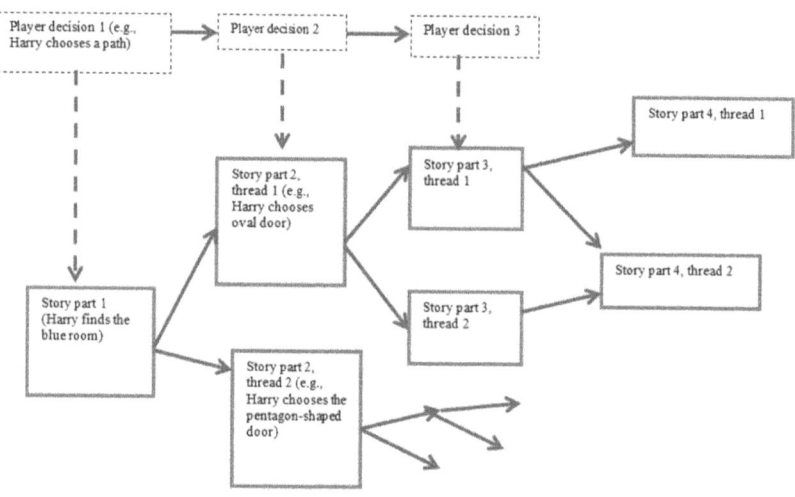

Figure 6.2. Multithread Structure of a Story

When designing traffic games to help drivers learn road rules, Sam's team developed the game *Splat!*, which incorporated problem solving into an imaginary world called Splatland. Sam wrote a letter to initiate the call to action of the game that provides a good example of how narrative can be interwoven to provide motivation and cognitive scaffolding. The letter reads as follows:

FROM: SPLATTERS@SPLATOPIA.SPLAT
RE: Thank you for helping Splatland!

Dearest Human,

I hope this letter finds you well. Thank you for agreeing to help us. Many of the humans we tried to talk with ignored us, perhaps because we are tiny, nano-beings? Macro beings, such as humans, sometimes feel skittish when we crawl in their ears to chat with them. Hearing voices like that is disturbing, apparently. So, we will agree to keep our communication through our Splat-Interface. Let me tell you a little about our world, a world that your scientists have never seen, because it is so small.

We are small fluid filled beings, called "Splats" and we call our land "Splatland." We live in little colonies, or communities. In the Days of "Before Discovery," we rarely ventured outside our own individual colonies and it was not unusual to spend your entire life there. But, there are always a few in any group who are not content. They had the desire to go on adventures and it was during these adventures that they discovered "The Ways," a means of travel from one colony to another. Travel through The Ways, back then, was a lonely, but fairly safe affair, because there were so few Splats travelling. However, once colonies discovered each other, wow. Trade developed, boy Splats met girl Splats from other colonies, and a desire to see how other people lived crept into the Splats' lives. Some colonies had waterslides, and you know how fun that can be!

So, over the years, more and more Splats took to traveling "The Ways." They grew impatient with the slow, leisurely travels that had been the hallmark of the previous generation, and now, arriving at the destination, and arriving quickly, became the preoccupation of the "Splats." The Ways are remarkably dull, after all, and you wouldn't want to spend any more time there than you have to. Unfortunately, this increasingly made The Ways unsafe. The problem? Splaccidents!

You see, due to an unfortunate happenstance, we Splats have not evolved a particularly thick skin. Once we reach a certain speed, if we ever touched another Splat, we explode. Although not fatal, reconstituting after these Splaccidents takes up valuable time, and, as you can well imagine, leads one to become somewhat cranky.

> *After much arguing, we in Splatland have agreed that what we need is wisdom, the wisdom of someone who can see the whole picture. We have agreed to try anything you suggest. If you give us a rule, we will follow it perfectly. We promise.*
>
> *Thank you for sharing your wisdom with us. We know that you will usher in a new age of Safe Travel on the Ways!*
>
> *Love,*
>
> *The Splaccident Reduction Committee*

Sam's letter from the Splaccident Reduction Committee immediately grabs players' attention. More important than gaining attention, this letter describes all the background information about the game, in addition to providing some operational rules.

Our experience of working with learners to design games illustrates that many students are motivated and enthusiastic about sketching stories to contextualize their games. However, one of the problems we encounter, as reflected in many of their games, is that a narrative is often used to frame the game but rarely goes beyond the initial call to action. In these games, once the role is assigned in the introductory stage, the functions of those roles are barely discussed in the subsequent phases. Although it is desirable that the storyline goes through the entire game, you may wonder how the narrations can be optimally blended into all phases of the game.

I describe next the story of Tim, an ESL teacher, in the Do It Yourself project. His *DDD* game provides a good example of how narratives can be organically integrated in different stages of game building. This game also exemplifies a multithread storyline. *DDD* was adapted from the existing board game *Dungeons & Dragons*, and this digital game was aimed at helping Tim's middle school ESL students learn English. *DDD* started with a narration to present the initial challenge that served as the catalyst of the storyline and the goal of learning. Leading up to this main challenge, Tim designed smaller obstacles and challenges, embedding resources and exemplars that students may encounter in real life. The game environment was also established in this fantasy setting at the specific geographic location. Narratives served to define the context and the overall mood and tone so that the players would have a clear sense of boundaries.

For example, "Palace of the Silver Princess" is an original *Dungeons & Dragons* adventure module. This module revolves around a country, except for the royal palace, frozen in time by a strange red light. The goal of the original *Dungeons & Dragons* game is to restore the flow of time and save the country (Palace of the Silver Princess, n.d.-b). Borrowing a map from the "Palace of the Silver Princess," Tim created a Smartboard game. The storyline of the game incorporated a baroness of Gullivan (Lady D'Mis) and a mountain (the Goblin Mountain) within the Thunder Mountains. In this game, players create their own avatars (e.g., fighter, wizard, cleric, thief). They move up in levels as they gain points by winning fights, discovering treasures, and collecting gold coins. Aiming to sustain students' interest in playing the game to complete the embedded educational objectives, Tim used parallel, intricate, and compelling storylines to engage students. The characters and geographic areas are well established through rich narrations. For example, Thunder Mountains are depicted as follows:

> ... low pine-covered mountains see the sunlight infrequently. Most of the time thick storm clouds linger on the mountaintops—clouds that often erupt into violent thunderstorms. An evil wizardess is rumored to live in the mountains in a giant hollow oak she uses as a lab. It is believed that it is she who keeps the thunderstorms alive, partly because she fears the light and partly because it keeps away the curious. Local people don't recall anyone ever going into the mountains, and if anyone ever did, they never returned to tell about it.

The introduction of the game is a very imaginative story about Lady D'Mis. Here is the first part of the game story:

> *About 3 weeks ago, Lady D'Mis' brother (Lord Thomas) went missing after he was seeking fame and fortune in the Thunder Mountains. He was expected back; however, a letter was found instead with scratchy writing on it. As soon as Lady D'Mis reads the letter, she is determined to destroy her enemy and capture her brother. She contacts the head of each guild in Gulluvia, and requests a party of brave adventurers to rescue her brother. This brave rescue will surely be dangerous, so Lady D'Mis will give a reward of 2000 gold pieces for the safe return of her brother. All exploits from the adventure may be kept by the adventurers.*
>
> Goblin Letter:
>
> *Lady Duh Missy,*
>
> *If you ever want to see your weakling brother again, you will pay 20000 gold pieces to his majesty, Goblin highness, Traco.*
>
> *We give you 1 week to reply!*

Do or else!

Slithering.

Allowing students to develop their game design documents can provide another opportunity to practice writing. In Tim's design document, he described the opening of the game:

> At the beginning of the game, you enter a cave. The cave's mouth opens up wide, like an animal's sharp teeth. The cave has jagged rocks that can crunch its player at any time. The cave, a great place to ambush people, narrows into a tunnel. There are four goblins hiding behind rocks and their job is to guard the cave and the mountain by fighting incoming enemies. You need to beat these goblins to advance to the different levels of the Dungeon complex, from level A to level Z. Each level contains different units. Each unit has a different setting. Depending on the unit being fought, you fight different enemies and or find different treasures. You can advance to the next level (e.g., from level A to B) after successfully exploring at least three units in a certain level.

For example, in the first level, there are eight different rooms: A1 to A8. If you enter room R7

> you will see that the room has 40 bunk beds lining the sides of the room. None of the beds are made! All of the bed sheets are also very dirty and ripped. There is a large table in the middle of the room with dirty plates and half-full glasses. There are 10 goblins in this room sleeping and playing cards. Five goblins are playing cards and five are sleeping. Each goblin has 10 Golden Coins. There is a portion of healing in one of the sacks. One of the goblins has a dagger. (Design document)

Level S contains 10 different rooms. Here is what you are told if you enter room R3:

> This room is obviously an exercise room. There is a wrestling ring and whips. Also, bags of dirt and rocks litter the ground. Wooden swords are neatly leaning against the north wall. Three goblins and two orcs (orcs are mythical human like creatures who are fierce and combative) are always training in this room. Each goblin has 10 Golden Coins and the orcs have 20 Golden Coins each. The orcs have a potion of healing in their sack. (Design document)

Moving up to level P, a total of seven units, P1– P7, is described. Unit P1 contains 11 prisons, and each prison is a 10-foot by 10-foot room:

> The strong doors are made of iron bars. Each room has a stool and some straw. These rooms obviously do not get cleaned nor do they have light. Screams can be heard from the various cells. The prisoners are all regular people that have been trapped or tricked by the goblins and used as slaves. They are not well fed and will scream for help if they sense that the party will save them. Lady D'Mis' brother, Thomas, is chained up in the last cell in the room and will not have to work for one more week or if the ransom is paid soon. (Design document)

In this game, Tim vividly described each scene and its associated story piece. Reading through the game design document, we can see that, depending on the paths chosen throughout each level, the player (or the avatar) can live different experiences, all in an effort to achieve the end goal: save Lady D'Mis's brother, Thomas. Therefore, each decision made by the player will determine the experience he or she will have in the subsequent stages of the game. Apparently, this is a multithread story that leads to various fun game ventures.

At the second level of the game, Tim gives another challenge to the player, again through narrative: "Lady D'Mis wants to move in with her army to attack the hordes of goblins. She therefore needs to map out Goblin Mountain. Your job is to help the lady to acquire an in-depth map of the mountain to seek her revenge upon the evil goblins."

Tim's ESL students learned a great deal of English without even noticing, because of the types of stories that are embedded in the game. In this case, English reading does not consist of boring lines of literature to be imposed on students. Rather, English here becomes a meaningful context of information needed to play and experience the game.

To further challenge students and promote creativity, Tim even integrated writing components into *DDD*. He asked students to create their own adventures to be played by their classmates. He offered the following scenario:

> The Goblin Mountain has uncharted territories that the Dungeon Master can expand to. To expand the dungeon, the Dungeon Master needs to open up the blocked passageways and add new and challenging dungeon levels. Many of the units have spaces for monsters, treasure, and or traps. Some examples have been given of how to stock these rooms in other areas. Design your own adventures so that the Dungeon Master can build the whole complex.

Due to time and technological constraints, Tim arranged these as paper-based instead of digital-based creative activities. Students start by creating small maps of houses and shops and then describe each room. This is followed by the development of storylines involving an adventure in one of the cities from a large, commercial *Dungeons & Dragons* map. Knowing that other people would play their games, the students became extremely excited and wanted to make the best adventure possible, as exemplified by Tim's description of one group: "I was astonished with their projects. These students had not gone above and beyond with any of their schoolwork to date, but they probably could have sold their adventures to a publisher."

In this case, students are given an opportunity to tell their own fantasy stories. Writing becomes a pleasurable experience of sharing one's own creative expression for others to explore.

· PART FOUR ·

Value

• CHAPTER SEVEN •

Enactivist Learning World and Value

This chapter looks at enactivist learning worlds in relation to value, demonstrating how students develop values of professional practices in such learning worlds: to value the things professionals think of as important, interesting, and meaningful. Further, it describes powerful learning in such a world through students' identity transformation. In addition to a discussion of the affective domain—a critical aspect of learning, focusing on emotions—this chapter also explores ethical issues, including questions related to privacy. Finally, the chapter concludes with a dialogue about important aspects of assessment.

Value and Identity

Effective learning occurs when learners participate in a social group or a learning community, and they take on new social identities. To borrow Gee's (2007) ways of explanation, I enjoy dancing in my leisure time and have joined different dance schools during the last several years. Although I have a lot of experience dancing and watching performances, my views about dance have been largely shaped and continue to be reshaped by the many social groups of which I have been a part (such as the dance schools with the dance teachers and students). How should I interpret a particular type of dance in certain contexts? When I receive feedback about my dance movements, how do my reactions affect my performance? When I wear a costume representing a certain nationality, how should my movements appear in order to reflect the culture of that ethnic group? Here, the established value, practice, knowledge, and skills of experienced dancers all come into play and largely shape my experience and views. Therefore, my dancer identity is formed and informed by the various communities of practices. My active participation in dance groups, and the new identities I have taken on as a member of such groups, have resulted in my deep learning and appreciation for all that dancing has to offer me.

When adapting learning by game design to establish an enactivist learning world, we need to consider how to best facilitate deep learning. If students buy into the ideas and take on the new identities, deep learning is most likely to occur. Just like my dance experience, when students value a new role, they are more likely to take on that role. Their commitment to take on such a role will lead to a heavy investment in what they do. This, consequently, will result in deep learning. The Games in Motion project is a great example of how students can take on new identities and learn from such experiences. The original task for students in that project was to develop digital games to teach others Newton's three laws. This task inspired these elementary students to take on the new identity of a teacher, a role they highly valued and through which they became heavily invested. Adopting their new role resulted in an extended commitment, a prerequisite of deep learning. For instance, students autonomously started teaching their parents and siblings not only Newton's laws, but also how to use Scratch (a programming language for game creation), even though the original task focused solely on Newton's laws. In fact, about one third of the students taught someone else how to use Scratch, demonstrating that they had inherited the new teacher role. Every day, many pleaded for more time on the computer and were reluctant to leave the lab. *What* they needed to do was no longer enough; rather, they wanted to learn *why* and make decisions as to *how* they should do what they needed to do. Evidence like this, along with our observations of these students, revealed their deep commitment to learning.

Having students design and build their own games to teach others meant that the students already owned their learning and were inherently buying in to the learning process. The teacher identity was so intriguing for some students that they started to project their own fantasies, desires, and pleasure onto this identity. For example, Martin and Rick used a hippo as the teacher character to teach others Newton's laws. In one of their games, the hippo tried to quiz the players on Newton's three laws. Martin and Rick spent lots of time discussing their ideas, programming the game, revising the rules, and getting feedback from others. The students' heavy investment in designing this game inspired them to create a Hippo Club. They developed a "hippo song," a "hippo dance," a series of "hippo games," a "hippo badge," and a "hippo rank." Martin and Rick became the Hippo Club leaders. They invited other students to join their club, and as a result, nearly every student in their class joined. For those two weeks of the summer camp, whether they were lined up for recess or walking to the computer lab, Martin would lead the line and Rick would march at the end of the line to direct the Hippo Club members as they sang their hippo song and danced their hippo dance. Martin's dad proudly told us the following:

> My son was very excited to talk about the computer games he was creating and brought the ideas generated there out of the game and into the classroom dynamics. For example, the character that leads the players to the quiz about Newton's laws became a club name for the kids in the class. He showed us the games and took us through them. He also wanted to show us how Scratch worked so that we could make games too!!! [final survey]

Apparently, these students had embraced new roles in this learning community and developed new identities. In a similar vein, designing games for educational purposes demands careful consideration of how to help learners, in this case, game players, cultivate their own identity both inside and outside the game. Identity plays an important part in how the gamer forms relationships with the characters and objectives of the game. Inversely, a player may project his or her unique self on his or her own learning as the game progresses.

One strategy in assisting players to naturally start developing their new gaming identity is to give players opportunities to create and customize their own avatars or characters throughout the game. In the Do It Yourself project, practicing teachers all realized how important it is to help players project their identity in the game. For instance, Iso, Linda, and Ela worked together to develop a game to teach primary math. They used a generic farmer at the beginning to set the stage for the development of the players' virtual identities. This was done in the hopes that players could relate the virtual character to a real-life person who is learning mathematics. David and Lisa used a multicharacter strategy to help players personalize their game play. Their role-playing game provided different characters from which the player could choose. They believed that role play would force players to process information according to the game design and make rational decisions that comply within the game's context. With the understanding of the importance of identity, some teachers felt that the players could use the games to assume alternate versions of their real-life identities, while other teachers wanted the players to reflect on and analyze their virtual selves as they progressed through the game. Jack developed a game to help players learn how to balance chemical equations. He believed that when "balancing chemical equations is presented as a game, students have a chance to break out of restrictive mounds of being strong or weak students in real-life and try out and assume new virtual identities regardless of previous academic standings."

In another game, *Samsara*, the players could develop their virtual identities through their avatars in the East Indian environment. They could see how their situation would change (e.g., getting better jobs, making more rupees, and progressing faster through the caste levels) as they progressed through the game. Assuming such virtual identities, the players gained a sense of what it might be like to live in India and experience a very wealthy or very poor environment. The players' identities evolved through their interactions with the game environment, which helped them gain deep understanding of the content knowledge.

Affective Domain and Ethical Questions

Emotions

Researchers and educators commonly accept the motivational value of digital game play. However, much of this acceptance may be hinged on the actual game play instead of game design and building. So what about when students build the games, not just play them? The truth is, when students design and create their own games, they take great pride and ownership of their learning. In every project we have conducted, whether it has been elementary students designing science games, high school students creating math games, or practicing teachers developing games for their own classrooms, the reactions have been overwhelmingly positive. Most of the time, the designers felt proud, excited, smart, and happy; rarely did they get bored or frustrated. The reward of a functional game that others may actually play is intrinsically motivating for students. Tricia, an elementary student in the Why Read If I Can Build project, had a fantastic experience designing her game. She was so enthused that she published it on the official Scratch website and it became the featured game. She was so excited and wrote the following on her blog:

> OH MY GOSH! OH MY GOSH!! OH MY GOSH!!! Do you know that my game is actually featured!!!! I have never dreamed that I would get FEATURED, even in my wildest dreams!!! It's 10:53 PM right now! I gotta remember that! I am shivering because I am so excited!!!

Value   157

The excitement, the pride, the sense of accomplishment, and the overall positive experience all powerfully transferred from her post to her classmates and teachers. A flurry of responses was posted on her blog, cheering for her and asking her specific questions or giving her feedback about her game. Such enthusiastic endorsements became a powerful force in promoting student achievement in this learning world.

I interviewed all 21 students enrolled in the Newton's Law summer camp project at the beginning, middle, and end of the camp. *Fun* was the term used by EVERY student when asked to articulate the most significant aspect of designing his or her games. David, a camp student, expressed the following: "... cause everything is really fun. EVERYTHING!"

When I interviewed Jean, the mother of another student, she confirmed the amount of fun that her son had during the process: "Gary talked about his games non-stop for a few days. He loved it and talked about it to anyone who would listen. His comments were—it was fun and cool!"

Students' engagement went beyond "of the moment" interest and fun. Their level of commitment to their projects indicated the extent to which they were engaged. Instead of trying to minimize the amount of work they had to do, students willingly spent their own time doing more work. Although not required, 13 of the 21 students (i.e., over 60%) autonomously downloaded and used Scratch at home. They also worked at home to perfect their games and/or to create additional games. All but one student told their parents about the software. Of the 21 students, 13 had created one game, 2 students built two games, and 6 students created three or more games, in less than two weeks.

The Run for Math project got secondary math students equally excited from the very beginning. When the game development software Kodu was introduced, students loved interacting with it. They found the tool interesting and rewarding. Each time they tried to program the characters, they would receive immediate feedback letting them know if what they were doing would work or not. Additionally, if their programming worked, the reward was "an operational game, as opposed to the boring teacher-marked 'right answer' only, Wohoooo ..." as stated by a student.

Flourish, the teacher, found that at the beginning of the project, the students preferred game building than typical schoolwork. Unlike in ordinary math classes, if she let students play with Kodu for a bit, they would do almost anything (math related) that she asked of them. Her blog showed her excitement:

> I am amazed to see that students become so excited about something in school and, more significantly math. Programming a game became such a good hook. Students were like 'I can make a game???' 'I can play it on my Xbox?' 'I can shoot things???' Yes, yes, and yes!

Flourish taught several groups of students at the same time. The largest group was the lowest performing class, in which students were learning probability. Many of the students, not surprisingly, had little confidence in their math abilities and negative attitudes toward math. It was a struggle to get them engaged in regular math classes. Yet, they became enthusiastic about designing and building games for this math course. Flourish pleasantly watched how the students' confidence soared with looks of pride and joy on their faces each time they completed more and more complex tasks. Such reactions did not occur often in her typical math class. According to Flourish, "observing such students' changes gave me a glimpse of what is possible with math if you work and push past the status quo."

In addition to enhanced motivation among her students, Flourish also noticed an improvement in students' thinking processes. Planning is an integral part of programming within the constraints of the game. For example, within Kodu, every command is a "when…do…" statement. If a student wants to do something in the game, he or she needs to think through all of the programming steps to make that happen. According to Flourish, it became evident that her students' ability to plan and execute a math problem improved greatly because of their experience with programming games. These programming skills were ultimately transferred to other skills, such as problem solving and logical thinking, which are necessary for enhanced understanding of mathematical ideas and concepts.

These examples and stories demonstrate that game building is intrinsically motivating. It is important to realize, however, that not all game design projects will result in a sustained high level of engagement. Carefully crafted instructional activities and procedures are essential for successful learning through game design approach. Next I describe some useful tips, mainly based on Schreiber's (2009) work, to facilitate the approach of learning by game building with sustained motivation.

Tip #1. As a teacher, you need to identify appropriate learning objectives for the game building activities. The experience designed for students should focus on achieving such objectives. Equally important, you need to provide meaningful and useful materials as guides for students' game building.

Tip #2. If students can work in groups, have one veteran member in the group if possible. This person can provide group members with guidance and decrease the anxiety level.

Tip #3. It is optimal to start the project by demonstrating a model or a sample prototype. This provides learners with something tangible to work with at the beginning, not only offering exemplars but also progressively presenting the main challenge.

Tip #4. Ask learners to build small games or modify existing games using the software before they create a major game. This will scaffold the game design process and the learning of the program language. Considering that learners want to see the end result of their project, we need to provide lengthy time for development but shorter time for prototyping. Do not spend time perfecting the appearance of the paper prototype, because prototyping only serves to identify potential problems.

Tip #5. As a teacher, you probably have limited time. It is nonetheless critical to ask students to play test as early and as frequently as possible and use the feedback for revising the product. These kinds of activities can be done in class and/or after schoolwork, depending on your design of the learning activities.

Tip #6. This tip continues the theme of time constraints. Since game building is a complicated process requiring a lot time, it is important to brainstorm ideas as early as possible. Having formal storyboard ideas before prototyping can save time in the long run. These ideas will contribute to the fun and enjoyment of the process.

Ethical Questions

Before introducing digital game designing to your students (or clients), it is worth some time to consider the ethical issues surrounding the gaming movement. There are many challenges and potential benefits of embedding the gaming environment into your instruction, and understanding both is critically important.

Mass media has often portrayed video games as evil. They claim that games, most specifically shooter games, promote violence. Consequently, popular opinion concludes that the increase in sales of violent video games must result in the increase in youth violence, especially in schools. In their book, Kutner and Olson (2008) discussed the correlation between game and violence. They argued, based on data from many research studies, convincingly against such popular opinion. According to them, numerous research studies have shown no connection between violent video game play and youth violent behaviour. We know that start from early 1990's, video games have gain more and more popular. Looking at the statistics, we can see that since 1993, juvenile crimes in United States have been constantly declining. In fact, arrests for murder, forcible rape, robbery, and aggravated assault dropped 49%. School violence has also decreased. Murder arrests plummeted 71% from 3,790 in 1993 to 1,110 by 2004 (Kutner & Olson, 2008).

This being said, a number of ethical questions must be addressed before we invite students to design and build games. Coincidentally, game playing and game building provide a perfect platform for open discussion about ethics, human rights, morality, and other important issues. Previously, I described the game *Samsara*, which was developed by Mike, an elementary teacher. The game's central theme is Indian culture, where players start as foreign travellers, fulfilling the personal obligations, callings, and duties of the traveller. Via working, learning, visiting temples, and helping others, they progress through a caste system. In the game, the players inevitably encounter negative experiences such as the contraction of a disease, the subjection to criminal activity, the injustice of child marriage, the need to protect themselves from taxi scams, or police corruption. Players need to make decisions about what they would do to address these issues. They are then provided feedback based on their decisions (e.g., players receive different points if they ignore child marriage vs. if they start educating the local people). Here, the built-in mechanism in the game teaches certain values and beliefs through the feedback. It also provides an excellent opportunity for open discussions about these ethical issues when students play this game. What should we do when we see police corruption? How do we proceed if we suspect child abuse? Open dialogs and debates about these ideas can help students develop a deeper understanding of morals and ethics.

Often, ethical questions about their favourite games or their preferred genre for game design naturally emerge during conversations with students. First-person shooter games, for example, are very popular. A large proportion of the preservice and in-service students I teach (e.g., graduate students) love to play shooter games like *Halo* or *Infamous*. We often engage in conversations about the possible negative effects of playing these games, which helps raise their awareness of issues at hand. Further questions are posed to guide their thinking about whether violence should be included in their game design, and if yes, how moral and ethical issues can be addressed. Sometimes, teachers find it challenging to combine their educational content with a particular game design and genre. Mary, an ESL teacher, shared her concerns:

> Sometimes it is not feasible to come up with a particular genre for game play like first person shooting as in an educational context it provokes violence and may not be ideal for children to get accustomed to. So even though I like first person shooter games I could not use this form of gameplay in an educational setting.

Other times, teachers creatively consider ways to organically integrate educational content with game genres. One way is to actually integrate violence elements. Many teachers believe that since their students are already familiar with video games, violent games such as shooting games are something students know, and have, in many ways, grown up with. Ignoring the genre altogether, therefore, is naïve. We can consider integrating violent elements into teaching and learning. Violent content, if carefully crafted into educational games, can enhance learning of the targeted content knowledge. Sam's *MythGiving* game, for instance, contains warriors and features fighting with violent components included. Yet these violent elements are purposefully designed in the game, avoiding the bloodshed but focusing on the teaching of ancient Greek culture and the improvement of students' understanding of that history. Similarly, Aileen developed a shooting game teaching middle school chemistry where players have to shoot falling chemical elements from the sky.

Adapting the learning by game design to establish an enactivist learning world in schools demands us to consider that students are still in a developmental stage physically, psychologically, and emotionally. Violence and video games are already part of the student vernacular. Integrating some elements related to violence, for example, fighting against evil dragons, to a game may enhance its playability and engage more students. It is critical, however, that we discuss purposes, audiences, and outcomes with students. Such an open-minded approach to address violence and other ethical issues, rather than prohibiting the use of any violent elements in students' game design, creates a greater opportunity for moral and character development.

Assessment

Successful adaption of learning by game design and building requires carefully crafted assessment plans and procedures. Assessing student-created games can provide valuable information that will allow us to better understand students' thought process and mechanical actions. Depending on the design of the learning experiences, the assessments can be formative or summative. Although traditional approaches tend to focus on assessments of learning, recent work has called for attention to assessments for learning and even assessments as learning. These three terms describe three assessment approaches, often for different purposes. Specifically, assessment of learning refers to teacher evaluation of students' learning outcomes for administrators and parents, which usually occurs at the end of the learning process. Assessment for learning concerns teacher evaluation practices that are ongoing throughout the learning process, often for teachers to collect information in order to improve their instruction. The current movement to assessment as learning approach differs from the previous two because the assessment as learning method engages students as active critical assessors of their own learning. Students' self-monitoring and self-adjustment are the main characteristics of this assessment approach, which is ongoing and can happen at any stage of the learning process (Torrance, 2007).

How do we assess students when they learn through game building? Since the focus is on learning, it is necessary to start with the learning objectives. That is, the assessment criteria should be applied to match the intended learning goals for the game building experience. When evaluating learner-built games, a frequently practiced approach is to use rubrics to assess such games. Rubrics should first consider how to assess whether students achieved the learning goals. Since the final outcomes are developed games, motivational and game design components may also be included in the assessment rubric. These components can include aspects like fun and ease of play. Another important consideration is that the assessment tools, like rubrics, need to be developed and shared early in the learning process so that students have a good understanding of what is expected. With a clear goal in mind, game building becomes more purposeful, prompting students to focus on learning the content. Teachers can also use the rubric as a guideline to assess the contributions of the students. Students and teachers work in tandem and review the rubrics at critical or fixed junctures, which can help students attain peace of mind before and during the process of design and development of the games.

For example, in the Call of Math project, preservice teachers learned pedagogy in a learner-centered, inquiry-based, and field-oriented context to prepare them to teach secondary math. Aside from various in-class and out-of-class tasks and assignments, one of the major components of the course work was to design, develop, and build a digital game that focused on topics in algebra.

Considering that rubric development is a valuable learning opportunity for preservice teachers, as the course instructor, I involved these teachers in the process of establishing evaluation tools. It turned out that the preservice teachers not only learned a wonderful lesson about how to assess but also what to assess and how to integrate assessment into teaching. More importantly, preservice teachers provided insights from learner perspectives, which consequently improved the quality of the assessment tool.

When developing a rubric to assess the games these preservice teachers created, our first priority was to align the rubric with the learning goals of the course. Since the main goal of the project was to help preservice teachers develop ways of thinking about mathematics to better facilitate inquiry-driven secondary mathematics classrooms, an important criterion was that games should move beyond a simple worksheet approach and promote inquiry, critical thinking, and exploration. Grounded in the existing literature in mathematics education (e.g., the national standards by the National Council of Teachers of Mathematics), we included in the rubric the following essential mathematics educational components: problem solving, representation, active learning, exploration and reasoning, connections, collaboration, bridging and scaffolding, assessment. Specifically, we operationally defined these categories:

- Problem Solving: We look for evidences that students draw on their knowledge to search for solutions, and through such a process, they develop new mathematics understanding. The game should encourage students to better understand math through problem solving. The game creates situations and contexts for students to apply and adapt appropriate strategies to solve problems and develop new mathematics knowledge.
- Representation: We search the process of capturing mathematics in some form. The game should encourage players to use representation to

communicate and organize mathematics, to model and make sense of physical, social, and mathematical phenomena, and to solve problems.

- Active Learning: We identify game components that encourage student's active engagement in thinking about what they are doing. Its antonym is inactive learning, which occurs when a student is just given a simple question and is asked to answer it via the use of routine, given procedures. Instead, active learning occurs when students develop their own questions and/or are presented with complex questions that require multiple, nonroutine steps (that are not laid out for the students) to solve. Players may have to think outside of the game, and the mathematics content is not necessarily overt.

- Exploration and Reasoning: We strive for events in games that provide rich problems through which students explore and reinvent solutions rather than solving by straightforward computations. The game allows for students to "make and investigate mathematical conjectures" (National Council of Teachers of Mathematics [NCTM], 2000, p. 56) and to look for and identify patterns and structures. Here we are looking for problems that allow students to further their understanding of the topic by delving into the problem and justifying their solution. The focus in this item is not on the method a student used (which is emphasized in "Problem Solving") but rather on students' mathematical explanations and justifications of their answers.

- Connections: We look for components of the game that relate the material to different areas in mathematics (e.g., linear function and geometry) or different subject areas (e.g., the game includes components related to physics or biology). Another way to think about this is through the connecting of math to real-world experiences that the students would be knowledgeable of and have experienced in their own lives (e.g., relating percentages to sales tax).

- Collaboration: The game provides and encourages ways for the gamer to work with other gamers or with objects and/or nonplayer characters within the game, for the purpose of emulating group work, connecting to the environment, and sharing knowledge with other gamers.

- Bridging and Scaffolding: The game builds on and bridges from players' previously known ideas and provides specific means for increasing the level of challenge and conveying knowledge in good measure, in order to stay within the knowledge competencies of the students while continually pushing the boundaries of their learning.

- Assessment: The game includes components that allow the gamer to reflect on his or her progress thus far and gauge one's own learning up to that point. This category is very close to scaffolding, but here the focus is on providing an explicit mechanism for the gamer to be able to understand his or her own progress, that is, to reflect on and self-assess one's development.

(Li, et al, 2013, p. 334-335)

In addition to the pedagogical and educational value, we believe that the motivational value of the games is critical. Hence we added, in the rubric, four game design and engagement components: strategy, participation, engagement/motivation, user-friendly and ease of play.

- Strategy: Within the game, do players have to strategize to win? This category focuses on game play and the elements that require players to make a plan in order for them to beat the game. For example, in the *Portal* games, you have to plan where to put your portals so that you can finish a level. This category focuses on game play.
- Participation: This category focuses on the problems posed; a game is well designed if both strong and weak students want to play it. The educational components of the game are set up in a way that they do
- not exclude weak students or bore strong students. That is, the problems are rich enough to allow students of all levels the opportunity to solve them.
- Engagement/Motivation: This category focuses on game play. Since games are typically used in schools because they are fun and students like playing them, we want to make sure the games themselves are enjoyable and engaging. This is a very difficult category to quantify, as it is fairly subjective. Here, we look for game elements that would interest students. Examples of components that could be considered engaging and motivating include (but are not limited to) an interesting narrative, working toward a goal, competition (with self or others), and increasing level of difficulty.
- User-Friendly and Ease of Play: An important component of good game design is making sure the objectives and instructions of the game are clear. If not, this can affect engagement and participation. Here we examine whether or not the game is frustrating when playing it. As a player, do you understand what your goals and objectives are? If you are told to accomplish a task, are clear instructions given on how that could be done? Is the level of the game reasonable for the target student population and/or mathematical concepts?

(Li, et al, 2013, p. 334-335)

Together, the nine components became the basis of the rubric, constituting the most important aspects of a game created in this context. Table 7.1 represents the developed rubric.

Formative and Summative Assessment

Both formative and summative assessments are vital components of student learning and therefore should be included throughout the game designing and building process. Perhaps the most important type of assessment in the game building process is the formative assessment, which should be ongoing instead of a one-time event. Continued feedback from both teachers and peers can significantly improve the quality of the games developed and student learning of the content. For example, students can provide feedback regarding each other's game design; they can also critique peers' paper model games and play test each others' prototype. These ongoing assessment activities provide valuable information to help teachers' instruction and improve students' learning.

Table 7.1. Pedagogical Rubric of Digital Games Designed by Preservice Teacher

Category	Below the Standard	Standard	Above the Standard
Problem Solving	No events* or one small event that showed problem solving.	One substantial event or two or three distinct small events that showed problem solving.	More than one substantial event or more than three distinct small events that showed problem solving.
Representation	No events or one small event that showed representation.	One substantial event or two or three distinct small events that showed representation.	More than one substantial event or more than three distinct small events that showed representation.

Value

Active Learning	No events or one small event that allowed for active learning.	One substantial event or two or three distinct small events that allowed for active learning.	More than one substantial event or more than three distinct small events that allowed for active learning.
Exploration and Reasoning	No events that allowed for exploration and reasoning.	One substantial event or two or three distinct small events that allowed for exploration and reasoning.	More than one substantial event or more than three distinct small events that allowed for exploration and reasoning.
Connections	No events or one small event that showed connections.	One substantial event or two or three distinct small events that showed connections.	More than one substantial event or more than three distinct small events that showed connections.
Strategy	No events or one small event that showed strategy.	One substantial event or two or three distinct small events that showed strategy.	More than one substantial event or more than three distinct small events that showed strategy.
Participation	Does not encourage most players to participate.	Encourages most players to participate.	Encourages all players to participate.
Engagement/ Motivation	Not interesting or fun to play.	Interesting and fun to play.	Really interesting and really fun to play.

User-Friendly and Ease of Play	Confusing or unclear objectives or instructions. Many elements that caused major frustration in play and may cause player to stop playing.	Clear objectives and instructions of the game. A few elements that cause minor frustration in play.	Very clear objectives and instructions of the game. No elements that cause frustration.
Collaborations	Does not allow any form of collaborations with other players or with other objects in the game.	Allows for some collaboration.	Encourages several collaborations, whether with nonplayer characters or with other gamers.
Bridging and Scaffolding	No scaffolding within the game. There is no support for progression of knowledge or concepts in the game.	Creates an adequate platform for scaffolding through tutorials or guides.	Goes above and beyond in setting up stages and levels that progress the concepts conveyed in an increasingly challenging way.

Assessment	No characteristics that help the gamer to assess the level or situation within the game. Gamers may feel lost when trying to understand their abilities and/or achievement in the game.	Provides tools (e.g., hit points, level-ups, gauges/meters, visual maps, messages, and alerts) to adequately assess the gamer's progression through the game.	Set up in a way that makes the gamer feel as though he or she knows how his or her character is doing, what levels have been achieved or need to be, and is able to make conjectures on the game play because of it.

*An event is defined as any component of the game. This can include explicit or implicit problems presented, strategies needed to solve the game, or anything else that is a feature of the game. A substantial event is a component of the game that would either take substantial game playtime to do (20% to 50% of game time) or is a primary component of the game (e.g., a theme that runs throughout the game but doesn't necessarily take up a lot of game play). This table was originally published in Li, et al (2013) in the *Journal of Research on Technology in Education*, reprinted by permission of the publisher.

Assessment can also be an integral part of learning in the game design process. In the Run for Math project, secondary students learned mathematics by designing and building digital games to teach others the math content they were learning. The games were used to replace the traditional unit test to demonstrate the students' understanding of the mathematics content. Here, students needed to create game stories and scenarios, develop mathematics questions, and provide answers. After completing the game, each student wrote a summary with the questions they asked in the game, their solutions, and reasoning for any wrong options provided in the game. Students had to justify their games as to why they could replace their unit test. That is, they rationalized why their games demonstrated at least equivalent information of their mathematics understanding as a unit test would.

This summary, along with the games created, allowed the teachers to better judge the extent to which the student understood the concepts and procedures. The teachers were also able to see if the students could clearly communicate mathematics with symbolical, graphical, and verbal presentations. For example, there are "good" wrong answers to a specific math problem that can be included in the games. Being able to articulate why something is a "good" wrong answer shows students' depth of understanding of the math content.

The teachers' concluding reflection suggested that this summary was a great experience for the students. Flourish, one of the teachers, indicated that the students showed phenomenal work that would not have been seen on traditional paper and pencil tests. The following segment, "Searching for Euphoria," describes Flourish's experiences in using assessment to encourage and deepen students' learning of mathematics during the Run for Math project.

Searching for Euphoria. Flourish has always had the desire to help her students search for euphoria. To her, being able to reach euphoria can build students' confidence and increase their engagement in learning. In her blog, she wrote the following:

> Many of us have the experience of seeking out euphoria. This feeling of euphoria often comes when we least expect it . . . even when we are in the midst of doing something we may or may not really enjoy, like math, or programming. But we do very well in them and we seem to be sucked in to it. For example, we try to solve a math problem. We work on it and work on it and work on it . . . until wham! We finally get it correct and we get hit with this feeling of euphoria—this amazing sense of accomplishment. This euphoria only comes with working hard, pushing our brain to the max, and accomplishing something that we thought we would not be able to do. Bringing students to this feeling of ecstasy in their own learning process would definitely increase their interest in learning, but how? They often don't even know they are searching for such a feeling. They may not even know that this feeling exists in the realm of school work, much less in classes like math or history, those traditionally perceived as boring subjects.

The Running for Math project provided Flourish with a wonderful context in which to experiment. She found that one way to help students search for such rewarding moments was to correctly establish assessment standards so that they were pushed to maximize their potential. At the beginning of the project, Flourish discovered that her students were excellent at programming but terrible troubleshooters. She realized that students tended to estimate the amount of efforts needed to build an excellent game and settled on "ok" and "operational" rather than seeking for excellence. She explained her frustration in her blog:

I'm not seeking excellence, this is their first foray into programming, but I am disappointed that they may miss out on this euphoria. I feel if they experience it here they may seek it out in other realms of school . . . one can dream!

Flourish had a discussion with the students and modified the rubrics so that the expectations were higher. She also added, in the rubrics (see Table 7.2), spaces to encourage students to reach higher. To promote students' creativity, the "Excellent" column in the rubric was not specified. The blank was intentional, indicating that the category would be beyond what the teachers could imagine, and the teachers were ready for wonderful surprises.

Sometimes students' programming/technical ability can be a hindering factor, especially if the subject matter to be learned is not technology or programming. Flourish felt that students should not be penalized because of their limited technical knowledge, unless that was the focus of learning. She then included, in one of her rubrics, "mark boosters" to encourage students to take risks and be creative. This rating rubric included three major components: task performance, understanding of concepts and procedures, and communication. The task performance focused on whether a student demonstrated consistently excellent work on routine and nonroutine tasks in both familiar and new contexts. This component served as the mark booster to inspire students to be more courageous by stepping out of their comfort zone and exercising their creative muscles.

Flourish found that more students experienced such euphoria when she adapted those modified rubrics. For example, David, a student with attention deficit and hyperactivity disorder, was originally building one probability problem where players had to seek out the correct apple (out of many) and give it to the correct avatar in order to progress in the game. The next time Flourish observed David, he had begun to work on a different problem: "Bring the correct coloured apples (out of many colours) to the correct pad, to kill a 'guard' and free the trapped fly fish." Flourish just thought that David had changed his mind. After some intense troubleshooting, David zoomed out the view of his game. Instead of one probability problem, he had actually created three for his game. According to Flourish, "He blew me away! I really feel that given the traditional probability context in math he would have done the work and moved on. Instead, in this game building project, he did in-depth exploration of the topic and went much further with it than in a traditional setting."

Table 7.2. Rubric for Math Games

Name: _____ / 20 points

Discussion	Needs Improvement (Max 1)	Satisfactory (Max 3)	Exceeds Expectations (Max 5)	Excellent (Max 5 additional points total)
Quality of Reflection	Missing all or some of the components required.	Provided all the required elements but lack of appropriate articulation for some or all components.	Provided extremely well articulated writing for all the required components.	
Quality of the Question	Little or no evidence of understanding of the math concepts involved.	Evidence of low-level understanding of the math concepts involved.	Evidence of higher-level understanding of the math concepts involved.	
Game Clarity	The game rules and goals are difficult to understand or follow. Cumbersome design.	You worked out a streamlined design. Rules somewhat clear and relatively easy to understand.	You have a very streamlined layout and design. The game goals and rules are very easy to understand.	

Note: The total defined points possible in this rubric is short of the total of 20. The rationale for this is that the instructor is unwilling to put a ceiling or limitations on "excellence" and wants to leave room for the "extras" and "enactivist learning" that often occur and that are indicated by the assignments. These go above and beyond what the instructor could predict. So, surprise the instructor!

The final sharing and playing of each other's games served both as a performance assessment and a celebration. This became the big AHA! moment for Flourish when she observed that every student was overwhelmingly proud of what they had done and were excited to showcase their work and see what other games people had developed. This was the "euphoric moment" she was looking for. The students were clearly "euphoric" over what they and their peers had accomplished.

After summer vacation, Flourish returned to school and was told that those students identified themselves as those who made games. When they talked to people, whether teachers or peers, they proudly announced that they were part of the GAME COHORT! In this independent study school, it was a big deal for these students to talk to teachers in a very proud way. When they required math help from teachers, these students made sure the teachers knew that they had done something "different" for math. "I need help on this question, but I really am a good math student because I was able to make a math game" was the way many of these students thought and conveyed. It further highlights, even after a summer break, that these students remained proud of what they had done. Flourish noted, "I have never heard of or seen a student identify themselves to a teacher as 'Oh I got 100% on ___ math test or ___ math assignment.' This behaviour and self identification is an anomaly."

Student Involvement in Assessment

In an enactivist learning world, students' involvement in both the development of evaluation tools and the process of evaluation is critical, although teachers may often still play a prominent role. Students' engagement in these processes has several benefits.

First, it can bolster students' interest in the game creation experience. When students are involved in the process of creating the assessment tools, they can provide insight into what they consider important. They also learn from the contributions of others, including teachers, about the critical components of the content they are learning. Being able to contribute to the evaluation instruments can promote students to take ownership of their learning.

Second, involving students in developing assessment tools can enrich the content and provide a broader understanding of the aspects being examined. For instance, in the Call of Math project, we used the Pedagogical Rubric of

Digital Games Designed by Preservice Teacher (see Table 7.1) to evaluate the mathematics games developed by preservice teachers. The categories "strategy" and "participation" were not included in the original rubric. In fact, no game play components were part of the original rubric. However, when preservice teachers played, reflected, and discussed the important aspects to assess these games, it became apparent that strategy and participation should be considered. The preservice teachers realized, through evaluating each other's games, that the games were testing more than just traditional education problems and that the games themselves might require strategies. From this, the strategy category was born. Working together to refine the rubric, we also found that some poor games were caused by certain preservice teachers' inadequate programming skills. Considering that the focus of the project was to enhance learning of pedagogy instead of the game itself, emphasizing their programming would be an unfair assessment. Hence, we created the categories of engagement/motivation, participation, and user-friendly and ease of play to avoid unfairly punishing preservice teachers' limited technical skills.

Third, student engagement in the assessment process can enhance their own understanding of the subject matters they are learning. Again, in the Call of Math project, when the task of developing a rubric to evaluate their self-created games was presented, the preservice teachers started to discuss what should be considered "essential knowledge" for secondary mathematics teachers. With the help of the professor, they realized the importance of grounding the development of the rubrics in the existing literature and the national standards. The rich discussions amongst the preservice teachers and professors enabled the preservice teachers to deepen their understanding of pedagogical knowledge. For example, mathematics teaching should focus on problem solving, connection, representation, reasoning, and active learning.

Students can be involved in every aspect and every stage of the assessment process. This includes, but is not limited to, the development of rubrics, peer evaluations, and play testing. While students playing each other's games and providing feedback is one form of assessment, teachers can evaluate students at another level by observing the performance of the students who play the games. They can then analyze both their observation and the peer evaluation/feedback to assess students' abilities. For example, in the project Why Read If I Can Build, sixth-grade students, working in small groups, first developed game prototypes based on different mathematics ideas. Then each group played the other teams' games and offered their comments on the games and game play. Table 7.3, adapted from the work of Gallegos and Flores (2010), provides some examples of student comments, teacher observations, and student abilities that were developed.

Table 7.3. Examples of Students' Ability Assessment

Student Comments	Teacher Observations	Ability Development
Playing this game, I learned how to add simple fractions. I think [the game] should provide some guides to better organize the objects.	Suggest strategies to improve.	Leadership
This game is fun. But I want them to add a structure, sort of like a help file, so we can reaffirm our understanding.	Provide creative ideas.	Innovation
I like how the game allows us to play together as a team. We help each other during the play. We feel we can easily learn the math concepts in a fun way.	Discuss how to take advantage of distributed talents.	Collaboration

Understanding Assessment in the Participatory Context

The development of technology tools leads to the emergence of a participatory culture. We actively create and contribute to our world through various venues rather than just passively consuming and accepting. This means that we change our ways of living, learning, playing, and assessing. Say, for example, you want to buy clothes from eBay. A legitimate question you would ask is, "Can I trust this seller?" You may first check the online rating for this seller and then make your decision. Or perhaps you bought something from Amazon.com and had really horrible service and you wanted to shop elsewhere. You might post your own review of Amazon's service in order to share your experience online with other potential buyers.

These are examples of assessments in a virtual world, newly created assessments that are part of the online participatory culture most of us have come to accept. Letting users rate products has become increasingly more common, and many stores have online rating systems for consumers to evaluate their experiences. In the game world, a typical way to know whether a game is successful is by how many downloads or copies are sold, as well as by the ratings from its players. Online rating has become such an important aspect of the modern business world that, sometimes, companies even give incentives to people who rate their products online.

In the field of education, this type of evaluation is practiced both online and in face-to-face environments. For example, in *Gamestar Mechanics*, a game focusing on game design, online rating is built in to assess you (the player), based on your abilities and contribution. In that game, you can advance levels by playing existing games, by building your own games, or by reviewing and rating other people's games. Like the Scratch website and many other websites dedicated to game building software, the *Gamestar Mechanics* website has a category entitled "Highest Rated Games," which is featured on the front page. These mechanisms provide a wonderful way to encourage various levels of participation from different perspectives, fitting into the needs of diverse learners. These powerful tools for assessment allow us to authentically evaluate students and, at the same time, actively involve our learners. Using these tools meaningfully, however, demands careful thinking and attentiveness to possible drawbacks.

The following story Sam shared in his blog is by no means unique. In fact, this story reflects a phenomenon in our virtual world in relation to collective assessment.

> Sam was using *Gamestar Mechanics* to teach fifth-grade students math and science concepts. He started by posting his own game, *Mt. Siepiski*, a very challenging game based on fractal, a mathematics concept. When finding out that his game was featured on the official *Gamestar Mechanics* website, Sam got very excited. Being a featured game, many people played *Mt. Siepiski* and some players gave it good reviews. Eventually, this game became a top-rated game, which further demonstrated Sam's success in creating the game. Sam's excitement, however, did not last long, for he noticed that his rating began to drop drastically. Why? He soon realized that this was a result of really low scores provided by some authors who

also had games on the top-rated pages. Those authors chose to "attack" the game as a strategy to help bolster the ratings of their own games. This eventually caused the *Mt. Siepiski* rating to decrease and fall below the other games on the top-rated page. Another trick some game authors employed was to trade top ratings with others (meaning if A gives B good review review, B will then rate A's game five stars). Using these unjust approaches, some games with poor quality were moved up to the highly rated games list. Sam acknowledged that the more people play a game, the game would be less affected by this kind of "attack."

Unfortunately Sam's *Mt. Siepiski* game continued to be impacted by erroneous ratings. This continued until a seemingly non-related incident occurred one day. That day, during recess, Sam accidently caught John, a student, doing a naughty thing. John got really upset and decided to retaliate. He rated all of Sam's games with one star (the lowest possible rating). The interesting thing, however, was that some of Sam's other students noticed this and responded by rating Sam's games five stars (the highest possible rating) in an attempt to undo the damage John's ratings caused. This event had two consequences that influenced the rating of Sam's games: First, the games had increased plays because more students knew about or got curious about Sam's games and wanted to play them. Secondly, the ratings of his games improved because many more students gave their fair evaluations. The result was a surprise for John: Sam's games had better evaluation results because of John's poor ratings, completely contradicting what John originally had hoped would happen.

(Modified from Sam's blog)

The significance of the lesson learned from this goes beyond what online rating and engaging learners in assessment can lead. It shows that the user rating system, as illustrated by this story, is in fact an ecosystem. At the superficial level, the system looks chaotic. Yet, if you look deeper and observe longer, you can see that people in the community interact dynamically and self-organize, eventually resulting in consistency. Engaging students in such a system helps them understand new ways of assessment in the context of a participatory culture. The enactivist learning world discussed in Chapter 1 endorses the method that lets students experience with the review ecosystems, observe how the systems evolve, and come to their own conclusions. While we can always take the direct approach by telling students to be honest and provide critical and constructive review, the enactivist approach of immersion students into the assessment ecosystem will mostly likely to lead to a better understanding of the pros and cons of such assessment tools.

· CHAPTER EIGHT ·

Vital Domains and Basic Tools

This chapter focuses on important domains related to values and mechanic aspects of implementation for the establishment of an enactivist learning world. It first discusses how to engage and motivate learners through game building, followed by a discourse on the new roles of teachers and learners. Then, it delineates popular game genres and specific game building tools that can be easily integrated into classrooms. Last, it offers methods of how to engage learners in the assessment process, including important issues of "what to" and "how to" assess in order to provide authentic learning experiences.

Learner Motivation and Engagement

Without learner motivation, learner game designing and game playing would not exist; the learner means everything. Students are often intrinsically motivated when designing and building games. In fact, we have worked with different groups of learners focusing on various subjects, from elementary students learning science, to high school students learning mathematics topics, to preservice teachers learning teaching methods, to practicing teachers learning pedagogy. When students learn content through game building, their high level of engagement is reflected regardless of the format of the settings: from formal elementary classrooms, to summer camp, to online graduate classes. Whether we collect data from surveys, individual interviews, face-to-face observations, or online interactions and documents, our analysis of data always demonstrates students' overwhelmingly positive emotions toward learning by game design and building.

For example, during the Games in Motion project (Li, 2010), students showed great interest and were very engrossed in the process of designing their games. Students' engagement went beyond "of the moment" interest and fun. Their commitment was another important dimension indicating the extent to which they were engaged in the process. Instead of trying to minimize their efforts to complete the tasks like they typically do with schoolwork, students willingly spent their own time doing more. They gave up lunch or recess time to work in the lab to refine or play their games.

The idea of publishing their games online for others to play was another factor that contributed to students' deep engagement of the experience. We often heard conversations amongst students as typified by the following exchange between two students: Bob and Peter:

> Bob: Peter, I want to play your game. Can you let me play it, pleeeeeeeeese?
>
> Peter: I am playing it now .... I've uploaded it on the Scratch website. Why don't you go online and play it from there?

Conversations like this demonstrated how much students were committed to their learning. Such commitment undoubtedly led to their learning at a deeper level. They were no longer limited to *what* they needed to do but more importantly were concerned about learning *why* and making decisions as to *how*.

Jenny, one of the only two girls enrolled in the summer camp, was just 7 years old. She had difficulties interacting with the other students and cried every day during the first week of the camp. However, she had great fun designing her own games and creating three different games in less than two weeks. In the lab, she always worked on or played her own games. She described her experience: "It [is] more fun to play my own games because I can change [the games] as much as I want." Her mother further added the following:

> My daughter did talk about the computer game, came home and downloaded the software at home the first day, showed us the games she created and started creating some new ones. She was very excited about it.

David, a sixth-grade teacher who participated in the Why Read If You Can Build project, observed how his students were completely engrossed in the game building process. He described in an interview how learning and class activities of math and science became exciting and interesting:

> Today when we did game project, students vibrate with energy that is just unbelievable...Most of the time if you take a worksheet with dot to dot drawings, nobody is going to be, 'Oh, I've got to get this finished. Is that the bell? I have to get it done before the bell! It's so much fun!' you never see that. But I had to kick kids

out of the room today [when we did the gaming project]. It's like 'the bell went, go for lunch.' As a teacher, you know that's when you've hit the jackpot, right? You always know when the bell does not matter anymore. You are doing something that is certainly capturing their attention and they are motivated to do.

Our observations of students also confirmed that such excitement occurred frequently. On one occasion, a small group was programming in an attempt to move a frog from one lily pad to another. Suddenly, one boy shouted out the following:

It works! It's exactly what I wanted to do! When I click on that frog, it's the only one that moves. It moves to where I want it to go. I just have to work on some stuff on collisions. You know I've been working on this for two hours and now it's doing what I want. I've managed to convince the computer to do what I want!

The students were so excited that they wanted to share it with the teacher and their friends. They had this instant desire to say, "Look at all of this stuff that we've managed to make happen!" This strong level of engagement in learning though game building and design happened so frequently in every project we conducted.

Designing and building students' own games to teach others means that students already own their learning and are inherently buying into the learning process. The novelty and challenge of programming their own games make students work harder at a higher engagement level.

Gamification?

How do we motivate students and get them excited about learning? These are two prevailing questions of which teachers have always sought answers. In a survey we conducted with over 120 preservice and in-service teachers, we found that the most important reason for the teachers to adapt a game-based learning approach is the idea of harnessing the motivational value of games (Li, 2013). This concept of using games to stimulate student interest falls loosely to the emerging field of gamification, an area focusing on the use of game thinking, game design approaches, and game mechanics to nongame applications and contexts to engage users.

Sam, the elementary teacher we met in Chapter 1, has employed the gamification approach for a long time. The following story, based on Sam's blog, tells how gamification can be played out in a classroom.

Years ago, Sam was teaching elementary music courses. He adopted a leveled music book to teach recorder, an instrument. The levels in that book are color-coded. Sam used a three-step approach for his teaching: first, he would briefly introduce a new level. Second, he would let students practice the related skill in the new level. Finally, when students thought they had mastered the skills in that level, they could go to Sam for a test. To inspire students, Sam awarded students a coloured piece of string to tie around the recorder if they pass each level test, similar to the colour belts idea in karate.

Although the idea was motivating, some students simply did not like testing. For these students, getting tested and the possibility of failure were nerve wracking. One day, Sam overheard a conversation between two 4th-grade boys. One boy was talking to the other boy, completely reframing the whole practicing-testing process. He said, "Treat Mr. Sam like he is the boss from Half-Life 2." Here, why the 9-year-olds were connecting his music class to a violent video game taking place in a virtual space fighting aliens ☺ is not important. What is important is that this conversation made Sam view students' learning and testing in a completely new light. Next day in class, Sam told all his students: "Imagine that we are fighting a Recorder Battle in Half-Life 2 and I am your evil music boss. Each music level is a chapter in that game." To spice up, he then started to speak in his deep evil voice: "Now Young music warrior, come and beat me in this Recorder Battle. You think you will be able to get to the next level? Do your worst. Mwahahahahaha...."

Now, students still went through the same process of practicing and testing, yet, the whole atmosphere of learning and assessing was altered. No longer did students perceive failure as significant. Failed this test? Students were not worried, "Oh, man. I will so get that note right next time, evil music boss." No more anxiety, no more being downhearted, and best of all, persistency became the norm.

Observing the magic result, Sam decided to adapt this strategy in every class since then. "Think of me as the boss in a video game," he would tell his students. "You may not beat me the first time, or even the first ten times. Each time you try to beat me, you are getting a little bit closer to getting it right." Using this approach, Sam has succeeded in every class, from kindergarten kids learning English to sixth-grade students learning algebra!

While such approach of transforming learning to game playing intrinsically motivated students, Sam exemplified another strategy to engage learners when he taught spelling. Once he taught the spelling unit to his fifth-grade class and created an online shell for advanced spellers. Loosely based on the Scripps National Spelling Bee competition, Sam used this online shell to inspire students' love of words and testing of spelling. At one point, Sam realized that although students enjoyed it, they progressed too slowly. He contemplated on how to improve this situation. One day, his students took a "Hard Words with a French Origin" test and

Mary received a perfect score. Borrowing the idea from games, Sam created this beautiful webpage of "Wall of Exceptional High Scores." On that virtual wall, he put, in fancy letters, a banner stating, "Mary, Master French Etymologist, 1st Rank". This seemingly minor change, according to Sam, had a huge impact on his students: "First, they realized that if they got 100% on their test, they would get a title and their name on the front page. Then they figured out that the rankings were first come first serve. If one wanted to be the first rank, he or she needed to be the first one to get the perfect score." The students were now greatly motivated to compete with each other to advance faster. The success of this strategy triggered Sam to apply this to all aspects of classroom life. A student in his class "could be 'Geographer and Cartographer' Marty, 'Master of Algebra' Amber, 'Creator of Five' Haiku, or even 'Honoured Sink Cleaner' Tony." Tony had to work diligently to clean the classroom sink to earn the Honoured Sink Cleaner title.

(Modified from Sam's blog)

You might have noticed that this was not limited to academic learning and this was intentional. Sam made sure that every student felt included and everyone could earn such an award. He even created an "Online Security Specialist" title for students who changed their password.

Sam's story is telling and provides an alternative way for us to look at teaching and learning. Borrowing the same idea when adapting learning through game design, we can honour students with titles like "Master of Scratch" (a game development software), "Programmer of the Year," "Best Game Prototype Creator," and "Gold Medal Winner of Game Design." The list can go on. We can also situate the game design and building experience to game playing scenarios. Imagine learning that a programming language like Scratch is beating the evil programming boss in a video game; all students need to do is master the commands until they can defeat the evil boss. Failing once, twice, or even ten times is no longer simple frustration but a way to improve skills. Understanding how one "boring" command works and for what purposes is no longer a chore of learning. Rather, students are sharpening their skills and weapons to conquer that evil boss! Let our imagination go wild, and we can certainly increase learners' motivation by leaps and bounds.

The Role of Teachers and Learners

In an enactivist learning world, both teachers and learners play different roles compared to those in a traditional classroom. Enactivists embrace the idea that the learning process and learning outcomes can never be fully predetermined because learners and the environment co-evolve and co-emerge. Such beliefs lead to the changing of teaching and learning practices. Teachers need to become more open minded and accepting of the fact that they do not and cannot control everything. Although possible learning goals can be set at the beginning, we need to understand that these goals will evolve during the process. Such goals, therefore, need to be constructed and modified with students along the way. This is not to say that our teaching is goal free. Instead, it stresses that goals should be framed in such a way that enough freedom is given for students to learn in their own way, and these goals should be adaptive to students' proclivities. Teachers need to focus on the creation of a world with a collection of stimulating learning conditions, whose functions are not entirely prescribed. The best ways for students to learn are determined on the fly, and this learning environment is potentially responsive to such spontaneity.

Teachers in the Why Read If I Can Build project have a lot to say about how such an enactivist learning world encouraged deep learning in student experience, a learning that went beyond simple academic knowledge acquisition. The Why Read If I Can Build project focused on sixth-grade students' learning of mathematics and science through their design of computer games. Three classes worked together, mixing students into different small groups. The structure was intentionally set with a high degree of freedom and ample opportunities for social interaction and team building within and across different classes. One of the teachers' favourite parts of the project was watching the collaboration amongst students and how reluctant students, those who usually did not succeed and were withdrawn, became successful and had a chance to be leaders. The experience of Johnny, a "below average" student, provided a perfect example to demonstrate this phenomenon. As teachers described, Johnny was introverted and eccentric and never had a chance to shine. While developing their games, students had many problems programming and sometimes teachers did not have all of the answers for them. Johnny, though, did have the answers. He understood Scratch very well and became extremely popular because he was able to create two small, yet complex games using Scratch. Realizing his knowledge about programming, students started to ask him questions, and soon enough he became a star in the class. My dialogue with David and Sam, two of the teachers, exemplifies this:

Value

David: I have never seen the sides of Johnny that I was in this project. He was more social; he became a real leader. I really like to see how proud he became of his own work. Like if you sit down and do a math worksheet, you do not walk away and say: "wow I really accomplished something!" But when you have twenty kids from a group of eighty students coming to you to ask you questions about your project? Man he [Johnny] was over the moon! He became the expert and even more than me. I would tell students: 'I do not know how you do that. Johnny knows how to do it though.' This balance of power in the classroom shifts because I am no longer the expert in this. We are going to work through this together as a team. The team building was unbelievable. The kids work together and [the teachers] become the guide. You figure out what you can do. You work to your limit and [the teachers] are here to support you along the way and give you what you need to get there. That is so unlike traditional learning. That cannot happen in a static environment. The thing is there is no net. So when things go wrong—and they do—then you have to be aware of [it] and you just have to deal with it and move on.

Qing: What do you mean things go wrong?

David: Technology can go wrong. Social relationships in groups and dynamics can go wrong.

Qing: Can you give me an example?

David: We had a few groups that had usual group dynamics of people do not get along. The strong powerful type meets the less powerful people. But the interesting thing is that is a valuable skill for them to learn because in the end you have to work it out. This is your group and you have to reach your gal and that is just as powerful as anything that is in the curriculum.

Sam: Another thing is the communication skills they exercise when working together. Heather in my room was working with Katie in [David's] room. Heather was pulling out her hair because Katie was assigned the art job but she was not doing it. She was saying to Katie: "you need to draw stick people in different colours and I still do not have stick people. Am I supposed to make the stick people too? Where does your responsibility, where do you come through with what you said?" Katie answered: "well, it is too hard and I cannot do it." I remember Heather just looking at Katie saying, "They are stick people! Are you saying you cannot do it because you need my pencil crayons?" Like we are not asking for the moon here. Katie then realized that she mistakenly thought the stick people had to be made on the software Scratch. Katie now understood she had a role in the project. She was all of a sudden like, "I can draw them on paper?" That was that moment between the two when they understand each other.

David: How much more powerful can you have of a skill of them being able to communicate with people? Especially people that you are not getting along with. Back to Johnny who has a zillion watts of energy and often it's misguided. His communication skills were not particularly strong. So it was incredible to watch what he is doing and see him to teach other people in a language that is foreign to all of them. And it became second nature to him. It's like, OK I am going to help this group because I already know how to do this.

From this conversation, one can see that the teachers were willingly and intentionally letting go of control in many aspects. They were comfortable about the shift of power, and they were happy to see students becoming empowered and largely in charge of their own learning. Such a high degree of freedom allowed deep learning to occur, learning that goes beyond subject matter. This learning is more about various lifelong skills such as logical thinking, ways of learning, communication, collaboration, and problem solving.

My further conversation with David and Sam focused on what they would change if they could adapt this approach again. Their consensus was that they would tweak the planning a bit. Now that they had experienced it, they had a better understanding of what is involved in this process. However, they also agreed that there was so much that they could not predict. David elaborated:

Looking in hindsight we got a lot out of the project . . . [some parts of the project] you do not see as much learning [of curriculum], but a lot of the social skills the stuff that I saw from the project I think ultimately what is really more valuable in the long term. I know there are always the curriculum goals, but some of the things that happened socially and the interactions between some of the students, you can't plan that. And it can't be forced. It just happened as a natural evolution and I think wow like I am seeing kids that don't normally get along, kids who don't know each other from the classes and that social bond that they create and the ability to communicate. I think that is one of the most powerful things through the project.

> *Even the most reluctant learners still were engaged with the curriculum and still were engaged in the dynamics of their groups. I like watching it just to see what the kids do with it because there were so many things that I saw them do that I would not have thought of anyway so how can I plan for that.*

My dialogues with these teachers, along with our observations of the students in this project, confirm the co-evolving of self, others, and the surrounding learning world. In an enactivist learning world, teachers are no longer simply playing the passive guide on the side role. Rather, teachers need to be organizers who strategically facilitate the learning process to involve varied ways of experiencing, thinking, and behaving. They need to be mediators who create opportunities for critical discourses and actions (Michie, 2004, April). They need to be orchestrators who provide multimodal learning configurations promoting both interpersonal and intrapersonal ways of seeking, evaluating, and applying knowledge (Gay, 2000). They need to be communicators who help name and make use of appropriate language. They need to be story makers who encourage and record the interactions between the learner and the learned. They need to be interpreters who assist learners in their making sense of the emerging patterns and understanding their involvement (Fenwick, 2000). They need to be learners who notice what is happening in the classroom and explore new possibilities to enhance learning. It is therefore important for teachers to realize their own enmeshment in the evolving systems of the learner and the learned, the knower and the known, and the self and the other.

So You Want to Build a Game?

Platforms

This book focuses on students' designing and building digital games whereby they learn a variety of skills and gain knowledge in multiple domains. Yet, the building of digital games requires appropriate software tools that can be used seamlessly to help students' content acquisition. Mastering the tools should be a simple enough task, whereby students can focus on the game building aspect rather than struggling through the syntax of a programming language.

There are many different platforms or software environments, let's call them "learn-by-design" software, that can be used for your digital game design and development. These learn-by-design software platforms often use a graphical design with built-in commands. Instead of obscure punctuation and commands of traditional syntax, learn-by-design software uses a process of drag-and-drop actions. Some learn-by-design software gives you a lot of functions to develop very sophisticated programming. This type of software, like GameMaker, is inherently more complex, with a deeper learning curve if you have limited prior programming knowledge. Other learn-by-design platforms, like Scratch or GameStar Mechanics, are easier to learn, but they may not allow you to develop sophisticated or very complicated digital products. Regardless, all learn-by-design software platforms provide sophisticated enough tools for the learning by game designing and building projects. Although the learn-by-design platform is usually best for students to learn content, it is possible to learn high level programming skills too, at least the logical principles that are fundamental for any programming language. Here, I discuss some of the learn-by-design software tools that can be used without prior programming knowledge. My description of the functions of all the software tools below is, for the most part, based on the information provided by the official websites of the software with links provided.

Scratch (http://scratch.mit.edu/) is a graphical language consisting of puzzle pieces, like blocks, to represent commands. It is free, downloadable software developed at the Massachusetts Institute of Technology (MIT). Programming in Scratch is a simple process of snapping together graphic blocks, thereby allowing students to pay attention to what the commands are doing rather than on the syntax. Scratch has an official website that promotes social interaction, because it allows users to easily download and remix existing media products, as well as publish their own games online where others can play them or even learn the scripts used to make the games. Scratch 2.0 was released in 2012 with some new features that could potentially have a pedagogical impact on teachers' and or students' use of the software. One advantage of Scratch 2.0 is that it is very easy for students to save and back up their drafts. Another benefit is that a school can host its own Scratch 2.0 website through a learning management system, thereby facilitating the development of a dynamic Scratch community within their schools. Additionally, Scratch 2.0 gives player the freedom to create their own syntax puzzle pieces, leading to unlimited possibilities.

Although Scratch is, for the most part, user friendly, it does require a certain level of skills that can best be learned by students in Grade 2 and above. Consequently, Scratch Jr. was developed, which is a simplified version of the Scratch program targeting preschoolers to Grade 2 students. This Scratch Jr. version has great potential, for it may provide younger children opportunities to acquire this new media literacy and give them other tools for self-expression.

Gamestar Mechanic (http://gamestarmechanic.com/) is another learn-by-design software that takes a slightly different approach in that it is a video game about designing video games. In the game, you are a player and at the same time a designer. As with most online games, you gain experience by completing tasks in four main areas: designing games, playing others' games, reviewing games, and being a good citizen. In essence, you can advance by building games or playing other people's games. If you want to advance to higher levels, not only must you build games, but you also must play others' games. Gamestar Mechanic places a lot of emphasis on helping players learn game design principles rather than programming. Consequently, it is really easy for novices to start building their games, because not much programming is involved. The trade-off, however, is that you are more limited in terms of how much you can customize your own game compared to other software like Scratch. In addition, you have minimum opportunities to learn and practice skills specific to programming or coding. Programming involves some very important skills, such as logical thinking, abstraction, multistep problem solving, analyzing, and attention to detail, that are essential for learning other subjects like mathematics, science, and engineering. In short, these skills are not really exercised in Gamestar Mechanics.

Kodu (http://www.kodugamelab.com/), developed by Microsoft, is also a learn-by-design programming language that is free and downloadable. In Kodu, you can use a computer or your Xbox to program, which provides you the flexibility for rapid design iterations using only a game controller for input. The games you create in Kodu can also be played on a computer or the Xbox. Compared to Scratch, Kodu is more intuitive and therefore easier for novice programmers to acquire and understand. However, Kodu is less sophisticated, with less built-in scenarios and features than Scratch.

GameMaker (http://www.yoyogames.com/gamemaker/) is a well-developed, free, downloadable platform for game building that uses simple drag-and-drop actions. The software allows you to easily make backgrounds, animate graphics, produce sound effects, and even make 3D games. It has a high degree of flexibility and a variety of features, enabling you to build professional looking games. The disadvantage is that GameMaker has a steeper learning curve for beginners, as compared to Scratch or Kodu. The trade-off is that the software allows you to create more sophisticated games.

Alice (http://www.alice.org/) is a 3D programming environment much like Scratch. Also free and downloadable, this software allows you to easily create animations, play a game, or create a video to share. As a multi-university initiative, this environment has a strong focus on education aimed at teaching students programming in a 3D world.

StarLogo TNG (http://education.mit.edu/projects/starlogo-tng) is another 3D programming environment for modeling and simulation. Built on the original Logo software developed at MIT, using this software you can make compelling games and simulations with 3D graphics. One cool feature of StarLogo TNG is its model importing function that allows you to import Google Earth models directly into your games or simulations.

The learn-by-design software platforms described here are great for teachers to adopt in their approach to learning by game building. In addition, there are commercial game building environments that can be used. For example, RPG Maker XP (http://www.rpgmakerweb.com/) enables you to easily create your own original role-playing games. 3D GameMaker (http://www.thegamecreators.com) allows you to build a uniquely playable game without prior programming knowledge or artistic skills. It contains over 12 billion gaming options so that you can easily develop your dream game. Game Studio (http://www.3dgamestudio.com/) is another game-authoring suite for both 2D and 3D media products. It contains 2D and 3D engines and a physical engine as well as terrain and model editors with libraries of objects. Depending on the situation, you can choose appropriate learn-by-design software that meets your unique requirements and needs.

Mechanics

When creating a learning world that adopts the approach of learning by game building, various instructional materials are needed. As discussed in detail earlier, gaming software is certainly necessary. Additionally, other resources are desirable in order to best support students' learning.

The first useful resource to share with students is examples of previous student-created games. These examples can be the entire game, or detailed screenshots and text, or even video clips of the game. If possible, samples of previous students' developed game design documents are also helpful. Providing examples can give students an idea of what is expected as well as what is possible. These examples can increase their confidence. Some teachers provide a range of examples by including the best, the ordinary, and the not-so-good products, along with an explanation or evaluation of the work. Letting students view the range of work can provide a big picture. But the possible negative consequence, on the other hand, is that some students may estimate how much effort is needed for creating an ordinary game versus an excellent game, and they may decide to go for mediocrity. To avoid this, some teachers only share exemplary games so that students can be inspired to achieve their highest potential.

The second useful resource is a "Best Tips" type of guide for designing a game. Depending on the student population, the guide should inform students about what is considered a good game design. For example, during our Call of Math project, preservice teachers developed games for secondary math students. The following tips, adapted from Schreiber (2009), were provided to these preservice teachers to assist in their design of educational games:

1. *Balance*: In your game, it is important to create a balance so that players are challenged and at the same time not overwhelmed. You also need to balance the amount of development work involved and the time you have to create your game.
2. *Educational value*: Carefully consider the educational value of your game and how learning objectives are embedded in your game: Where is the math learning and what else do students learn in this game? Players are usually more intrinsically motivated when the learning objectives are skilfully hidden rather than overtly displayed in the game.
3. *Creativity*: You need to let your imagination go wild. Your creativity in the game will have unexpected power to engage your learners in their learning. Try your best to avoid cloning existing games.
4. *Simplicity*: You need to make sure the game is easy to learn and play by designing a user-friendly interface and controls. Conventions can be your best friend. For example, use hot keys like arrow keys or A, W, D, X, the way they are used in a typical game.

5. *Focus on players*: The players are the ones who give life to your game, so you need to know your audience. You should consider players' experience and interest so that your game can engage both new players and seasoned players. One way to achieve this is to make highly adaptive games with different levels.
6. *Engagement*: Is your game exciting and interesting? Try adventures, problems, and puzzles, so that players can explore their turf and discover excitement.
7. *Play testing*: Play testing is the most effective way for you to identify problems and improve your game. It is essential to play test and revise your games according to the feedback collected.

While this list of tips is useful for secondary math teachers, parts of it may not be appropriate if we are implementing learning by game building in an elementary social studies classroom. Therefore, the tips need to be tailored to specific audiences.

A third useful resource is a list or cheat sheet of the strategies needed for paper prototyping. According to Brathwaite and Schreiber (2009), these strategies can include information such as what should be included in the paper prototype. For example, the paper prototype should focus on the underlying mechanic of your game play and ignore all the apparatus of your interface like the sound or visual splendour. It is also important to remember that you are not modeling the actual finished game play experience in your paper prototype; it would be too convoluted to do so. Rather, you put emphasis on the aspects to answer your design questions.

It is always useful to have cheating codes, which is a fourth useful resource to share with students. The cheating codes can be lists of keystrokes, strategies to create objects, and/or popular commands to program actions (Katie & Zimmerman, 2003). Providing these cheat sheets and making them easily accessible can greatly reduce students' anxiety level and enhance their learning.

Scaffolding

The learning process that takes place through designing and building digital games is a complex one that involves various challenges. The most prominent and consistent challenges across different age levels and topics are the technical ones. Many students, particularly those who have no prior experience with programming, have difficulty mastering the game development software. Even though the learn-by-design game building software, as discussed earlier, is user-friendly and can usually be understood without any prior knowledge, the actual mastering of it to build a sophisticated game idea can be difficult. In all the game building projects we have conducted, whether with elementary camp students, or high school math students, or preservice or in-service teachers, we asked the same question: "What are the challenges you faced during the project?" We used different methods of collecting participants' answers to this question, ranging from interviewing, to surveying, to analyzing their written documents. A common answer has been this: "One challenge is how to get [the software] to do what I want it to do."

The prevalence of the technical challenges learners encounter suggests that we should pay close attention to address this issue. When students become too frustrated, it can potentially hinder their learning and decrease their enthusiasm about game building. In our Do It Yourself project, Tim, a participating teacher, described his feelings about the learning journey of building his own game:

> I can honestly say that I have learned the most through the game design and building process while simultaneously being extremely frustrated with my learning. . . . I felt that I had taken on an unfeasibly large "plate of programming" with my limited game designing skills. However, through bad moods and nervous twitches, I managed to create a larger Smart Board game and three smaller Scratch games that stem from my paper version game.

Although Tim was able to find some solutions to partially implement his game design, the fact that his game idea could not be fully realized in digital format hampered his progress and satisfaction. So how should this problem be addressed?

There are two important strategies that can be used to help students overcome technical difficulties. One approach is to encourage collaboration in the learning community. For example, students can work in small groups to complete the activities. Teachers can also identify a few students as the programming experts in class and give them opportunities to help other students. In addition, many of the programming environments discussed earlier are community based, meaning that they often have a large virtual learning community where members actively engage in learning and using the software. Students can take advantage of these virtual communities and find support in them. For instance, the Scratch forum (http://wiki.scratch.mit.edu/wiki/Scratch_Wiki:Table_of_Contents/Forums) contains rich information ranging from ideas to teach with Scratch to suggestions for addressing technical glitches.

The second approach is to properly scaffold students' learning of the programming language. For example, it's a good idea to give students small tasks, gradually increasing the difficulty levels. In our Why Read If I Can Build project, the teachers created a series of tasks to scaffold students' Scratch skills. They developed "Scratch Challenges" booklets, dividing the tasks into two difficulty levels: the basic challenges and the super challenges. The cover of the booklet reads as follows:

> *In this book are a series of challenges. See if you can write a program for each challenge. Your teacher has the answer if you get really stuck.* **Talk with other teams if you need help! Use trial and error.**

Each of the subsequent pages poses a programming challenge with some graphic representations. For example, the first challenge is to change the color of an object in Scratch: "Programming so that when you press a key, the colour of a sprite would change."

Challenge number 4 is "Follow the Mouse." Students need to program so that a sprite in Scratch "is following the mouse. Make a cat chase the mouse."

Challenge number 5 is to make an "Interactive Whirl" in Scratch. The students' task is to "whirl a photo by moving the mouse. Not a click this time. Can you make the photo whirl by moving your mouse around the screen?"

Challenge number 7 asks students to program the "Glide" motion in Scratch. Students need to make a sprite to "move smoothly from one point to another. Think about what the word 'Glide' means."

Challenge number 10 is about making a surprise button. Students need to make their own button in Scratch so that "each time you click on the button, you get a random sound and the color of the button change!"

Challenge number 11 is to keep score. In this challenge, students are asked to add a scoreboard to a Scratch game.

These tasks involve relatively simple programming skills, with one building on another. In completing each task, students learn how to better navigate and program. After students have mastered these first level skills, they can work on the one of the following three "super challenges."

Scratch Super Challenge #1: Make a Virtual Musical Instrument
Requirements:
1. Create a Virtual Musical Instrument that uses pitch or non-pitched sounds.
2. Users can click or press keys on the computer to activate the sounds.
3. Build a colourful and interesting User Interface that allows the user to select sounds.

Scratch Super Challenge #2: Timer Game
Requirements:
1. Create a "Main Sprite" (e.g., the cat) to play a sound and measure in seconds how fast the user can click the space bar.
2. Display the user's time in seconds.
3. Ask the user if s/he wishes to play again.

Scratch Super Challenge #3: Quiz Game
Requirements:
1. Choose a quiz topic (examples: colours, parts of a cell, vocabulary words).
2. Create a list of possible answers.
3. Create a Sprite to "ask the question."
4. Allow user to type in an answer.
5. Compare user's answer to question.
6. Provide user feedback to tell the user if they are correct or incorrect.

Using these smaller tasks with different levels of difficulties, teachers were able to scaffold these elementary students' learning. Scaffolding helped students acquire the needed programming skills in a friendly and gradual manner, thereby minimizing possible frustration caused by technical challenges. This approach can also be modified and repurposed for other levels of learners, from high school students to practicing teachers. In fact, Sam found this to be so useful that he later developed a website that contained all the information.

When we worked with teachers, either graduate students or undergraduate students, we found that scaffolding through a period of time worked well. In each class, we would first give a brief instruction on a particular command and then allow the students time to complete a small task similar to the basic Scratch challenges described earlier. This would take only about five to ten minutes per class. We would also build in small assignments to further improve students' programming skills. One of the assignments, for example, was to ask students to create their own name game. Adapted from an activity originated from an online forum (http://scratch.mit.edu/discuss/), this is the assignment they were given:

Create an animation of your name so that each letter does something different when a letter is clicked or when that letter is pressed on the keyboard. Try different visual effects on your own name game:
- colour
- mosaic
- whirl
- movements, e.g., rotation, bouncing around the screen.

Another assignment teachers found helpful was to allow students opportunities to modify (i.e., modding) existing games. For instance, I would ask the teachers to find a game such as a *Pong* game and then modify it using at least five new commands that were not used in the original *Pong* game. They could also change at least five parts of the *Pong* game if they wished. Such game modding exercises greatly reduce the teachers' level of programming fear as well as let them practice and become familiar with new commands.

This kinds of scaffolding provides students a safety net or a parachute for them to take risks and explore, rather than simply letting them blowing in the wind. Scaffolding can be the link that connects great teaching to euphoric learning.

PART FIVE

Conclusion

• CHAPTER NINE •

Learning by Game Building in the Twenty-first Century

Our world is changing. The emergence of virtual worlds, for example, the massive multiuser online game environments where millions of people live out a collective existence, is quickly changing the landscape of our world. Using Castonova's (2009) ways of describing, for example, you can become immersed for hours and hours in a virtual world. In such a world, you, through your avatar, may see green trees, blue sky, and puffy white clouds. You may hear birds chirping, music playing, or even tigers roaring. You may live in a fancy house by the ocean beach with big coconut trees planted in your front yard. You may talk with your neighbours in this virtual village through texting, chatting, tweeting, or having a video conversation. You can practice various skills ranging from blacksmithing to yoga. In short, you can play, experience, learn, and interact with characters run by other human beings or by the system's artificial intelligence engines. In other words, you can live with people in this virtual world just as if you were in a real world.

The number of people immersed in this virtual frontier is growing rapidly. Increasingly we live, work, socialize, and play in a virtual world. For example, according to Wikipedia, *World of Warcraft* was launched in 2004, and by 2012 over 10 million subscribers (World of Warcraft, n.d.-c). Facebook, a social media site, had one million subscribers at the end of 2004, and has 1.19 billion monthly active members in 2013 (Facebook, 2013). The Pew report (Hampton, Goulet, Rainie, & Purcell, 2011) indicates that since 2011, Facebook has connected at least one-eleventh of the world population on a single website. McGonigal (2011) listed some impressive statistics, which she collected from various sources:

> Globally, the online gamer community counts more than 4 million gamers in the Middle East, 10 million in Russia, 105 million in India, 10 million in Vietnam, 10 million in Mexico, 14 million in Central and South America, . . . 100 million in Europe, and 200 million in China. (p. 3)

Society's fascination with the virtual world and digital games is ubiquitous. At first glance, one may not appreciate the gravity or significance of how widespread virtual engagement has become. Yet, the impact of virtual worlds, including digital games, is quite salient, affecting how we live, work, and play. The sheer volume of people who spend so much time and energy immersed in virtual game worlds, however, has resulted in a combined effect that is much like the advent of a new country (Castronova, 2007). It impacts our economy, policy, and life. Our current educational systems are also challenged by such changes.

Furthermore, although technology has become ever-present in the world around us, unfortunately a gap still exists between students' experiences with technology usage in and out of their classrooms. Youth quickly and effortlessly learn how to navigate the web on their own. They access tremendous amounts of information from the Internet; they are avid consumers of media; and some of them have become devoted digital media creators. However, As Klopfer (2008) has argued, even with their notable skills, this does not guarantee that the vast majority of our students will have what they need to be successful contributors to society. For starters, not all students have access to the latest technologies and other resources. It is imperative that strides be made to close the digital divides that are so pervasive throughout our world. Second, accessing information is not equivalent to understanding information. Students may know how to retrieve vast amounts of data, but many still have limited understanding of how to use the data purposefully. Third, many of our children are still passive digital content consumers and have never created digital media products. In an effort to include our youth in the participatory culture that evolved as a result of the virtual worlds, it is important for us to include their voices in various online communities. Fourth, even for those who have been active participants and contributors in the technological world, they may have difficulties transferring their technological skills acquired through their use of technology in their personal lives to other fields. Schools should help prepare our students to be able to navigate in this complex and challenging intellectual landscape (Klopfer, 2008).

Throughout this book, I have presented enactivism as a feasible framework for us to reconsider education. Specifically, I have described how learning by game building, grounded in enactivism, can be manifested in educational settings, from informal out-of-school programs to formal school classrooms. My position is supported by the work of other researchers and scholars (Gee, 2007; Kafai, 2006; McGonigal, 2011; Papert, 1993). Learning, through game design and building, in a well-crafted environment, offers a number of advantages when it comes to connecting the current landscape of school learning to the real world in the context of a participatory culture. The nature of such an approach promotes active knowledge and digital media creation and sharing, rather than passive content consumption. It affords unique opportunities that can help our children learn 21st-century skills. From the lessons we have learned from our own projects and those of others, we can see that such an approach is beneficial in the following ways:

Flexible focus: Game design and building can focus on any content, therefore providing a very flexible approach to teach. When students design their own games, we can easily tailor the focus of their game design to fit into our curriculum demands. For example, we can ask students to build games using Scratch to teach any subject, from mathematics to babysitting.

Learning as game designing: Designing and developing a game demands different kinds of skills than playing a game. For example, our creative muscles and logical thinking skills are exercised frequently when we design a game. The game making process is complicated and requires designers to plan well and construct ideas and resources in a logical way. The experience of game design and development therefore offer learners rich opportunities to practice these 21st-century skills.

Game design as a mind tool: We can design learning activities that engage students in designing and developing digital games such that the students can organize their knowledge, build dynamic models, interpret information, and collaborate with others during the game's development process. That is, the game development tools can be mind tools for students to practice analytical skills and systems modeling as well as build knowledge.

No doubt, our students are in an Internet culture, a participatory culture, a game culture, in short, a culture that still requires parents, teachers, and community leaders to be in charge and do their part in bridging the gap between kids' casual use of information to their meaningful employment of what the web has to offer them. Their participation should be deep and built on understanding. Learning by game building provides a wonderful means to help students achieve in this way. By engaging students in well-crafted, rich experiences that integrate authentic challenges and social participation, students can grow with a deep understanding of these 21st-century skills. In fact, McGonigal (2011) has posited that "game design isn't just a technological craft. It's a twenty-first-century way of thinking and leading" (p. 13). This endorses the bright future of learning by game design and building. Game design and development can involve people of any age to learn almost anything. Game design can take place in any setting and for any subject. As we saw in the instances of our Games in Motion and Why Read If I Can Build projects, game design was embedded in various in-class and out-of-class activities, not only in formal classrooms but also in summer camp programs. A similar experience was created around Sam's story of developing his *Splat!* game, where learning game-based design principles were intertwined with gaining knowledge of good driving rules. Being successful at designing games means carefully thinking about the content behind it and strategically embedding the knowledge into game situations. You ask, where and when should we adopt learning by game design? My answer is, here and now. The real question is, are you inspired?

References

Abt, C. C. (1970). *Serious games*. New York, NY: Viking Press.

Armstrong, S. (1979). The natural learning project. *Journal of Experiential Learning and Simulation, 1,* 5–12.

Bateson, G. (1972). *Steps to an ecology of mind*. New York, NY: Ballantine Books.

Begg, A. (2000). Enactivism: A personal interpretation. Retrieved from http://www.merga.net.au/documents/RP_Begg_1999.pdf

Borgman, C., Abelson, H., Dirks, L., Johnson, R., Koedinger, K., Linn, M., . . . Szalay, A. (2008). *Fostering learning in the networked world: The cyberlearning opportunity and challenge*. Washington, DC: National Science Foundation.

Brathwaite, B., & Schreiber, I. (2009). Challenges for Game Designers: Non-digital Exercises for Video Game Designers. Boston, MA: Course Technology.

Caillois, R. (2001). *Man, play, and games* (M. Barash, Trans.). Champaign: University of Illinois Press.

Capra, F. (2002). *The hidden connections: A science for sustainable living*. London, England: HarperCollins.

Castronova, E. (2009). *Exodus to the virtual world: How online fun is changing reality*. New York: Palgrave Macmillan.

Costikyan, G. (1994). I Have No Words and I Must Design. *Interactive Fantasy, 2*. Retrieved May 28, 2013 from http://www.rpg.net/oracle/essays/nowords.html

Crawford, C. (1984). *The art of computer game design*. Columbus, OH: McGraw-Hill.

Crayon Physics Deluxe. (n.d.). Wikipedia, 2012(Dec. 6). Retrieved from http://en.wikipedia.org/wiki/Crayon_Physics_Deluxe

Csikszentmihalyi, M. (1996). *Creativity: The work and lives of 91 eminent people*. New York, NY: HarperCollins.

Csikszentmihalyi, M. (1997). *Finding flow*. New York, NY: Basic Books.

Davis, B., & Sumara, D. (1997). Cognition, complexity and teacher education. *Harvard Educational Review, 67*(1), 105–125.

Davis, B., & Sumara, D. (2006). *Complexity and education: Inquiries into learning, teaching and research*. New York, NY: Routledge.

Davis, B., Sumara, D., & Luce-Kapler, R. (2008). *Engaging minds: Changing teaching in complex times* (2nd ed.). Mahwah, NJ: Lawrence Erlbaum.

Dede, C. (2008). A seismic shift in epistemology. *EDUCAUSE Review, 43*(3), 80–81.

Dewey, J. (1933). *How we think*. Boston, MA: Heath.

diSessa, A. (2000). *Changing minds: Computers, learning, and literacy*. Cambridge, MA: The MIT Press.

Facebook. (2013). Facebook Reports Third Quarter 2013 Results. Retrieved from Facebook: Investor Relations website: http://investor.fb.com/releasedetail.cfm?ReleaseID=802760

Fenwick, T. (2000). Expanding conceptions of experiential learning: A review of five contemporary perspectives. *Adult Education Quarterly, 50*(4), 243–272.

Gallegos, I., & Flores, A. (2010). Using Student-Made Games to Learn Mathematics. *Primus: Problems, Resources & Issues in Mathematics Undergraduate Studies, 20*(5), 405-417. doi:10.1080/10511970802353644.

Games, A., & Squire, K. (2011). Searching for the fun in learning: A historical perspective on the evolution of educational viedo games. In S. Tobias & J. D. Fletcher (Eds.), *Computer games and instruction* (pp. 17–46). Charlotte, NC: Information Age Publishing.

References

Gardner, H., & Hatch, T. (1989). Multiple intelligences go to schoo: Educational implications of the theory of multiple intelligences. *Educational Researcher, 18*(8), 4-10.

Gay, G. (2000). *Culturally responsive teaching: Theory, research, & practice.* New York, NY: Teachers College Press.

Gee, J. (2007). *What video games have to teach us about learning and literacy* (2nd ed.). New York, NY: Palgrave Macmillan.

Gee, J. (2008). Learning and games. In K. Salen (Ed.), *The ecology of games: Connecting youth, games, and learning* (pp. 21–40). Cambridge, MA: The MIT Press.

Gee, J. (2009). *Good video games + good learning.* New York, NY: Peter Lang.

Gilmore, B. (1971). Play: A special behavior. In R. E. Herron & B. Sutton-Smith (Eds.), *Child's play* (pp. 311–325). New York, NY: John Wiley & Sons.

Gros, B. (2007). Digital games in education: The design of game-based learning environment. *Journal of Research on Technology in Education, 40*(1), 23–38.

Habgood, J., & Overmars, M. H. (2006). *The game maker's apprentice: Game development for beginners.* New York, NY: Apress.

Hampton, K., Goulet, L., Rainie, L., & Purcell, K. (2011). *Social networking sites and our lives: How people's trust, personal relationships, and civic and political involvement are connected to their use of social networking sites and other technologies.* Washington, DC: Pew Research Center's Internet & American Life Project.

Holzman, L. (2010). Without creating ZPDs there is no creativity. In C. Connery, V. John-Steiner, & A. Marjanovic-Shane (Eds.), *Dancing with the muses: A chat approach to play, meaningmaking, and creativity.* New York, NY: Peter Lang.

Hunicke, R., LeBanc, M., & Zubek, R. (2004, July). *MDA: A formal approach to game design and game research.* Paper presented at the Nineteenth National Conference on Artificial Intelligence, San Jose, CA.

Jenkins, H. (2007). Confronting the challenges of participatory culture: Media education for the 21st century (part two). *Nordic Journal of Literacy, 2*(97-113).

Jenkins, H., Clinton, K., Purushotma, R., Robison, A., & Weigel, M. (2006). Confronting the challenges of participatory culture: Media education for the 21st century (p. 66). Washington, DC: John D. and Catherine T. MacArthur Foundation.

Johnson, D., & Johnson, R. (1989). *Cooperations and competition: Theory and research.* Minneapolis, MN: Interaction Book Company.

Jonassen, D. H. (2001). Objectivism versus constructivism: Do we need a new philosophical paradigm? In D. Ely & T. Plomp (Eds.), *Classic writing on instructional technology* (vol. II, pp. 53–65). Englewood, CO: Libraries Unlimited.

Kafai, Y. B. (1995). *Minds in play: Computer game design as a context for children's learning.* Cambridge, MA: The MIT Press.

Kafai, Y. (2006). Playing and making games for learning: Instructionist and constructionist perspectives for game studies. *Games and Culture, 1*(1), 36–40.

Kahn, K. (1996). ToonTalkTM-An animated programming environment for children. *Journal of Visual Languages and Computing, 7*(2), 197–217.

Klopfer, E. (2008). *Augmented learning: Research and design of mobile educational games.* Cambridge, MA: The MIT Press.

Klopfer, E., & Begel, A. (2003). StarLogo under the hood and in the classroom. *Kybernetes, 32*(1/2), 15–37.

Klopfer, E., Scheintau, H., Huang, W., Wendel, D., & Roque, R. (2009). The simulation cycle—Combining games, simulations, engineering and science using StarLogo TNG. *E-Learning and Digital Media, 6*(1), 71–96.

Kutner, L., & Olson, C. (2008). *Grand theft childhood: The surprising truth about violent video games and what parents can do*: New York, NY: Simon & Schuster.

Li, Q. (2010). Digital game building: Learning in a participatory culture. *Educational Research, 52*(4), 427–443.

Li, Q. (2012). Understanding enactivism: A study of affordances and constraints of engaging practicing teachers as digital game designers. *Educational Technology Research & Development, 60*(5), 785-806. doi: DOI: 10.1007/s11423-012-9255-4

References

Li, Q. (2013). Digital games and learning: A study of preservice teachers' perceptions. *International Journal of Play, 2*(2), 101-116. doi: 10.1080/21594937.2013.817105

Li, Q., Clark, B., & Winchester, I. (2010). Instructional design and technology grounded in enactivism: A paradigm shift? *British Journal of Educational Technology, 41*(3), 403–419.

Li, Q., Lemieux, C., Vandermeiden, E., & Nathoo, S. (2013). Are you ready to teach secondary mathematics in the 21st century? A study of per-service teachers' digital game design experience. *Journal of Research on Technology in Education, 45*(4), 309-337. `

Li, Q., Tay, R., & Louis, R. (2012). Designing Digital Games to Teach Road Safety: A Study of Graduate Students' Experiences. *Loading...,, 6*(9), 17-35.

Li, Q., Vandermeiden, E., Lemieux, C., & Nathoo, S. (in press). Digital game building in high school mathematics classrooms. *Computers in the Schools.*

Lieberman, H. (2001). *Your wish is my command: Programming by example.* Burlington, MA: Morgan Kaufmann.

Liikkanen, L. A., & Perttula, M. (2010). Inspiring design idea generation: Insights from a memory-search perspective. *Journal of Engineering Design, 21*(5), 545–560.

Linda07. (2007). Essentials of a good online game. Retrieved from http://www.giveawayoftheday.com/forums/topic/2189

Maturana, H. R., & Varela, F. J. (1980). *Autopoiesis and cognition: The realization of the living.* Dordrecht, Holland: D. Reidel Publishing.

Maturana, H. R., & Varela, F. J. (1987). *The tree of knowledge: The biological roots of human understadning.* Boston, MA: Shambhala.

McGonigal, J. (2011). *Reality is broken: Why games make us better and how they can change the world.* New York, NY: Penguin.

Menary, R. (2006). Introduction: What is radical enactivism? In R. Menary (Ed.), *Radical enactivism, intentionality, phenomenology and narrative: Focus on the philosophy of Daniel Hutto* (pp. 1–13). Philadelphia, PA: John Benjamins Publishing.

Michie, M. (2004, April). *Teaching science to indigenous students: Teachers as culture broker or is it something else?* Paper presented at the meeting of the National Association for Research in Science Teaching, Vancouver, Canada.

Mitra, S., & Dangwal, R. (2010). Limits to self-organising systems of learning—The Kalikuppam experiment. *British Journal of Educational Technology, 41*(5), 672–688.

Mitra, S., Dangwal, R., Chatterjee, S., Jha, S., Bisht, R. S., & Kapur, P. (2005). Acquisition of computing literacy on shared public computers: Children and the "Hole in the Wall." *Australasian Journal of Educational Technology, 21*(3), 407–426.

Mitra, S., & Rana, V. (2001). Children and the internet: Experiments with minimally invasive education in India. *British Journal of Educational Technology, 32*(2), 221–232.

National Council of Teachers of Mathematics [NCTM]. (2000). *Principles and standards for school mathematics*. Reston, VA: Author.

Nijstad, B. A, & Stroebe, W. (2006). How the group affects the mind: A cognitive model of idea generation in groups. *Personality and Social Psychology Review, 10*(3), 186–213.

Noss, R., & Hoyles, C. (2006). Exploring mathematics through construction and collaboration. In R. K. Sawyer (Ed.), *Cambridge handbook of the learning sciences* (pp. 389–408). New York, NY: Cambridge University Press.

Papert, S. (1980). *Mindstorms: Children, computers, and powerful ideas*. New York, NY: Basic Books.

Papert, S. (1993). *The children's machine: Rethinking school in the age of computers*. New York, NY: Basic Books.

Partnership for 21st Century Skills. (2004). A framework for 21st century learning. Retrieved from http://www.p21.org

Pellegrini, A., & Holmes, R. (2006). The role of recess in primary school. In D. Singer, R. Golinkoff, & K. Hirsh-Pasek (Eds.), *Play=Learning: How play motivates and enhances children's cognitive and social-emotional growth* (pp. 36-53). Oxford, England: Oxford University Press.

References

Piaget, J. (1962). *Play, dreams and imitation in childhood.* New York, NY: Nortion. (Originally published in French in 1945).

Proffitt, D. R. (1999). Perception: Ecological versus inferential approaches. In R. J. Sternberg (Ed.), *The concept of cognition* (pp. 447–473). Cambridge, MA: The MIT Press.

Proffitt, D. R., Bhalla, M., Grossweiler, R., & Midgett, J. (1995). Perceiving grographical slant. *Psychonomic Bulletin and Review, 2*(4), 409–428.

Reid, D. (1995). *The need to prove* (Doctoral dissertation, University of Alberta, Edmonton, Canada). Retrieved May 28, 2013 from: http://www.acadiau.ca/~dreid/publications/davesweb/start.htm

Riener, C. R., Stefanucci, J. K., Proffitt, D. R., & Clore, G. (2011). An effect of mood on the perception of geographical slant. *Cognition & Emotion, 25*(1), 174–182. doi:10.1080/02699931003738026

Salen, K., & Zimmerman, E. (2003). *Rules of Play: Game Design Fundamentals.* Cambridge: MIT Press.

Schell, J. (2008). *The art of game design: A book of lenses.* New York, NY: Morgan Kaufmann.

Schreiber, I. (2009). Game design concepts: An experiment in game design and teaching. Retrieved May 28, 2013 from: http://gamedesignconcepts.pbworks.com/f/Game+Design+Concepts+0-5.pdf

Suits, B. (1990). *Grasshopper: Games, life and utopia.* Toronto, Ontario, Canada: Broadview Press.

Tapscott, D. (2009). *Grown up digital: How the net generation is changing your world.* New York, NY: McGraw-Hill.

Torrance, H. (2007). Assessment as learning? How the use of explicit learning objectives, assessment criteria and feedback in post secondary education and training can come to dominate learning. *Assessment in Education, 14*(3), 281-294.

Trump, J. (1970). *A school for everyone. Design for a middle, junior, or senior high school that combines the old and the new.* Reston, Virginia: National Association of Secondary School Principals.

Varela, F., Thompson, E., & Rosch, E. (1991). *The embodied mind: Cognitive science and human experience.* Cambridge, MA: The MIT Press.

Vygotsky, L. (1976). Play and its role in the mental development of the child (C. Mulholland, Trans.). In J. Bruner, A. Jolly, & K. Sylva (Eds.), *Play: Its role in development and evolution* (Vol. 6, pp. 6–18). New York, NY: Penguin.

Vygotsky, L. (1978). *Mind in society: The development of higher psychological processes.* Cambridge, MA: Harvard University Press.

Weinsheimer, J. (1985). *Gadamer's hermeneutics: A reading of "Truth and Method."* New Haven, CT: Yale University Press.

Wikipedia. (n.d.-a). Crayon physics deluxe. Retrieved from http://en.wikipedia.org/wiki/Crayon_Physics_Deluxe

Wikipedia. (n.d.-b). Palace of the Silver Princess. Retrieved from http://en.wikipedia.org/wiki/Palace_of_the_Silver_Princess

Wikipedia. (n.d.-c). World of Warcraft. Retrieved from http://en.wikipedia.org/wiki/World_of_Warcraft

Wilensky, U., & Reisman, K. (2006). Thinking like a wolf, a sheep or a firefly: Learning biology through constructing and testing computational theories. *Cognition & Instruction, 24,* 171–209.

Williams, L. E., & Bargh, J. A. (2008). Experiencing physical warmth promotes interpersonal warmth. *Science, 322,* 606–607.

Willis, J. (2006). *Research-Based strategies to ignite student learning: Insights from a neurologist and classroom teacher.* Alexandria, VA: Association for Supervision and Curriclum Development.

Index

21st century global civilization, 10
21st century skills, 50-65, 121, 201
    Learning and Innovation Skills, 50, 51, 56
    Information, Media and Technology Skills, 50, 59, 60, 61
    Information Literacy, 59-61
    Media Literacy, 59, 60, 61, 189
    ICT Literacy, 60
    Life and Career Skills, 50, 61-62
    Communication and Collaboration, 51, 114
    Critical Thinking and Problem Solving, 51
    Critical Thinking and Analytical Skills, 56
    Creativity and Innovation, 50, 51
    Perseverance, 63-64
36 learning principles, 21

A

Abstract thinking, 19
Active learning, 117-119, 163, 164, 167, 174
Activity theory, 18
Action, 74
Agentsheets, 35
Alice, 190
Allen's design, 78, 87, 92
Animal Crossing, 42
Art of Game Design, The, 49
Assessment, 77, 78, 79, 90, 117, 118, 119, 125, 126, 128, 153, 162-178
    Formative assessment, 166
    Students' ability assessment, 175
    Summative assessment, 166
Assessment tools, 162, 173, 178,

Autopoiesis, 14
Awesome Adventure, 62

B

Balance, 191
Bateson, G, 12, 14
Behaviourism, 3,
Blizzard Zone, 101-103
Bodily-kinaesthetic intelligence, 98
Brain's Coming Back, 97
Brain's Return, 72
Brainstorming sessions, 82, 89
Bridging and scaffolding, 163, 164, 168
Buggy Jump, 122

C

Capra, F., 14
Caste system, 110, 111, 160
Catch It!, 140
Call of Duty, 42, 104
Call of Math, 22, 23, 24, 25, 53, 58, 61, 62, 96, 163, 173, 174, 191
Callois, R., 37
Cartesian system of coordinates, 101
Challenge, 94, 95
Cheat mode, 85
Cheats, 52-53
Chess, 41
Children's Machine, The, 20
Chocolate Covered Broccoli games, 29, 78
Clark C, A., 36,
Co-emergence, 14
Cognition, 3, 4, 6, 8-16, 18, 20-32, 126, 127, 136
    Cognitive development, 18, 19, 39, 124
Collaboration, 25, 50, 52, 58, 59, 94, 105, 112, 114, 117, 118, 120, 121, 123, 124, 125, 126, 127, 128, 129, 130,

132, 136, 139, 167, 168, 172, 179, 187, 189, 196
   Collaborative learning, 109, 121-128
   Collaborative skills, 6, 126
   Collaboration principle, 114
   Group processing, 123, 124, 128
   Individual accountability, 123, 124, 128
   Interaction, 123,126-128
   Interpersonal and small group skills, 123, 124, 128
   Positive interdependence, 123, 124, 127
   True collaborative learning, 123-129
Common Core Standards, 142
Community building, 109, 138
Conceptual abilities, 19
Conflict, 36, 37, 38, 42
Connections, 114, 117, 118, 163, 164, 167
Constructivism, 3, 12, 15, 16, 17, 18, 20, 22
Constructionism, 19, 20
Content knowledge, 33, 35, 53, 70, 76, 79, 82, 115, 124, 156, 161
Crayon Physics, 3, 7, 8, 9, 32, 36
Crawford, C., 37,
Creativity, 43, 44, 49, 50, 51, 52, 53, 54, 88, 93, 96, 114, 119, 149, 171, 191
Cycles of expertise, 21

D
Dede, C., 113, 114
Designer, 4, 28, 32, 33, 49, 62, 69, 90, 104, 105, 125, 139, 189
DDD, 98, 146, 149
Dichotomy, 14
Digital game, 3, 4, 18, 19, 21, 22, 29, 35, 43, 49, 67, 81, 84, 85, 88, 99, 110, 118, 132, 146, 156, 159, 163, 188
   Digital game-based learning, 3, 18, 19, 22,
   Digital game design, 22, 35, 49, 88, 188,
   Digital game building, 99,
Discovery, 9, 19, 31, 94, 96, 119, 131, 139, 145

Do It Yourself, 23, 24, 54, 64, 70, 84, 85, 101, 103, 110, 117, 125, 141, 146, 155, 193
Drag-and-drop, 188, 189
Driven, The, 23, 25, 66, 70, 78, 86, 91, 112, 125, 127, 128
Driven for Life, 72
Dualism, 10, 17
Dungeons & Dragons, 98, 146, 147, 150

E
Educational value, 165, 191
Edutainment, 34
Eggcellent Math, 71
Elena's Dragon, 72
Embodied Mind, The, 10
Embodiment, 10, 12, 13, 55
Emotions, 13, 64, 106, 142, 153, 156, 179
Empowered learners, 21
Enactivism, 3, 4, 6, 8, 9, 10, 11, 12, 14, 15, 16, 17, 18, 20, 22, 24, 26, 27, 28, 30, 32, 65, 66, 114, 135, 137, 200
Enactivist approach, 55, 177
Enactivist learning approach, 54
Enactivist learning world, 27, 29, 33, 49, 81, 106, 109, 110, 124, 138, 142, 153, 173, 177, 179, 183, 184, 187
Enactivist learning world and culture, 109
Enactivist learning world and value, 153-178
Enactivist principles, 32
Enactivist view, 15, 66
Enactivist world, 29, 114
Enactivist world for 21st-century learning, 114
Engagement/motivation, 117, 118, 165, 167, 174
Epistemology, 1-45
ESL, 70, 98, 146, 149, 161
Ethics, 112, 160
Exploration and reasoning, 117, 119, 163, 164, 167
Expression, 94, 95, 113, 120, 139, 150

F
Facebook, 113, 199
Fantasy, 91, 92, 93, 94, 95, 96, 98, 146, 150
Feedback loops, 140,141
Fellowship, 94, 95, 96, 139
Fibonacci sequence, 53

Index

Find It, 71
Fish tanks, 21
Flash, 70, 84, 127
Flexible focus, 201
Flickr, 113
Flow, 38, 42, 44, 147,
Focus on players, 192
Fortress, 72
Fraction Mahjong, 97
Fraction Town, 58
Freedom principle, 115

G
Gamification, 181
Game
    Action/Platform games, 70
    Adventure games, 34, 70, 78, 117
    Board games, 4, 23
    Commercial games, 143
    Educational games, 20, 34, 36, 60, 70, 77, 78, 81, 82, 161, 191,
    Edutainment games, 34
    Fighting games, 70, 117
    Mobile games, 4
    Off-the-shelf entertainment games, 60
    Puzzle games, 37, 69
    Role-playing games, 4, 70, 78, 190
    Sandbox games, 37
    Shooter games, 69, 159, 160, 161
    Simulation, 35, 38, 190
    Speed-based games, 42
    Sports games, 70
    Strategy games, 70, 117
    Traffic games, 86, 144
Game clarity, 172
Game design and building, 27, 34, 35, 36, 45, 49, 50, 56, 57, 58, 61, 81, 106, 114, 118, 125, 129, 142, 156, 162, 179, 183, 193, 201, 202
Game design as a mind tool, 201
Game design elements support the skills, 51, 60, 62
Game dynamics, 138-141
Game elements, 36, 40-44, 69, 75, 76, 100, 165
    Gamer profile, 54,

Resource management, 40
Rules, 34, 36, 37, 38, 39, 40, 41, 42, 43, 44, 52, 54, 58, 66, 67, 68, 69, 70, 76, 77, 83, 86, 90, 91, 102, 105, 111, 122, 125, 127, 138, 139, 140, 142, 144, 146, 154, 172, 202
    Sequence, 17, 40, 42, 53
    Player interaction, 40, 42
    Objectives, 9, 17, 28, 37, 40, 147
    Storylines, 42, 94, 95, 96, 97, 142, 147, 150,
    Narratives, 40, 42, 94, 95, 98, 106, 138, 142, 143, 146,
Game Maker, 35
Game mechanics, 51, 54, 66, 76, 83, 101, 137, 138, 154, 179, 202
Game mechanism, 66
Games in Motion, 23, 26, 52, 56, 64, 116, 135, 137, 154, 179, 202
Gamestar Mechanics, 22, 24, 83, 176, 188, 189
Gee, J.P., 3, 18, 20, 21, 77, 142, 201
GeoGebra, 84
Get Crack'n, 72
Go, 40, 41, 42, 139
Goblin Mountain, 71, 98, 147, 149
Google, 65, 114, 190
Group roles, 125

H
Halo, 160
Harry Potter fan fiction, 113
Hatchet, 97
Hole in the Wall, 5, 7

I
Idea generation, 81, 83, 86, 88, 89, 93
Identity, 21, 22, 33, 92, 153-156
Imparting events, 79,
Infamous, 160
Information on-demand and just-in-time, 21
Innovative pedagogy, 53
Interaction, 6, 7, 13, 14, 37, 40, 42, 65, 66, 69, 74, 76, 101, 112, 121, 122, 123, 124, 126, 127, 128, 138, 184, 188
Iterative process, 84

J
Jeopardy, 93
Juvenile crimes, 160

K
Karate Kid, The, 90, 91
Keep Up with the Joneses, 71
Kudo, 24, 97, 129
Kutner, L., 159, 160

L
Learn-by-design software, 188, 190
Learning by game building in the twenty-first century, 199, 200, 202
Learner-built games, 162
Learner Design Education Model, 81-88
Learning
    Learning by digital game designing and building, 4
    Learning by making, 36
    Learning Environment, 9, 23, 27, 128, 137, 184
    Learning in informal settings, 4-7
    Learning Theory, 9
    Learning through game building, 36, 49, 81
    Self-instructed learning, 6
    Teacher-instructed learning, 6
Learning communities, 127, 135-137
Learning objectives, 158, 162, 191,
LeBlanc, M., 93
Little Big Planet, 42, 62, 63, 83, 94
Little Cashier, 71
Little Sprout, 73
Logarithmath, 130
Logo, 20, 34, 35, 190

M
Macarthur Foundation, 35
Manipulation and distributed knowledge, 21
Mario Kart, 42, 94
MathBlaster, 36
Mathematia, 71
Math Fair, 25
Mathematics education, 10, 163
Meaning as action image, 21
Mediating tools and signs, 18
Merleau-Ponty, M, 10, 12
Mindstorms, 19

Mitra, S., 5,6
Mt. Siepiski, 176, 177
MythGiving, 101, 161

N
Narrative, 94-96, 98, 102, 106, 143, 144, 146, 149, 165
Negotiation, 42, 129
Newton's laws, 52, 53, 57, 135-137,154, 155
Next Gen, 73

O
Objectivism, 12, 15, 16
Olson, C., 159,160
Oregon Trail, The, 34, 36

P
Pac-Man, 40, 41, 139
Papert, S., 3, 18-20, 34,201
Participation, 24,74,117, 118, 153,165, 167,174,176, 201
Participatory culture, 50,63,109, 112-114, 116,120, 175-177,200,201
Pedagogical design, 77
Pedagogical rubric, 166, 173
Peer assessment form, 126
Periodic Table, 73
Play, 38-40
    Play of experience, 40, 74
    Play of pleasure, 40, 74
    Play of meaning, 40, 74
Play testing, 23, 30, 56, 58, 60, 81, 85, 87, 98, 101-106, 125, 174, 192
Pleasantly frustrating, 21
Portal, 36, 165
Principles,8, 20, 21,24, 32,36,49, 53, 65, 66, 74, 77, 81,82,84, 86,88,90,92,94,96,98,100,102,104,106,112,116,117, 137,142, 188,189, 202
    Creativity, 43, 44,49-54,88,93,96,114,119,149,171,191
    Graphics and sound, 43, 44
    KISS, 43
    Smooth control, 43
    Skill development, 43, 44
Problem-solving, 33, 64, 90
Programmer, 62, 83, 123, 125, 133, 183
Project manager, 125
Proffitt, D. R., 13
Profile That Gamer!, 54-56

Index

Prototyping Model, 81

Q
Quadratic Commander, 84, 85
Quality of reflection, 172
Quality of the question, 172
Quest for Elvis's Guitar, 141

R
Race to the Top initiatives, The, 142
Reasoning, 117-119, 163, 164,167, 169, 174
Reconstruction of constructivism, 20
Reflection principle, 116
Reflective process, 85
Replayability, 75
Representation, 12, 37, 38, 90, 118, 163, 166, 174
Riener, C. R., 13
Rubric for Math Games, 172
Rules, 41-43
        Operational, 41, 42, 68, 86,146,157,170
        Implied, 41, 42
Run for Math, 23, 25, 64, 129, 130, 157, 169, 170

S
Salen, K.,35, 37, 39, 40, 109
Samsara, 110-112, 156, 160
Sandboxes, 21
Scaffolding, 18, 21, 28,29, 43, 90, 106, 115, 117, 118, 122, 144, 163,164, 168, 192,195,196
Scaffolding principle, 115
Schreiber, I., 36-39, 140, 142, 144, 191
Scratch Cards,25
Scratch Intro Facilitorial, 25
Searching for Euphoria, 170
Sensation, 40, 94, 95
Sharing principle, 116
Sims 3, 4 ,21, 33, 36, 37
SimCity, 36, 37
SimFant, 72
Simplicity, 191
Situated learning, 18, 20, 142
Skills, 6,15,18,21,24,25,39,44,49-51,56,58-64,76,96-99,110,113,114,119-121,123-129,131,133-136,141,142,153,158,174,182,183,185-190,193-195,199-201

Skills as strategies, 21
Small group learning, 129, 131
Smartboard, 8, 9, 147
So You Think You're Canadian, Eh?. 73
Social and cultural processes, 18
Social City, The, 91
Social development theory, 18
Splat!, 67 ,68, 69, 90, 91, 144, 202
Stagecast Creator, 35
StarCraft, 36, 42, 94
Student-created games, 162, 190
Systems thinking, 21, 49, 51, 65, 66
Square Up, 96, 98
StarCraft 2, 42
StarLogo TNG, 35, 190
Strategy, 52, 70, 88, 89, 105, 117-121, 131, 155, 165, 167, 174, 177, 182, 183
Storytelling, 34, 138, 142, 143
        Linear storytelling, 143
        Multithread Structure of a story, 144
Submission, 94, 95
Super Mario, 41, 94

T
Tacit knowledge, 12
Taxonomy, 95
Teacher design games, 117
Testing events, 79
Tetris, 75
Toontalk, 35
Thompson, E., 10
Trading, 42
Traffic rules, 70

U
Unintentional Learning, 7
Usability test, 83,84
User friendly/ease of play, 117

V
Value, 53,105,131,153-178,181,183,185,187,189,191,193,195
Vault, The, 72
Varela, 10, 12, 14
Violence, 159, 160, 161
Visual literacy, 99
Vygotsky, L., 3, 18, 19, 22, 39

W

War, 30, 101
Where in the World Is Carmen San Diego? 34
Why Read If I can Build, 23, 24, 29, 121, 132, 140, 156, 174, 184, 194, 202
Wikipedia, 41, 65, 66, 113, 199
Web 2.0, 27, 28, 33, 112, 113
Well-ordered problems, 21
World of Warcraft, 40, 199

Y

You Auto Know, 73
Youtube, 4,113

Z

Zimmerman, E., 37, 39, 40, 74, 109, 192
Zone of Proximal Development (ZPD), 18

Colin Lankshear & Michele Knobel
General Editors

New literacies emerge and evolve apace as people from all walks of life engage with new technologies, shifting values and institutional change, and increasingly assume 'postmodern' orientations toward their everyday worlds. Despite many efforts to take account of such changes, educational institutions largely remain out of touch with the range of new ways of making and sharing meanings that increasingly mediate and shape the lives of the young people they teach and the futures they face. This series aims to explore some key dimensions of the changes occurring within social practices of literacy and the educational challenges they present, with a view to informing educational practice in helpful ways. It asks what are new literacies, how do they impact on life in schools, homes, communities, workplaces, sites of leisure, and other key settings of human cultural engagement, and what significance do new literacies have for how people learn and how they understand and construct knowledge. It aims to challenge established and 'official' ways of framing literacy, and to ask what it means for literacies to be powerful, effective, and enabling under current and foreseeable conditions. Collectively, the works in this series will help to reorient literacy debates and literacy education agendas.

For further information about the series and submitting manuscripts, please contact:

>   Michele Knobel & Colin Lankshear
>   Montclair State University
>   Dept. of Education and Human Services
>   3173 University Hall
>   Montclair, NJ 07043
>   michele@coatepec.net

To order other books in this series, please contact our Customer Service Department at:
>   (800) 770-LANG (within the U.S.)
>   (212) 647-7706 (outside the U.S.)
>   (212) 647-7707 FAX

Or browse online by series at:
>   www.peterlang.com

www.ingramcontent.com/pod-product-compliance
Ingram Content Group UK Ltd.
Pitfield, Milton Keynes, MK11 3LW, UK
UKHW021327180426
11947UKWH00017B/1483